SPRING

SUMMER

FALL

WINTER

The Field Guide to

WILDLIFE HABITATS

of the

EASTERN UNITED STATES

JANINE M. BENYUS
ILLUSTRATIONS BY GLENN WOLFF

A FIRESIDE BOOK
PUBLISHED BY SIMON & SCHUSTER INC.
NEW YORK   LONDON   TORONTO   SYDNEY   TOKYO

FIRESIDE
Simon & Schuster Building
Rockefeller Center
1230 Avenue of the Americas
New York, New York 10020

DESIGNED BY BARBARA MARKS
Manufactured in the United States of America

10 9 8 7 6 5 4 3 2 1

Library of Congress Cataloging in Publication Data
Benyus, Janine M.
   The field guide to wildlife habitats of the eastern United States
/ Janine M. Benyus ; illustrations by Glenn Wolff.
      p.   cm.
   "A Fireside book."
   Bibliography: p.
   Includes index.
   1. Habitat (Ecology)—United States   2. Biotic communities—
United States.   I. Title.
QH104.B46   1989
574.5'0974—dc19   88-37243
                                                     CIP

ISBN 0-671-65908-1

FOR MY PARENTS,

JOAN AND DANIEL BENYUS,

WHO TAUGHT ME

TO LOVE LEARNING.

This book, like an aspen sprout, is connected to a vast network of underground roots generations older than itself. The groundwork for these pages began with the first explorer-naturalists who eloquently recorded their impressions of the New World. Since then, thousands have carried on the inquiry, wading into bogs, scratching through thickets, and taking to the treetops for a glimpse of wild lives. Their insights illuminate this book, and to them I am grateful.

I am also indebted to the biologists and researchers in the United States Forest Service, where I have worked for the past nine years. I relied heavily on their individual "search images" as well as their published data about wildlife-habitat relationships.

A special thank-you goes to the professionals who were kind enough to review all or part of the manuscript: Dorothy Allard, Regional Ecologist, Southern Region of The Nature Conservancy; Dr. Robert Bucksbalm, Coastal Ecologist, Massachusetts Audubon Society; Anita Cholewa, Herbarium Director, University of Minnesota; James Dickson, Research Wildlife Biologist, U.S. Forest Service; The Interpretive Staff of Everglades National Park; John Kricher, Jennings Professor of Biology, Wheaton College, Massachusetts; Margaret Kohring, Executive Director, Minnesota Chapter of The Nature Conservancy; John Moriarty, Herpetologist, Bell Museum of Natural History, Minnesota; Karen Williams, Seaville Station Manager, New Jersey Marine Sciences Consortium; and Cindy Witkowski, Vegetation Ecologist, Southern Region of the U.S. Forest Service.

Glenn Wolff, the talented illustrator who created a world within each habitat drawing, has been an inspiration to me as well as a friend. I feel lucky to have worked with him.

ABOUT THE AUTHOR

Janine M. Benyus has been exploring and writing about the natural world for ten years. Her publications include *The Wildlife Watcher's Guide To Habitats Of The Northwoods,* which she wrote while working for the research branch of the U.S. Forest Service. She writes books and articles on natural history from her home in St. Paul, Minnesota.

ABOUT THE ILLUSTRATOR

Glenn Wolff is best known for his illustrations in the "Outdoors" column for the *New York Times.* His work has also appeared in numerous magazines and journals, including *Sports Illustrated* and *Audubon,* as well as many books for various publishers. He currently lives in northern Michigan with his wife and two children.

Contents

WILDLIFE/HABITAT PROFILES 47

Preface

I've always been comforted by the notion that somewhere out there, beyond the crime lights and car horns, there are dark, dewy habitats humming with life. As I plan my escape to these havens, I take it for granted that they will be there when I arrive.

But lately, I've been wondering. I have a friend who works for the National Forestry Project in India. She keeps referring to this book as a historical document, a picture of something that may not exist a lifetime from now. In her country, so many forests have been stripped for fuel or fodder that only 12 percent of the land remains adequately covered by trees. A book describing India's habitats as they were even thirty years ago would be an archive piece today.

But could this kind of devastation happen in the United States? Actually, it's not that farfetched. The settlers who first saw this country could not have imagined that the endless eastern forests would one day be completely cleared away. Nor could they believe that the sun-blocking clouds of passenger pigeons would be reduced to a single stuffed specimen in a museum. Likewise, as we unwrap our fast-food hamburgers, we find it hard to believe that the beef was fattened at the expense of millions of acres of tropical rain forest. Half of all rain forests will be gone in a few years, and their loss could dramatically upset the world's climate. What would rising temperatures do to the robe of vegetation that clothes our continent?

Although we can't recreate habitats once they are gone, we can recreate our behavior before it is too late. Forty years ago, a naturalist named Aldo Leopold called for a land ethic that would have us treat the land—plants, animals, soil, etc.—as we would treat one another. Instead of appointing ourselves as conquerors, we would take our place as plain citizens of the natural world, expanding our circle of kinship to include all forms of life.

As a planet of people, we've already proven that we can enlarge our concept of social ethics. Consider, for example, that men and women were at one time enslaved as a matter of course. The sanctity of property eclipsed any consideration of human rights. Today, while slavery is still practiced in some parts of the world, most cultures view it as an atrocity. Perhaps someday, people will also view land abuse as a violent and antisocial act. In such a world, we wouldn't have to pay landowners to treat their land decently; the rewards of doing the right thing would be payment enough.

This kind of commitment to the land cannot be legislated. To endure, a social change of heart must be forged in the fires of personal change. As Leopold said, "We can be ethical only in relation to something we see, feel, understand, love, or otherwise have faith in." Visiting the places you read about in this book is the first step to seeing, feeling, and understanding them. The affection and faith will blossom in its own time.

In India, a small group of women began what is now a national conservation movement called Chipko, which means to hug or embrace. They began with the simple act of hugging trees to protest their removal. It is my hope that after reading this book you will also be filled with a desire to embrace the habitats of your own country, and keep them from falling into the hands of those who would abuse them.

How to Use This Book

Shhhh . . . What could that be?

Have you ever wondered what kind of animal might be rustling in the dark just outside your tent? Given the several hundred birds, mammals, amphibians, and reptiles found in the eastern United States, you could be flipping through field guides until your flashlight burns out. Unless, of course, you have a "search image" for that habitat—a mental laundry list of the wildlife you could expect to see there.

People who have lived or worked in the woods for a lifetime carry this sort of search image in their head. When they step into a habitat, they notice the kind of plants blooming underfoot and the type of trees spreading overhead. They have come to associate this vegetation with a certain community of animals. Under a ceiling of northern needleleaf trees, for instance, they know to look for porcupines, red squirrels, redbelly snakes, and brown creepers. They also know where in the habitat to look—on the ground for snakes, on the trunks for creepers, and in the canopy for porcupines and squirrels.

If you haven't had the pleasure of living in the wild, take heart. This book puts the insiders' knowledge of wildlife habitats in your pack. With it, you can visit any woodland or waterway east of the 98th meridian and easily know which habitat you're in and what kinds of wildlife you're likely to see. More important, you'll find out why wildlife live in certain habitats, and what would happen to them (and to us) if these places suddenly disappeared.

You don't need technical training to use this book. The latest scientific studies have been transformed into simple stories that will stick with you. In your own wanderings, you'll uncover thousands of other stories enacted every day in the habitats around you. There are entire worlds to explore in every teaspoon of soil and every roothole full of rain—enough to feed your curiosity for years.

Before you go exploring, read the What Is a Habitat? section to find out why animals "choose" to live where they do. Knowing this, you'll be able to size up a habitat from an animal's perspective and predict which species would be likely to settle there. The Observation Tips section offers tricks of the trade that will better your chances of coming face to face with the wild residents. You'll learn how to think like an animal, how to lure, stalk, and hide from wildlife, and how to read their signs and signatures in the snow and mud. To help time your visits so you're out when the animals are, consult the Wildlife Events Calendar (see page 33).

Once you're outside, take a good look around. Are you in a forest, an opening, or a wetland? Is the water fresh or salt? Are the trees broadleaf or needleleaf? Use the Habitat Key (see page 46) to narrow your choice to one of the 20 habitats. To verify your choice, compare the habitat illustration (there is one for each habitat) with what you see around you. The drawing includes characteristic leaves, flowers, and fruits, as well as wildlife and their signs you should be on the lookout for. A sampling of places where you can see the habitat (national parks, forests, and refuges) follows each illustration.

Now that you know where you are, read the habitat profile to find out why that habitat is unique, how it changes, and what it offers to wildlife. A checklist of indicator plants accompanies each habitat profile.

At the end of each habitat profile you'll find a Wildlife Locator Chart— a matrix that groups resident wildlife according to where they feed and nest. So, for instance, if a furry head pops up near your canoe, you can turn to the lake and pond habitat, and look in the column marked "Feeds Underwater" to find out which animal it might be. Or, if you spot a nest in the branches along shore, look in the row marked "Nests in Tree Canopy." Many characteristic species are listed in each chart, giving you a complete "search image" for each habitat.

The habitat's most typical animals are illustrated in the art above each chart. For more technical renderings, you may want to consult identification guides. This book is not meant to replace these guides, but rather to put a shelfful of plant and animal information into a community context—the way you actually experience it in the field. In many cases, the illustrations you find here will be all you need to start enjoying the natural world around you.

After each chart, you'll find life history profiles of three key species— a bird, a mammal, and either a reptile or an amphibian—that are strongly associated with that habitat. You'll learn how each animal is adapted to its habitat and what to "look for," "smell for," and "listen for" to find it at different times of year. By learning how these animals excel in their environment, you'll also be learning about the community as a whole. Other animals that share the habitat will have many of the same survival adaptations.

Now you're on your way. You've learned the secrets of watching wildlife and you know how to identify the places where they live. If you'd like to know more, dip into the Resources for the Curious section at the back of the book. The Recommended Readings include some of my favorite sources, representing just a drop in the ocean of natural history literature. One of the great things about wildlife study is that amateur naturalists like you can add valuable information to our growing body of knowledge. If you'd like to be a part of the discovery, contact the groups listed in the Getting Involved section.

The deeper you delve into habitats, the more amazed you'll be. In each community, thousands of plants, animals, and microorganisms have evolved over eons to work together as one fantastic organism. I invite you to stand respectfully in their midst and come to realize how much a part of them you are.

What Is a Habitat?

A PLACE TO LIVE

A habitat is an animal's home—the place where it finds what it needs to survive. A livable habitat should offer a tolerable climate, a varied terrain, ample space, and a dependable supply of food and water. It should have safe places for feeding, playing, hiding, resting, and raising young. A habitat, in effect, is the sum total of an animal's everyday needs.

These needs may change throughout a year, or throughout the animal's life. Salamanders that swim in ponds during the early months may spend the rest of their lives crawling on the forest floor. Similarly, winter quarters for white-tailed deer (northern white-cedar swamps) are rarely sought out in the summer. Even in the course of a day, an animal may visit more than one habitat to fulfill all its needs, just as you may work in one town and shop for groceries in another.

Very often, one of these habitats is the "preferred" one. This is the place where the animal spends most of its time, and gets most of its important needs fulfilled. Often, it is where it breeds and raises its young. In this book, animals are matched with their preferred habitats—where you'd be most likely to see them during spring, summer, and fall, when you're apt to be out looking.

The fact that you can predict where a species might spend its "working hours" is no coincidence. As you will see in the next section, an animal's preference for a certain habitat is the result of a long evolutionary journey.

WHY ANIMALS PREFER CERTAIN HABITATS

Animals are driven by the desire to eat, pass on their genes, and avoid being eaten. Through millions of years of trial and error, the survivors have become more efficient in their quest. They have developed physical traits and behaviors that help them get the most from their environment with the least amount of effort or risk. Naturally, animals gravitate toward places where their survival traits can really shine. In these preferred habitats, they have an edge over other animals that may not be as specialized to compete there.

You can predict where animals might live by looking for adaptations such as bill design, body size and color, skin or fur consistency, or even the kind of feet they have. The toes of treefrogs, for instance, have large round disks to help them hang onto the slick surfaces of leaves. In contrast, the toes of bullfrogs, ducks, and beavers are connected by webbing, which, though not particularly helpful in trees, is designed to give them a good push in the water. Tree-climbing squirrels, porcupines, and woodpeckers have sharp, bark-gripping claws, while the hooves of deer and moose are blunt and horny for pounding terra firma.

ADAPTIVE CHARACTERISTICS

Through the transforming power of natural selection, species develop traits that help them survive. Here are some of the physical and behavioral adaptations that link animals with their habitats.

In the Water:
Common Loon: heavy bones good for diving; webbed feet set far back for paddling power; can empty air sacs and push all air from feathers to sink straight down like a submarine; can shuttle oxygen to important organs when submerged for long periods.
Water Shrew: air bubbles under bristly feet allow shrew to run on top of water.
Beaver: special "goggle" layer over eyes; waterproof fur; webbed feet; valved nostrils; lips close behind teeth so it can dine without drowning.
River Otter: sleek shape; muscular body flexes up and down for speedy swimming; webbed feet.
Green Frog: long kicking legs with webbed feet for "push"; eggs

protected from cold temperatures by jelly mass; eyes placed on top of head so it can keep a low profile in water yet still see.

Spiny Softshell (Turtle): can disappear under sandy river bottom by moving shell back and forth; long, sinuous neck allows it to keep nostrils above water while laying on the bottom.

In the Soil:

American Woodcock: long, probing bill "reads" the underground vibrations of earthworms; eyes set far back on head so it can keep watch when its bill is buried.

Star-nosed Mole: fleshy feelers around nostrils curl in to keep dirt out, open in water to "read" the environment; forelimbs extend horizontally from body like flippers; clawed fingers are flattened like paddles; shoulder blades are enlarged; powerful chest muscles are the "hydraulics" of digging.

Thirteen-lined Ground Squirrel: elaborate burrows; can sense change in air pressure when burrows are invaded or caved in.

Southeastern Pocket Gopher: narrow hips ease tunnel transit; two-way hair lays flat when backing up; touch-sensitive tail acts as rearview mirror; lips close behind teeth to keep dirt out of mouth when digging; fur-lined cheeks turn inside out for cleaning.

Eastern Hognose Snake: upturned snout helps it dig out prey; light sandy coloring for camouflage.

In the Snow:

Ruffed Grouse: grows combs between toes to keep from sinking into snow; dives into snowbank to sleep or escape predators.

Snowshoe Hare: extra fur creates "snowshoes" on long hind feet; winter coat is whitish with a slightly lighter underbelly to soften shadows under the hare and help it blend with backdrop of white.

Mice and Voles: build tunnels under the snow that are relatively warm, safe from predators, and close to food on the forest floor.

Ermine: coat turns white in winter; tail tip stays black to encourage predators to strike at the tail, not at the vulnerable torso.

Lynx: wide, floppy mops on paws help it float on top of snow; tufts on ears keep tips from freezing and may amplify sound.

In Tall Grasses:

American Bittern: vertical markings on chest look like reeds; behavior serves as camouflage too—stretches bill up to sky and sways when breeze moves the reeds.

Rails: vertically flattened bodies are "thin as a rail" to slip between grasses undetected.

Blackbirds: can perch between vertical stalks by balancing one foot on each of two stems.

Smooth Green Snake: bright green; when it straightens out, it looks like a fallen grass blade.

On Leafy Forest Floor:

Ovenbird: plumage looks like fallen leaves; builds a leafy "Dutch oven" nest that is almost impossible to spot.

White-tailed Deer Fawns: speckled coats look like sunspecks on forest floor; odorless to elude keen-nosed predators.

Wild Pig: piglets are striped like the leafy shadows.

Eastern Box Turtle: orange, black, and brown shell looks like dead leaves.

On Trunks or Limbs:

Woodpeckers: "grappling hook" claws for traction; stiff tail feathers for stability; reinforced skull bones for pounding. Extra-long tongue is stored in curved recesses of skull, then extended for remote-crevice probing. Tongue brushed with sticky barbs for pulling out insects.

Virginia Opossum: opposable "thumb" for clasping branches; tail can curl around branches.

Gray Squirrel: wide range of peripheral vision; memorizes routes through trees; tail acts as rudder; sensing hairs along body act as antennae.

Porcupine: backward-pointing quills dig into bark like spurs; strong thigh muscles clamp like a vise; paw pads roughened for a good grip.

Rat Snakes: belly scales adapted for climbing tree trunks; heart, lungs, and cells adapted to prevent swelling in lower body and speed blood back to head.

In the Leafy Canopy:

Wood Duck: narrow wings allow it to maneuver through the canopy at high speed; claws on webbed feet allow it to perch on branches.

Scarlet Tanager: bright plumage blends with the sun filtering through leaves.

Treefrogs: enlarged, sticky toe pads "glue" them to leaves; tips of toes jointed to hook around twigs; body flattened to distribute weight; skin the color of leaves or bark.

Populations develop these special adaptations through the process of natural selection, colloquially known as "survival of the fittest." Natural selection favors the better-adapted individuals in a population. These individuals tend to live longer and produce more offspring than poorly adapted ones. As their adaptive genes are passed on again and again, the population as a whole begins to reflect an affinity for the habitat.

For some species, this affinity becomes very strong indeed. The animal that can satisfy all its needs in one habitat may never wander to another. It may become so specialized that it can't survive anywhere else. Many of our endangered species, such as the red-cockaded woodpecker of the southern pines and the Kirtland's warbler of the northern pines, fall into this restricted group. Their very existence depends on the health of one kind of habitat.

For other animals, habitat flexibility may be the key to survival. The ability to switch into new and different habitats allows species such as the red-winged blackbird to multiply rapidly. These "jacks of all trades, masters of none" have parlayed their generalist tendencies into large populations.

HOW DO ANIMALS "CHOOSE" WHERE TO LIVE?

When an animal walks or flies through an area, how does it "know" whether this would be a good place to raise a family or find food? For some species, it's a simple matter of returning to where they were raised. Others must colonize new areas, relying on instinct to help them pick a good spot. Structure, patchiness, edge, size, special features, and other organisms are some of the factors that animals "consider" when choosing a habitat. There are, no doubt, more subtle clues that we don't yet understand. Next time you go into a habitat, try seeing it through an animal's eyes. Ask the following questions to discover why an animal might "choose" to live there.

Structure. Are the plants the right shape, height, and leaf density for nesting, feeding, resting, and singing? How many vertical layers are there? Is the midstory open enough to fly from perches and catch insects? Are the understory and ground layer sparse or dense?

Bird researchers believe that birds key in on the structural "look and feel" of a habitat—the outlines and density of vegetation taken together. The species of plant is not as important as how it grows: whether it is a spreading shrub, flowering herb, vertical grass, or mature tree.

Each of these life forms (grass, herb, shrub, tree) represents a vertical layer in the forest profile. Each layer provides a place for nesting, hiding, or feeding that differs slightly from the site above or below it. Different heights in a forest canopy, for instance, have different temperatures, humidity levels, insect populations, and food resources. Over the span of evolutionary time, species have come to specialize in one or more of the layers, thus dividing up the resources the way newspaper reporters cover separate "beats."

The more layers there are in a habitat, the more opportunities there are for these specialists. That's why a dense, tangled forest has a longer role call of species than a simple, "clean" plantation.

Patchiness. Is the dense shade of the forest relieved by occasional openings? Are there trees and shrubs of all ages, sizes, and conditions? Are there grasses, succulent plants, and varying amounts of forest litter?

In addition to vertical zones, there are also different horizontal zones that can entice an animal to live in a habitat. A river, for instance, is made up of riffles, deep pools, and slow, wide stretches, all of which have different combinations of food, water, space, and cover.

Natural disturbances such as windstorms, fires, insect infestations, and rockslides can create a gap in a large block of habitat and add a patch of an earlier stage of development. This mosaic effect gives wildlife a sunny field of berries, for instance, right in the middle of a dense, secure pine forest. A combination of patches allows animals to meet all their needs without traveling very far—a convenience factor that may mean the difference between life and death.

Edge. Are there zones of transition between two different types of habitat, such as field and forest, or marsh and shrub swamp? Is the contrast between the two sharp or gradual? How many miles of edge are there in this area? Are the perimeters of fields scalloped to provide more edge?

The junction between two different communities is one of the most heavily trafficked places in the outdoors, thus one of your best bets for wildlife watching. Here, animals from each community can be found together, along with "edge species" that specialize in this transition zone.

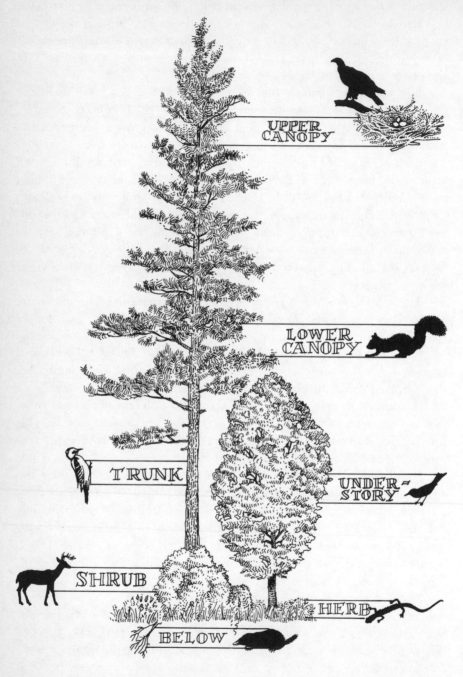

UPPER
CANOPY

LOWER
CANOPY

TRUNK

UNDER-
STORY

SHRUB

HERB

BELOW

Zoning: Each layer of the forest belongs to the animal best suited to survive there. By dividing up the forest's riches, animals can coexist while ensuring that none of the resources go to waste.

The edge, where two habitats meet, is one of your best bets for wildlife watching. You'll see residents of the forest and the field, as well as those specially adapted to live in this in-between zone.

The result is a community more diverse than either of the adjacent ones.

Habitats that are patchy have plenty of this edge environment. A gradual, shrubby transition between tall trees and short grasses will conceal wildlife as they move from one environment to the other. The vegetation along rivers (one long edge) also provides safe corridors that are essential for wildlife, especially when the river winds through miles of agricultural fields.

Size. Is the habitat large enough to roam in without having to cross roads or run into people? Is the center far enough away from the edges, where predators can enter?

Certain species of wildlife need large areas of unbroken terrain to roam in. Area-sensitive birds such as ovenbirds often build their nests deep in these extensive forests. If the center is too close to the edge, predators have easy access to these nests, and the ovenbirds may not be able to successfully raise their young.

Large mammals such as wolves and bears need a wide range of feeding territory to support themselves. Gray wolves are especially sensitive to the intrusions of humans, and can be found only where wild lands stretch for miles.

Suburban sprawl has begun to chop up the once remote parts of our country. Biologists are concerned by this "forest fragmentation." They notice that there is a wider variety of species on large blocks of habitat, and a simpler, less varied clientele on small habitat "islands." When these islands are isolated in a sea of shopping centers and subdevelopments, there may be no way for new species to move in and replace those that die. The wildlife roster gets simpler and slimmer, until only a few people-adapted species (such as gray squirrels and American robins) are left.

Special Features. Is the habitat close to water? Are there enough old trees to form cavities for nests? Are there perches for singing? Is the soil loose enough for easy digging?

A habitat may be generally ideal, but if it doesn't provide a particular ingredient essential to the lifestyle of an animal, the species can't survive there for long. If the soil is too hard for the American woodcock to probe, or the trees too young for nest cavities to form, or the water too stagnant for the mudpuppy to breathe, it must move on to other haunts. When you read the life histories of wildlife, keep their special requirements in mind. This will help you narrow down the habitats you can find them in.

Other Organisms. Will competition from similar species be too stiff? Will predators be too abundant to travel safely? Will there be enough of the right foods to eat? Will parasites plague the young nestlings?

No organism is an island; each lives in an environment that is influenced and changed by the fact that other organisms share the space. Eastern bluebirds, which have bills too weak to peck out their own homes, depend heavily on the advance work of woodpeckers. Snail kites wouldn't survive a month in a marsh that didn't have a good population of apple snails, their favorite food. On the negative side, pressure from competitors, predators, disease organisms, and parasites can make an otherwise ideal site inhospitable.

WHAT HAPPENS WHEN A HABITAT CHANGES?

Once animals have settled into the habitat they are best suited to, what happens when it changes? Natural communities are in a constant state of flux, changing and transforming in a process called "succession." In succession, communities succeed one another, each one better adapted to the conditions of the site.

Consider the slow parade from bare ground to dark forest, for instance. Annual weeds grow from seeds and make the soil fertile enough for grasses and perennial plants to get started. These stabilize and enrich the soil so that shrubs can break in. The shrubs shade the grasses and make room for tree seedlings, which finally shade out the shrubs. Even these sun-loving trees are not fated to remain for long, however. As they mature, an understory of shade-tolerant trees rises and eventually overtops the pioneers. Although this "climax" community is more stable than most, it is far from static. One lightning strike on a dry day can start the process all over again.

Each of the plant communities has its associated animal communities that wax and wane along with it. The ousted species survive by moving to another habitat that meets their needs. If there is one.

When humans alter habitats, it doesn't necessarily signal the beginning of a natural change. By pouring concrete, dumping wastes, introducing exotic pests, draining wetlands, or spraying chemicals, we often trigger an irreversible change. If the change affects a large area, there may be nowhere for sensitive species to turn. Other habitats may already be occupied or may lack elements that are critical for survival. Crowding animals into less-than-ideal habitats will diminish their populations, until, on a local level, they may become extinct.

When we lose a species, we also lose the free service that it performs in the ecosystem. Perhaps the lost species was a soil burrower, creating tunnels that rodents, toads, or insects used for shelter. Or perhaps by burying its food, it inadvertently "planted" acorns that grew into large oaks. If it was a predator, its prey may suddenly explode in number, stripping large swathes of food plants from the area, and forcing other species to seek new habitats.

EXTINCTION IS FOREVER

When extinction occurs on a worldwide level, the loss is even more profound. Species are the unique result of millions upon millions of years of genetic improvement. Once this carefully crafted template is lost, it can never be recreated. On a purely selfish level, we humans have much to lose when a species fades to extinction. Nearly half of our medicines come from plants and animals, yet only 2 percent of all species have been tested for their usefulness. If extinction rates continue as they have, nearly one-fifth of the species on earth today will be gone by the end of the century.

Forfeiting the opportunity for breakthroughs in medicine, agriculture, pest control, and environmental monitoring is actually one of the lesser dangers of extinction. The real menace is the tear in the intricate fabric of the worldwide ecosystem. A tear that starts small tends to run, and soon the fabric no longer covers or insulates as well as it once did. By weakening the ecosystem, we sabotage its power to heal, nurture, and replenish all life, including human life.

It's important to make a distinction here between natural extinction, which has been occurring for eons, and the relatively recent cases of human-caused extinction. In the past, as one species succumbed to a slowly changing environment, a better-adapted species evolved to take its place. This changing of the guard took place gradually, and for the most part, there were more new species than there were species going extinct. The result was a slowly growing pool of organisms.

Ecologists Anne and Paul Ehrlich compare this process to a faucet running new species into a sink, while extinction drains them away. As we overexploit organisms and whittle away at their habitats, we are actually widening the drain, and allowing species to go extinct more rapidly. At the same time, we are clogging the faucet up above, interfering with the ecosystem's ability to produce new heirs. By some conservative estimates, we are now losing one species a day, and that rate may increase to one an hour by the year 2000. At that rate, new species cannot possibly evolve fast enough to keep the level of the pool from sinking.

Extinction is the drain through which we lose unique, irreplaceable organisms like those in the margin. Human pressure on habitats has so widened this drain that new species cannot evolve fast enough to keep pace with extinction.

OUR NEW RESPONSIBILITY

Humans are changing the face of the earth. Armed with superhuman technology and a snowballing appetite for resources, we could conceivably make changes that would rival the ice age glaciers in their violence and scope. With this capacity comes a heavy burden of responsibility. Restraint

Most animals depend on a variety of habitat types to meet their daily needs. The best of all worlds is an area that has patches of old and young trees, both needleleaf and broadleaf, relieved occasionally by clearings and sources of clean water. This kind of diversity is healthy for the whole ecosystem. A diverse habitat, like a diversified economy, is less likely to crash when one element fails.

and wisdom are the emblems of an ecological conscience that we are finally beginning to form.

It is too late for us to step away from land management and simply "leave the land alone." We've made an indelible mark on the raw wilderness that was once the eastern United States. Some parcels of wilderness have, thankfully, been set aside as living laboratories, examples against which we can assess the health of our populated lands. But that is not to say that we can't live respectfully on settled lands.

National forests are "working" forests; they are professionally managed to provide wood, water, forage, recreation, and wildlife on a continuing and renewable basis. Each forest charts its future activities in a document called a "forest plan," which is subject to public review and comment. Your suggestions and objections must be considered before a single tree is felled or a foot of pipeline laid. In the same way, your city, county, and state lands are also managed with your tax dollars, and therefore can be influenced by your voice.

Surprisingly, though, the largest percentage of forest land in the eastern United States is privately owned. Strung together like a giant green necklace, the woodlots of hundreds of thousands of people make up the habitats you will read about in this book. How these people elect to use their land will affect us all.

While we can't go backward and make our lands as diverse as they once were, we can at least try to maintain all the habitats that we now have. As Aldo Leopold reminded us, the first rule of intelligent tinkering is to save all the cogs and wheels, assuming each is important in its own way. On a planet as small and as fragile as ours, this simple respect for the land is much more than a courtesy; it's a matter of survival.

Observation Tips

THE WILDLIFE ARE WATCHING

It's the sleepy end of a long day in the outdoors, and your campfire is crumbling into embers. Suddenly, you get the feeling you're being watched by a tiny pair of eyes just beyond the ring of light. Chances are it's not just your imagination. After all, you've been under observation all day!

Wildlife are the world's most astute wildlife watchers. Whether they are hunting or trying to avoid being hunted, animals keep their ears pricked and their eyes peeled. They sniff the air for strange scents, and even use their tongue and whiskers to investigate their world. To outfox their enemies, they have also become masters of evasion. Their coat, feathers, scales, and skin are patterned to help them blend into their habitat, and their every move is calculated to keep them from being seen.

Into all this cleverness, we humans come, with our eager intellects and our average set of senses. The wild disguises tend to work on us, especially if we are not accustomed to watching wildlife. As a result of our "training," we are more apt to see an approaching car than we are to see a bat fluttering by. But like athletes who learn to sense a ricocheting racquetball behind them, we can train ourselves to see "invisible" wildlife in the woods. The first part is simple: be where the action is when the action is most likely to occur.

LOOK IN THE RIGHT PLACE

Animals tend to spend most of their time in areas where all their needs can be conveniently met. The animals you'll meet in the wildlife profiles were chosen for their special affinity to that habitat. Be aware, though,

31

that habitat needs change from winter to summer as well as during different phases of the animal's life. For instance, many ducks that you'd normally look for on open water will take to the densest parts of marshes during the late summer when they shed their flight feathers and are suddenly vulnerable. Again, a look at the life history of the species will help you know where to look for it in any season.

It also pays to look up, down, and all around. Hikers who only watch the trail before them will tend to miss the owls roosting overhead, the martens chasing red squirrels in the branches, the woodpeckers poking out of tree holes, or even the warblers nesting at eye level just off the trail. Each of the layers in a community is occupied by animals that are specially suited to find food or cover at that level. Knowing which "piece of the pie" the animal specializes in can help you direct your search and spot the animal more easily. To find out where certain animals nest or feed—underground, on the ground, in shrubs, in the upper canopy, or in the air—consult the Wildlife Locator Chart for each habitat.

LOOK AT THE RIGHT TIME OF YEAR

Wildlife use different parts of their habitat at different times of year. If you know what critters are likely to be doing in any one season, you'll be more likely to find them. The following calendar can help you plan your outings to coincide with these peak periods.

Spring: Migrants return north to breed. Hibernators wake. **Summer:** *With life in full bloom, summer is a season-long feast—a good time to raise a family.* **Fall:** *Migrants head south for warmer climes. Overwintering animals store food for the long haul.* **Winter:** *Some animals hole up for the winter. Predators feed on animals weakened by winter hardships.*

Wildlife Events Calendar—Spring

Birds:

Migrating birds begin to return in waves, each week bringing a new species to paint the branches with color. They are in full breeding plumage—singing and performing conspicuous displays in hopes of being noticed by a potential mate. This may be their most vocal and viewable time of the year (especially before the leaves pop out).

Mammals:

Hungry mammals are browsing on succulent buds, shoots, and grasses, especially along roadsides and openings where the snow melts first. Moose and deer, starved for sodium after their spartan winter diet, often head for ponds where salt-rich aquatic plants grow. Hibernators such as black bears, weasels, and chipmunks are down to only a fraction of their normal weight. Once they regain their strength, the yearlings shove off to find new territories and the adults begin to breed.

Amphibians and Reptiles:

Amphibians are moving en masse from their hibernating spots to ponds for breeding. Many wind up flattened on highways that lay between their winter homes and their breeding ponds. The frogs and toads that reach the ponds fill the air with impressive trills in an effort to attract a mate. Meanwhile, salamanders, the quiet amphibians, are mating on the bottom of ponds, and hanging their eggs under logs, roots, or in the water.

Snakes tend to be rather groggy when they first emerge from their rock-crevice hibernacula. It takes a few days of basking in the sun to warm their temperature back up to the point where they can be fully active. Look for them on rocky, southwest-facing slopes, in the dust of unused forest roads, or on sunny logs. After they warm up and mate, they will move off into the woods or fields for the summer. Water turtles bask on half-submerged logs to warm themselves, sometimes piling on top of one another.

NORTHERN
RED
SALAMANDER

Wildlife Events Calendar—Summer

Birds:

In the North, late-arriving birds begin to nest, taking advantage of the fuller leaf cover. After one or more broods, they spend the summer foraging, becoming noticeably quieter. In late summer, some waterfowl shed their flight feathers and retreat to dense marshes where they can hide from predators. Early migrants begin to stage together in late summer, fueling up for the long journey south. Their restlessness at this time of year is called "zugunruhe," which means travel urge.

Mammals:

Young mammals are being raised and taught to fend for themselves. Summer is a good time to see family groups traveling together. White-tailed deer are feeding heavily in brushy openings in preparation for the autumn breeding season (called the rut).

Amphibians and Reptiles:

Many amphibian adults leave their breeding pond and disperse into woods and fields, most of them sticking to moist, humid places where they can keep their permeable skin moist. Young salamanders (newts) and tadpoles spend several weeks in the water, metamorphosing into adults that will seek land later in the summer. Watch the highways during warm summer rains; the moisture encourages frogs and salamanders to go out foraging.

Snakes spend the summer eating, shedding skin, basking, and avoiding predators. Land snakes may seek deep shade or burrows during the hottest part of the day. Turtles that grow too warm atop their basking logs simply slide into the water to cool down.

MARSH RABBIT

Wildlife Events Calendar—Fall

Birds:

As early frosts begin to kill insects and brown up the vegetation, many birds start to wing their way south, where food resources are still plentiful. Noisy flocks of migrants may descend on your area to feast on wild berries and grain for a few days. One morning when you wake, they will be gone. Wetlands along traditional flyways are great viewing spots, offering food and rest to hundreds of thousands of ducks, geese, and swans.

Mammals:

Hibernators are busy gorging on the fall crop of nuts and berries, gaining fat that they will live on for the next several months. Squirrels, beavers, and chipmunks are stockpiling enough to get them through the coldest days. Male deer and moose, full of the sap of the rut, are pawing and snorting through the woods, neck engorged and antlers itchy with velvet. Once their racks harden, they may lock horns with other males over the right to mate with a doe.

Amphibians and Reptiles:

Frogs and salamanders can be seen moving overland and across roads, heading for their winter quarters (hibernacula). They burrow beneath roots, rocks, or in the mud at the bottom of ponds—deep enough so that frost doesn't reach them and they can keep ice from forming in their tissues. Turtles burrow under ponds and in the soil, while snakes crawl into rock crevices and ant mounds.

MALLARD

Wildlife Events Calendar—Winter

Birds:

The southern United States is a balmy winter home to many of the birds that northerners call "theirs." Some birds remain up north, however, adding color (cardinals), sound (woodpeckers), and vivaciousness (chickadees) to snow-muffled forests. When food supplies in Canada fail, rare "irruptions" of boreal species such as the great gray owl make for exciting birding.

Mammals:

Deep snow sends deer and moose to wind-shielded evergreen swamps, where they tromp down a network of trails for easy travel. Other mammals are curled tail-to-nose in their dens, breathing and metabolizing at a fraction of their normal rates. Look for plumes of water vapor rising like smoke signals from the chimneys of muskrat and beaver lodges. Under the snow, chambers open as the frozen crystals give up their water and begin to shrink. In this subnivean world, moles and shrews scurry along runways, feeding on seeds and paralyzed insects. On the surface, lynx chase snowshoe hares, both running on "snowshoes" of extra fur that grow on their paws.

Amphibians and Reptiles:

Frogs are waiting out winter beneath the ground, breathing through their skin. Those at the bottom of ponds breathe a sort of muddy oxygen. Snakes are hibernating, sometimes in large groups of many kinds of species. Turtles under the ice breathe through their skin and through an all-purpose opening called the cloaca. A lining of sensitive tissues acts like a gill, filtering oxygen out of the muddy water and into their blood.

ARCTIC
SHREW

There are several "shifts" in the wildlife workday. Activity peaks at dawn and dusk, when the "changing of the guard" brings daytime animals in contact with those of the night.

LOOK AT THE RIGHT TIME OF DAY

Daytime. Early and late in the day are the best times to look for wildlife in the summer. High noon is usually too hot for most activity, and many animals are in day beds at this time. This may change in the winter, when some animals shift their activity to the warmest, middle part of the day.

Dusk and Dawn. Activity usually peaks in the twilight hours. Songbirds greet the dawn as night hunters catch one last meal. At this changing of the guard, animals of the daytime and nighttime mingle with those that are active only just at sunrise and sunset. Tracks are fresh, winds are still, and sounds are likely to carry far at this time of day.

Nighttime. A whole world comes alive behind the mask of night. Owls and flying squirrels with their huge, light-gathering eyes are deftly sailing through the air. Four-footed carnivores are zigzagging back and forth, noses pressed to the trail of some hapless prey. Nights with a full moon are especially active. Use the moon as a searchlight or as a backdrop against which you can watch the silhouettes of high-flying migrant flocks.

HOW TO LOOK—NEW WAYS OF SEEING

Once you've mastered the wheres and whens, the real challenge of wildlife watching begins. Now you must learn *how* to look—how to see things beyond your normal set of experiences. In this quest, it's important to use not only your eyes, ears, nose, mouth, and fingertips, but also your imagination. As successful wildlife watchers will tell you: to find an animal, it helps to think like one.

Putting on the Skin of an Animal. Indian hunters used to dress in the skin of the animal they were stalking in order to get close to it. In the same way, you can crawl into an animal's mind to predict how it might behave. What would your day be like if you were a frog or a weasel or a hummingbird? Imagine how you would elude your enemies, stalk prey, find a place to sleep, and protect your young from the elements. Where would you run for shelter? Where would you bury food to last you through the winter? What would you do if a human entered your territory? To help answer these questions, find out as much as you can about an animal's lifestyle—the role it plays in its habitat and what it needs in order to survive. Books like this one are a good place to start, but better yet, get outside and watch animals being themselves in habitats near you.

See the Forest, Not Just the Trees. Watching wildlife is sometimes like being at a three-ring circus. So as not to miss any action, focus on the center ring attraction for a few minutes, then scan the surroundings to get a sense of context. Focusing and expanding every few minutes will enable you to see the whole show, not just a part of it.

What's Wrong with This Picture? Wildlife are intimately familiar with every stick and stone in their territory, and will easily notice something out of place, just as you might notice if someone moved a lamp in your living room. Try to see their world as they do; memorize the backdrop so anything new stands out. Watching how fast leaves fall on a breezy autumn day, for instance, can help you discern something moving at a different speed.

Use Peripheral Vision. Quick. How much of your surroundings can you see without turning your head? Using your peripheral vision outdoors will allow you to notice more, while actually getting you closer to wildlife. Animals are often threatened by a head-on stare, since this gesture signals aggression in most wild codes. Keeping your gaze averted may cause animals to relax or even approach you. To help strengthen your powers of sideways vision, practice seeing colors and distinguishing shapes at the very edge of your sight.

Extend Your Senses. In the early days of natural history study, someone who wanted to identify a bird flying by would simply shoot the specimen. Today, thank goodness, you can get a close look at a living animal, even if it's way across the lake. Technology allows us to see like a hawk, hear what a bat hears, and find our way in the dark like an owl. Here are a few ways to improve on your natural equipment:

Sharper Eyes

Use binoculars, a tripod-mounted spotting scope, or the zoom lens on your camera to bring a distant speck into sharp focus. Most birders use a 7 × 35 or an 8 × 40 power binocular with a central focusing mechanism. The trick to getting a bird in your sights is to (1) find it with your unaided eye, (2) keep watching it as you raise the binoculars to a spot just below your eyes, (3) sight the bird over the top of the barrels, and, (4) without moving your head, bring the binoculars to your eyes.

Use a tilting mirror mounted on a telescoping pole to see the canopy world above you. Be careful not to disturb birds in their nests. Nest snooping is especially hazardous to rare or endangered species!

Better Ears

Use a parabolic reflector and headphones to pick up faint sounds. A tape recorder can capture them so you can bring the sounds of the outdoors indoors.

Keener Nose

Train your dog to follow scent trails and point out animals you may not be able to see.

In the Dark

Cover the end of your flashlight with a red filter (theatrical supply houses often have red gels that work well). Many animals see red as black and will go about their business without noticing your light.

Sprinkle fluorescent powders on the ground along wildlife trails. The tracks they leave with every footfall will show up brightly under a black light.

Underwater

Strap on a mask, snorkle, flippers, or even scuba equipment to get eye-to-eye with aquatic wildlife.

GETTING WILDLIFE TO COME TO YOU

Get a Front Row Seat. Like us, wildlife are creatures of habit. They often use the same trails day after day, and fall into a routine that you can almost set your clock to. Water borders, trail intersections, raised knolls, natural springs, scent stations (where they leave droppings or scent marks), and den sites are likely to be high-traffic areas. Another good place to watch and wait is near the carcass of a large animal. Sit facing an area you haven't walked through; if it is upwind, wildlife may not yet be aware of your presence. Make sure there are shrubs or thick grasses for safe travel; wildlife won't cross unsafe, open areas to get to you. Sit with the sun at your back so the animal has to squint to see you (you'll also get a better photo this way).

Try to Blend In. Remember that wildlife are sensitive to anything new in their surroundings. To minimize your strangeness, dress in natural colors, cover your face and hands (with camouflage netting, gloves, or face paint), and make only slow, measured movements. Be aware that your eyeglasses can glint like a beacon in the sun; cover them somehow or leave them at home. Mask your scent by storing your clothes with a sachet of pine and bayberry (or better yet, natural fragrances from that particular habitat), and avoid scented soap and shampoo. If you sit out in the open to wait, flatten yourself against a tree or rock so your outline is not so obvious. If you stand, make sure a long shadow or your reflection in the water won't betray your presence.

Use the Habitat to Hide You. Find something large enough to hide behind: upturned roots, downed logs, cattail clumps, boulders, etc. To see wetland animals, try wading into a marsh with cattails and other water plants tied onto your clothes. Or, camouflage yourself with leaves and go out on a limb to see warblers, kinglets, vireos, and other canopy birds.

Build a Blind with a View. Once you find a rewarding observation site, try rigging an artificial blind that you can use for the whole season. Place it out at least ten days before you first use it so wildlife will have time to get used to it. When you finally go in, have a friend accompany you. While you duck in, have your friend keep on walking. Wildlife can't count, and if they believe the human presence has passed, they may venture out sooner. A blind up in a tree may give you a good vantage point for watching larger animals that rarely look up for danger.

Do Animal Impersonations. If you don't have a blind, train yourself to sit comfortably, with eyes averted and muscles relaxed. Try "grooming" or "preening" as other large animals do. This "behavioral blind" technique has allowed many large-animal researchers to be accepted as one of the herd. You can also impersonate the call of a bird, and if you're good enough, the bird will respond in kind. It sings to let you (who it thinks is an intruding bird) know that this is its territory. With a baleful enough wail, you might even get a wolf pack to respond. You can also get frogs to chorus by imitating their voices. Tape recordings of animal calls can also be used, but require some caution (see Good Manners Are Good Form, page 42).

Sound the Alarm. Try imitating the alarm call of songbirds by saying the word "pish" a few times through clenched teeth. Curious birds may come to investigate the cry, especially if it's during breeding season when males are quick to defend their territories. Pishing works best when the birds are already giving chip calls, signaling their concern over your presence. Predators such as foxes, raccoons, coyotes, bobcats, owls, and hawks may come running if you imitate the squeaks and squeals of a rodent in its death throes. Kissing or sucking the back of your hand may be just as effective as a store-bought caller. You're liable to get the most response in April, May, and August during the three hours before dark.

Rattle Up a Buck. You'll need a set of deer antlers for this one. Rattle the tines of the antlers together, scrape in the litter, and beat the bushes to imitate the sounds of two bucks fighting for a doe. During the autumn rut, you might get a curious buck to respond to your rattle.

Wave Something Colorful. Animals such as bobcats, ground squirrels, minks, and gray jays are incurably curious. Keeping yourself well hidden, try waving a scrap of colored cloth or a piece of aluminum to lure them into view.

STALKING WILDLIFE

1. Follow in Their Footsteps. Look for wildlife "highways" of all sizes, from vole-sized runways chewed in the grass to well-rutted deer paths. On dewy mornings, look for a dry trail in the grasses. Following these might take you to a favorite feeding ground, a watering hole, or a den.

2. Keep the Wind in Your Face. Smells will be fanned out behind you, rather than into the keen nose of the animal you are walking toward.

3. Keep the Sun at Your Back. The animal will have to squint to see you. If the sun is in your eyes, you may not be able to pick out shapes and colors as easily.

4. Play "Red Light, Green Light." Like the backyard game, wait to move until the signal is green, that is, when the animal is busily engaged in grooming, eating, etc. At the slightest sign that it is listening—tensing,

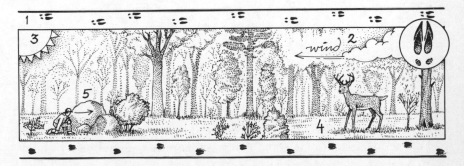

The numbers in the illustration correspond to the stalking tips in the text. Try using these techniques to get close to wildlife without alarming them.

ear twitching, raising its head—you should freeze. When it goes back to its task, you can advance again. You may be able to get within a few feet of a drumming ruffed grouse this way.

5. Move from Hiding Place to Hiding Place. When you do move, keep vegetation between you and the animal so it doesn't see your silhouette. If you take a peek, look around and not over the bush or boulder. Slink low to the ground when on hilltops.

6. Be the Creature from the Black Lagoon. Wildlife won't expect you to be coming from the water (not a typical human habitat). Try floating like a turtle, with just your head above the waterline, to get up close to animals on shore.

READING THE TRACES OF WILD LIVES

Wildlife stories are full of drama—hair-raising tales of chase and capture, braving the elements, and defending their young against all odds. These stories are recorded not only in books but also in the habitats that wildlife visit. The inscriptions are subtle—a shed antler, a drop of blood, the panicky imprint of a wing in the snow. These signs and signatures literally fill forests and meadows, and can tell you much about the sequestered lives around you.

The size, depth, and condition of tracks, for instance, can tell you how large the track-maker was, whether it was limping or running, and if it was alone or in a group. Claw marks and scrapes on the ground are "bulletin boards" where wildlife post messages to one another. Cast-off body parts such as snake skins or antlers tell you something about the age and condition of the animal. Animal droppings can reveal what they've been living on. Soft summer "cowpies" reflect a diet of berries and fruits, while a meat diet will produce droppings filled with hair and bones.

Try piecing together the comings and goings of the wildlife community by looking for the types of clues in the Sign Chart.

GOOD MANNERS ARE GOOD FORM

There's a fine line between just observing wildlife and being intrusive. Even well-intentioned wildlife watchers like you can cross that line without meaning to. Here are some tips to help you admire wild animals without alarming them.

Don't Bankrupt an Animal's Energy. Most animals perceive you as a possible threat. They are willing to let you get just so close before they feel

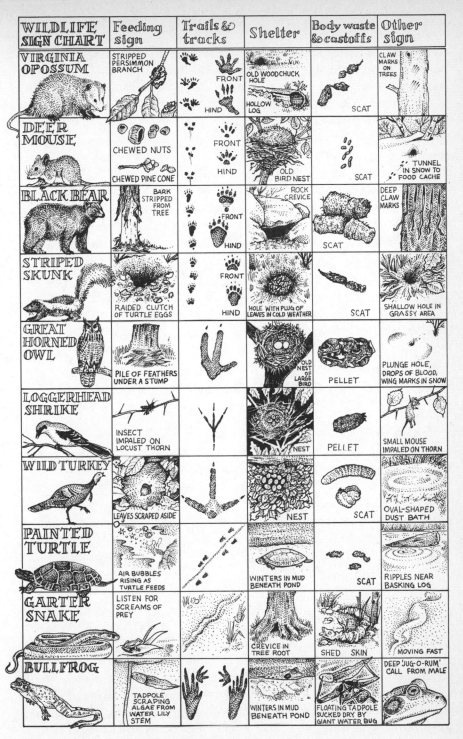

WILDLIFE SIGN CHART	Feeding sign	Trails & tracks	Shelter	Body waste & castoffs	Other sign
VIRGINIA OPOSSUM	STRIPPED PERSIMMON BRANCH	FRONT / HIND	OLD WOODCHUCK HOLE / HOLLOW LOG	SCAT	CLAW MARKS ON TREES
DEER MOUSE	CHEWED NUTS / CHEWED PINE CONE	FRONT / HIND	OLD BIRD NEST	SCAT	TUNNEL IN SNOW TO FOOD CACHE
BLACK BEAR	BARK STRIPPED FROM TREE	FRONT / HIND	ROCK CREVICE	SCAT	DEEP CLAW MARKS
STRIPED SKUNK	RAIDED CLUTCH OF TURTLE EGGS	FRONT / HIND	HOLE WITH PLUG OF LEAVES IN COLD WEATHER	SCAT	SHALLOW HOLE IN GRASSY AREA
GREAT HORNED OWL	PILE OF FEATHERS UNDER A STUMP		OLD NEST OF LARGE BIRD	PELLET	PLUNGE HOLE, DROPS OF BLOOD, WING MARKS IN SNOW
LOGGERHEAD SHRIKE	INSECT IMPALED ON LOCUST THORN		NEST	PELLET	SMALL MOUSE IMPALED ON THORN
WILD TURKEY	LEAVES SCRAPED ASIDE		NEST	SCAT	OVAL-SHAPED DUST BATH
PAINTED TURTLE	AIR BUBBLES RISING AS TURTLE FEEDS		WINTERS IN MUD BENEATH POND	SCAT	RIPPLES NEAR BASKING LOG
GARTER SNAKE	LISTEN FOR SCREAMS OF PREY		CREVICE IN TREE ROOT	SHED SKIN	MOVING FAST
BULLFROG	TADPOLE SCRAPING ALGAE FROM WATER LILY STEM		WINTERS IN MUD BENEATH POND	FLOATING TADPOLE SUCKED DRY BY GIANT WATER BUG	DEEP 'JUG-O-RUM' CALL FROM MALE

Here are some telltale signs of wildlife. With practice, you can learn to read them like calling cards to know which animals are at large in the habitat.

they must take action to defend themselves. Even the simple act of freezing and listening can be taxing. Their heart beats faster, they use up their food faster, and while they are watching you, they lose valuable foraging time. If you get too close for comfort, they will have to flee, which can burn up quite a bit of energy. One disturbance won't harm them, but repeated episodes might begin to cut into energy reserves that they need for raising young or keeping themselves warm. You can help by making your visits short and observing the animals from a distance they consider safe.

Keep Your Distance. How close is too close? If the animal shows the following signs (in ascending order of irritation), you are in the "disturbance range" and should sit quietly or slowly back away. Remember that binoculars and spotting scopes can bridge the distance between the two of you without unnerving the animal.

Birds
• Head raised, looking at you.
• Skittishness.
• Excessive preening, bill wiping, or pecking at food.
• Alarm calls, repeated chirping and chipping.
• Distraction display, e.g., dragging broken wing or spreading tail.

Mammals
• Head raised, ears swiveled toward you.
• Skittishness.
• Moving away or lowering its head, with ears back in preparation for a charge. Hairs on its neck and shoulders may stand up.
• Playing dead.
• Aggressive behavior, e.g., boring its teeth, charging, snorting, or slapping the ground with its paw.

Reptiles
• Hissing or rattling.
• Playing dead.
• Snakes raise their upper body, open their mouth.
• Striking.

Tiptoe Around Nurseries. Nesting animals are especially sensitive to disturbance. As you admire the nest, parents may be hanging back, while eggs chill or nestlings become dangerously hungry. If disturbed often enough, parents may abandon the nest, or young animals may leave before they are ready to fend for themselves. Remember also that predators may be following your scent trail, which takes them to nests they might otherwise have overlooked.

Before approaching a nest, always scan the area with your binoculars to see if the female is around. Use stalking techniques to keep her from being alarmed. If you are taking pictures, don't be tempted to trim back vegetation to get a better shot. The foliage you remove might have been shading the nest or screening it from winged predators. Better to leave the vegetation in place and limit your stay to no more than fifteen minutes.

Turn Rocks and Logs Back Over. When uncovering reptiles and amphibians, be sure to replace the debris you turn over. You're lifting the roof off their home! Leaving them exposed will subject the residents to the elements and predators.

Keep an Eye on Pets. A rambunctious dog or cat can do much damage by chasing wildlife or digging up their eggs, food stores, or burrows.

Cut Motorboat Speed Near Shore. Besides frightening wildlife, a speeding boat can cause serious erosion on shore. Boat wakes are tidal waves to breeding snakes, turtles, salamanders, frogs, emerging hibernators, and wading shorebirds. A whole raft of eggs may be washed away in one crest.

Don't Tempt Wildlife with Food. Bears and other so-called dangerous animals are rarely interested in fighting with you, but they are interested in your food. Never bring it into your tent with you, and before turning in, tie it up between two trees, well out of their reach. Making wildlife dependent on handouts does them no favors, and may lead to their untimely death. What if the next person they approach has a gun instead of a piece of bread?

Don't Be a Hero. There may come a time when you inadvertently get between a mother and its young, or a hungry animal and its dinner. Naturally, this will be seen as a threat. Don't run, and don't stare directly at the animal, as this can be interpreted as aggression on your part. Instead, avert your eyes and back away slowly—the wildland equivalent of "crying uncle."

Respect the Rights of Your Own Species. Many landowners will gladly waive their no trespassing policy if you let them know why you're there. Keep relations smooth by walking the edges of fields rather than through crops. And if you run into other rapt observers, stay still so you don't spook the wildlife they are watching.

HABITAT KEY

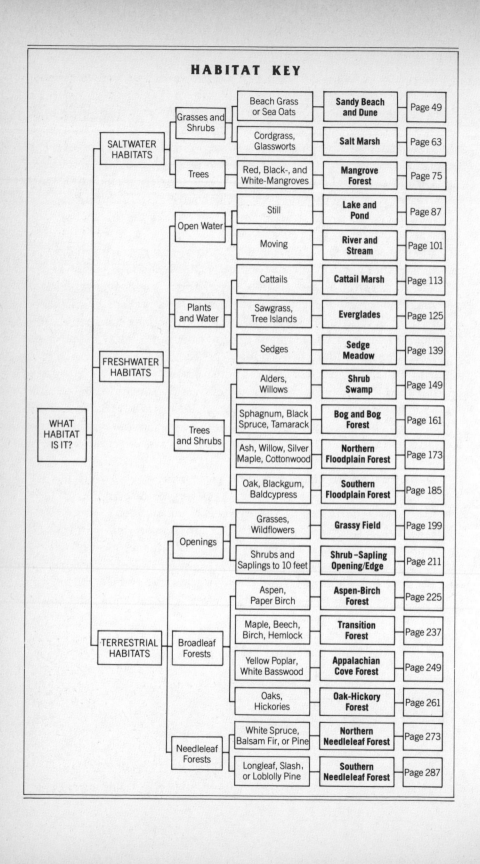

	Grasses and Shrubs	Beach Grass or Sea Oats	**Sandy Beach and Dune**	Page 49
SALTWATER HABITATS		Cordgrass, Glassworts	**Salt Marsh**	Page 63
	Trees	Red, Black-, and White-Mangroves	**Mangrove Forest**	Page 75
	Open Water	Still	**Lake and Pond**	Page 87
		Moving	**River and Stream**	Page 101
	Plants and Water	Cattails	**Cattail Marsh**	Page 113
		Sawgrass, Tree Islands	**Everglades**	Page 125
		Sedges	**Sedge Meadow**	Page 139
FRESHWATER HABITATS	Trees and Shrubs	Alders, Willows	**Shrub Swamp**	Page 149
		Sphagnum, Black Spruce, Tamarack	**Bog and Bog Forest**	Page 161
		Ash, Willow, Silver Maple, Cottonwood	**Northern Floodplain Forest**	Page 173
		Oak, Blackgum, Baldcypress	**Southern Floodplain Forest**	Page 185
	Openings	Grasses, Wildflowers	**Grassy Field**	Page 199
		Shrubs and Saplings to 10 feet	**Shrub–Sapling Opening/Edge**	Page 211
TERRESTRIAL HABITATS	Broadleaf Forests	Aspen, Paper Birch	**Aspen-Birch Forest**	Page 225
		Maple, Beech, Birch, Hemlock	**Transition Forest**	Page 237
		Yellow Poplar, White Basswood	**Appalachian Cove Forest**	Page 249
		Oaks, Hickories	**Oak-Hickory Forest**	Page 261
	Needleleaf Forests	White Spruce, Balsam Fir, or Pine	**Northern Needleleaf Forest**	Page 273
		Longleaf, Slash, or Loblolly Pine	**Southern Needleleaf Forest**	Page 287

WHAT HABITAT IS IT?

WILDLIFE HABITAT PROFILES

DAYTIME   DUSK · DAWN   NIGHT

Dusty Miller

Bayberry

GREAT
BLACK-BACKED
GULL

BLACK
SKIMMER

SANDERLING

Beach Plum

Beach Pea

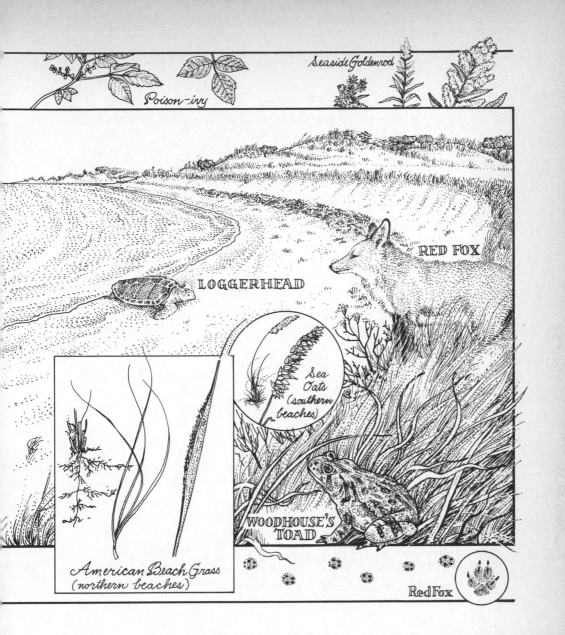

Poison-ivy

Seaside Goldenrod

RED FOX

LOGGERHEAD

Sea Oats (southern beaches)

American Beach Grass (northern beaches)

WOODHOUSE'S TOAD

Red Fox

Sandy Beach and Dune

WHERE TO SEE THIS HABITAT:

Florida: Canaveral and Gulf Islands national seashores; Merritt Island and St. Vincent national wildlife refuges

Georgia: Cumberland Island National Seashore

Louisiana: Delta and Breton National wildlife refuges

Maryland: Assateague Islands National Seashore

Massachusetts: Cape Cod National Seashore; Monomoy, Nantucket, and Parker River national wildlife refuges

New Jersey: Gateway National Recreation Area, Sandy Hook Unit

New York: Fire Island National Seashore; Gateway National Recreation Area, Jamaica Bay Unit

North Carolina: Cape Hatteras and Cape Lookout national seashores; Pea Island National Wildlife Refuge

Rhode Island: Block Island and Ninigret national wildlife refuges

South Carolina: Cape Romain National Wildlife Refuge

Texas: Padre Island National Seashore; San Bernard National Wildlife Refuge

Virginia: Back Bay and Chincoteague national wildlife refuges

Sandy Beach and Dune

BEGINNINGS

Beaches are what mountains become. The grains skittering across your beach blanket were once imprisoned in solid bedrock miles and miles inland. Millions of seasons of rain and snow, freeze and thaw loosed these grains and sent them journeying, via river, glacier, and wind, to the sea. Each day, an endless procession of waves fans up the beach, bringing some of the grains back to dry land.

Imagine that you could somehow mark a single grain of sand and follow it for a day. Early in the morning, the grain is dredged from the sea floor and carried landward in one of the 14,000 roiling waves that strike the beach each day. The wave approaches obliquely, slides up the beach at an angle, and drains straight back to the sea, thus drawing an arc. If the grain is light enough, it will stay suspended in wave after wave, creeping up and along the beach in a series of these arcs. At some point, the grain may be caught in the "longshore current" flowing parallel to the shore.

After many wave trips up the beach and conveyor trips along the coast, your grain may finally be caught by a particularly powerful wave that tosses it far up on the beach. The returning wave sinks into the sands, loses energy, and is not strong enough to drag the grain back. As the tide falls, the wet sand begins to dry out. Once the cohesion of water is gone, a single onshore gust can pluck thousands of grains from their resting place and move them hop by hop up the barrier dunes.

This process, repeated by the trillions, takes sand from one part of the coast and transports it to another. In the meantime, for each grain removed, another is brought in to take its place. New sand arrives daily through rivers and through the action of waves plucking and abrading coastal bluffs.

THE BEACH-BUILDING PLANTS

Beach plants are the lion tamers in this circus of wind, water, and waves. Without them, the restless sand could simply ride the wind inland, smothering everything in its path. Instead, the sand mounds into dunes, and is bound in place by a framework of plant fiber.

A dune begins when an obstruction (a rock, a bit of driftwood, etc.) breaks the stream of wind and causes sand to drop out in the "windshadow" on the leeward side of the object. A seed or a fragment of American beach grass (or sea oats on southern beaches) lands on this dunelet and rapidly sinks its roots. It sends up pointed, vertical blades that arch gracefully away from the stem, forming a drooping green fountain. These blades bring sand-laden winds to a halt, forcing them to drop their cargo around the stem of the plant. As the dune grows higher, so does the plant, apparently stimulated by being buried in sand.

In the meantime, the grass is spreading like an underground wildfire by means of "runners." Every few inches along these horizontal stems, a new tuft of roots gives rise to another clump of sand-stopping grass. Even-

CHARACTERISTIC PLANTS:

Upper Beach:
sea rocket
seabeach sandwort
seaside spurge

Foredune:
American beach grass
beach pea
dusty miller
sea oats
seaside goldenrod

Hollow Between Dunes:
bayberry: northern and southern
beach plum
crowned earthstar
old man's beard
poison-ivy
red crest lichen

Backdune:
beach heather
evergreen bearberry
golden asters
prickly pear cactus
reindeer moss
wild indigo

Dune Thicket and Forest:
cherries
hollies
Japanese honeysuckle
maples
oaks
pitch pine
sassafras
sheep sorrel
wild sarsaparilla

tually, an internal skeleton of roots, runners, and fallen blades crisscrosses the dune and keeps it whole.

Above the sand, the blades must endure near-desert conditions. In the shimmering heat, their edges curl in until the blade is a skinny trough. Long ridges on the surface are squeezed together like the bellows of an accordion, forming a seal over the pores that keeps moisture from escaping.

Other plants that work alongside beach grass are also adapted for the extreme life of the foredune. Dusty miller leaves are covered by fine white hairs that reflect the sun while trapping dew and conserving moisture. Other plants have waxy coverings, or tilt their leaves away from the sun to reduce evaporation. The seaside goldenrod has a thick, knobby stalk that actually stores water for dry times.

In the sheltered hollow behind the foredune, winds are usually not as intense, and woody plants such as southern and northern bayberry and beach plum provide shade for other plants. Older dunes farther inland are carpeted with beach heather, evergreen bearberry, and various lichens such as reindeer moss. Poison-ivy can grow almost anywhere in the back dunes, appearing as a trailing vine or even a woody shrub. Sixty species of birds feed on the berries. Even farther back, where a convex "lens" of fresh groundwater lies above the heavier layer of salt water, sassafras, hollies, pitch pines, oaks, and maples can sink their roots. Even here, their topmost branches can be pruned by salt-spray aerosols, giving rise to the short, sheared "pygmy forests."

WHAT'S IN IT FOR WILDLIFE?

As we humans snooze on the beach, millions of living things are fighting for their lives in the habitat around us. Those closest to the roar of the surf must endure the pounding pressure of breakers, the drag of the backwash, and the alternate wetting and drying caused by the tides. Farther up the beach, there are pelting winds, stinging salt spray, high temperatures, and a very dry surface layer. Add to this the constant changes wrought by storms and seasons, and you have a habitat more challenging than most.

And yet life adjusts and prevails here. Consider the swash, the strip of wet sand that is constantly washed by waves. Each wave brings a fresh buffet of foods to the swash: particles of dead fish, scraps of kelp, bits of shellfish and sponges, innumerable microscopic plants and animals, even swarms of exhausted insects that have blown offshore. Before the wave can drain back to the ocean, an army of organisms picks through this stew. Buried shellfish and worms siphon the water or eat the flooded sand, "seining" for the small edibles hidden there. Hundreds of tiny mole crabs buried around them hoist their feathery antennae in unison. Their timing is critical. They must snag scores of microscopic plants and animals with their antennae, then comb them into their mouths and duck beneath the sand before the wave retreats and exposes them. Sanderlings and plovers are racing the wave back to the sea, hoping to pick up disoriented crabs that don't make it under in time. Another wave is close on their heels, bringing a fresh serving to the swash.

With each wave, a ridge of flotsam is cast up along the high-tide line, looking as if it were swept there by a giant broom. Long-legged sandpipers, turnstones, and plovers regularly cruise these graceful arches, stopping occasionally to pluck a morsel from the tangle of seaweed, driftwood, and shells. Boat-tailed grackles, fish crows, and other scavenger birds feed here too, fighting among themselves for carcasses thrown up on the "graveyard" of the beach. At night, raccoons and striped skunks waddle down from the dunes, sharing the flotsam feast with swarms of sandhoppers—shrimp-like creatures that can number 25,000 to the square meter. When daylight comes, these sandhoppers scurry back to the upper beach, digging into burrows at an astonishing rate. They can drill through 6 feet of sand in 10 minutes, the equivalent of you digging a 60-foot hole with your bare hands in the same amount of time.

In spring, late summer, and fall, throngs of shorebirds visit our beaches while en route to their northern nesting ranges or their southern wintering haunts. Migrant watching can be spectacular, especially on the outermost barrier islands and points like Cape Cod that reach out into the sea. Some birds, such as willets, killdeers, and oystercatchers, stay during the summer along with the ever-present gulls, which you can find all year long.

You'll begin to notice, after watching these birds for a while, that different species concentrate on those zones of the beach to which they are best adapted. Plovers and sandpipers have short bills that are just right for pulling surface burrowers out. Others, such as willets, have long bills for

WILLET

retrieving deeply buried species. American oystercatchers are equipped with blunt, chisellike bills that are perfect for prying open shellfish.

Separate feeding techniques allow birds to use all the food on the beach without too much competition between species. Black skimmers "troll" with their beaks in the water beyond the breakers, while flying terns keep their eyes on the shallows. Gulls fly or stroll along the high-tide mark, looking for crabs and clams that have been jostled from their ocean homes. When herring gulls snag a hard-shelled morsel, they fly off looking for a solid surface on which to crack open their dinner, such as a bed of rocks or even a parking lot. Notice how they gauge their height; they must be high enough to cause the shell to break upon falling, but close enough to be able to retrieve the juicy insides before their hungry counterparts can.

Day and night are separate "zones" as well. Ghost crabs wait in their upper beach burrows until their foes (daytime birds) have roosted for the night. Under cover of darkness, thousands of these comical, sidestepping crabs zigzag down to the sea like lightning streaks, eyes bobbing on periscopelike stalks. Though these crabs live almost entirely on land, they have enduring ties with the sea. Every now and then they have to journey down to the edge of the surf and refill the chamber that keeps their gills moist. If you are quick with a flashlight, you may see them filling up or bringing food to their mouth with both front claws. Once they realize you are there, you'll see why they are called ghost crabs.

Turtles are also in transition between land and sea. Those that live otherwise marine lives must return to the land to dig a hole and lay their eggs. These eggs are relished by land creatures such as raccoons, skunks, foxes, and snakes that journey from the forests to the surf for seaside delicacies.

In between the forest and surf, the grassy dunes provide food and shelter for small ground-dwelling rodents such as meadow voles, meadow jumping mice, and eastern cottontails. Burrowing species such as eastern hognose snakes and Fowler's toads find the loose soil to their liking. Overhead, northern harriers (daytime) and short-eared owls (nighttime) sail in search of this small prey.

In the hollows between dunes, slightly moister conditions may nuture clusters of bog plants and low-growing bushes, which, in turn, provide nesting sites for birds, cover for small rodents, and food for both. Yellow-billed cuckoos and brown thrashers will sometimes fly to dune thickets to feed on tent caterpillars nesting in the black cherries. Migrating American robins and cedar waxwings fatten themselves on cherries, while tree swallows and yellow-rumped warblers head for the bayberries, an important winter food. Poison-ivy berries become important to northern flickers and

BROWN PELICAN · WILLET · PIPING PLOVER · RUDDY TURNSTONE · CASPIAN TERN · SANDWICH TERN · RING-BILLED GULL

WILDLIFE LOCATOR CHART—SANDY BEACH AND DUNE

	Feeds from Air	Feeds in Dunes	Feeds on Wet Sand or Beach	Feeds at High-tide Mark	Feeds in Water
Nests in Tree Canopy or Shrubs	Brown Pelican Osprey	Yellow-billed Cuckoo American Robin Cedar Waxwing		Fish Crow Boat-tailed Grackle	
Nests in Trunk		Downy Woodpecker Northern Flicker		Raccoon	
Nests on Ground	Northern Harrier Gull-billed Tern Caspian Tern Royal Tern Sandwich Tern Common Tern Least Tern Black Skimmer Short-eared Owl	Eastern Cottontail	Black-bellied Plover Wilson's Plover Semipalmated Plover Piping Plover American Oystercatcher Willet Sanderling Semipalmated Sandpiper Dunlin Laughing Gull Ring-billed Gull Great Black-backed Gull	Ruddy Turnstone	
Nests Beneath Ground or Debris		Oldfield Mouse Meadow Vole Meadow Jumping Mouse Six-lined Racerunner Eastern Hognose Snake (also feeds in burrows)	Mole Skink	Island Glass Lizard Red Fox Striped Skunk	Loggerhead
Nests in Fresh Water		Fowler's Toad			

NOTE: *Some animals that feed on beaches and dunes may nest elsewhere.*

downy woodpeckers in the winter when their preferred insect foods are killed by the cold.

Great Black-backed Gull

Gulls have elaborate social lives that will reward you over a lifetime of behavior watching. They feed, rest, and breed in mixed flocks that include herring gulls and terns. From the bird's point of view, there is much to recommend this flocking way of life.

Birds in a flock bask in the safety of numbers. Because more eyes are on the lookout for predators, each bird can safely spend more time with its head down, feeding. Also, large crowds of birds tend to discourage predators that normally wouldn't think twice about accosting a solitary bird. Biologists believe there may also be some information sharing that goes on in roosting flocks. Perhaps gulls notice neighbors that seem fat and satisfied after a day of good eating. Come morning, they are likely to fly off with these birds in hopes of cashing in on a good find.

For the burly black-backed gull, the flock itself can be a source of food. Blackbacks are considerably larger than the birds they flock with, and can easily wrestle a hard-earned meal away from one of the lesser birds. They will sometimes harass a bird in flight, forcing it to drop the morsel from its bill, or even to regurgitate a meal it has already eaten.

At the nesting sites, blackbacks feed like kings on eggs, on young chicks, and even on adult birds sitting on nests. They have been described as ferocious in their attacks, and have enough brawn to take down a full-grown rabbit, or to swallow a nestling in one gulp.

They are equally well equipped to catch food from the sea. Their 5½-foot wingspan carries them high above the water, where they wheel on updrafts, searching below for floating food or schools of fish. Humans have created new feeding grounds for the gulls. Large flocks gather at open dumps or behind commercial fishing vessels, filling the air with their raucous screams and cries. These new food sources have enabled this once Arctic breeder to extend its range southward. Now, blackbacks can be found nesting as far south as the Carolinas.

Look for great black-backed gulls—soaring above water, mud flats, or garbage dumps in pursuit of a meal. Gulls fly with their bills straight out; terns point their bills down. Look for roosting flocks on extensive open areas that give them a good all-around view for early detection of predators.

Length: 28–31 inches.

Look for nests—on coastal islands and high cliffs along the northern coast, or in salt marshes from New Jersey south. The nest is a hollow depression in the ground lined with seaweed, grasses, mosses, feathers, and sticks. The adults feed their young by regurgitating—the red dot on their bill is the "doorbell" that chicks peck at to prompt their parents to open up and feed them.

Listen for—loud, sharp cries or ravenlike croaks, especially on the nesting grounds when they are at their noisiest. Their long drawn-out "keeaaw" is in a lower key than the cry of herring gulls. Also listen for a rapid "kow-kow-kow" and hoarse laughter.

Red Fox

If you're lucky enough to find the sandy den of a red fox family, you'll see the kits roughhousing, chasing each other, and leaping on every leaf that blows by. It looks like sheer play, but is actually a way to rehearse hunting moves that will later determine their survival. One day, the leaf they are leaping on will be a prey animal intent on escape.

Red foxes size up their prey from a distance. Then, from a frozen crouch, they launch into a gracefully arcing leap, landing forepaws-first on a startled vole, frog, or mouse. Foxes can cover 15 feet in one leap—a giant step compared with kangaroos that leap only 3–4 feet and bullfrogs that reach a little over 6 feet.

Foxes' hind legs are long, well muscled, and can be doubled up like a frog's to exert the maximum push-off force for the longest period of time. They are a trim animal, with extra light bones, reinforced in the perforated center much like bird bones are. Their stomach is also small, holding only 1 ounce of meat at a time. This keeps them light, but requires them to eat more often than other carnivores. (Gray wolves, for example, can eat 20 ounces at a sitting and then go for 2 weeks without food.) The noshing fox stores what it can't eat in a cache, returning when its stomach is empty again.

Look for red foxes—emerging from the dune forests at twilight for a night of hunting along the high-tide line. They return at dawn, traveling along the dune thickets for protection. Trotting at 6 miles per hour, they seem to float along like "thistledown on their feet." In late winter, courting foxes travel together, leaving intertwined tracks in the wet sand or snow. In early spring on remote beaches, you may see a female out during the day, searching for food to feed her hungry pups. Try kissing the back of your hand (sounds like a squealing mouse) to coax a curious fox out of hiding.

Length: Head and body, 22–25 inches; tail, 14–16 inches.

Look for dens—at the forest-dune border or deep in the woods, on a well-drained slope with sandy, loamy soil and a nearby source of water. They may dig their own or simply redecorate an abandoned woodchuck burrow. There may be several 10-inch-wide entrance holes, with a sandy apron of soil spilling from them. Young kits, born in the spring, have charcoal-colored coats to blend in with the dark interior of the den. At five weeks, when they begin to venture out onto the apron for play, buff-colored fur replaces the charcoal. Use your binoculars to watch the growing family; coming too close may cause the female to move her young, a costly use of her energy. After the foxes have finished raising the family, study the apron to find the bones of prey, hair, feces, and tracks.

Look for day beds—patches of worn-down vegetation in overgrown ditches, thickets, long grass, or among tangled tree roots. In the winter, foxes look for sunny spots that will warm them.

Look for food caches—mounds of meat 6–12 inches across, covered with grass, leaves, or snow.

Look for scat, urine, and fur—along fox trails at raised bare spots, gaps in hedges, forest edges, or other conspicuous spots. The scat is 2–3 inches long, twisted, and pointed at both ends. Unlike scats of domestic dogs, fox droppings contain bone chips and hair. Look for balls of fur that foxes "comb" from their coats while grooming.

Look for tracks—a perfectly dotted line, with each four-clawed paw placed in front of the other. You may see an occasional brush mark from the tail. Foxes have a series of established routes: water jumps where they always cross a creek, or trails leading to dens, food caches, or favorite hunting places. Fox tracks are more no-nonsense than domestic dog tracks. Our pets tend to wander and romp more in the woods, perhaps because they don't have to worry about enemies or catching their dinner. Foxes are conscious of saving their energy, and will travel along ridges or trails so as to avoid obstacles such as deep snow or wet swamp. To help you "read" their trails, remember that foxes usually beeline straight ahead when traveling between two points, zigzag when they hunt, and circle around when they are looking for a place to sleep.

Listen for—whimpering, chirring, and whining of courting foxes. They may stand on their hind legs, performing a sort of dance with one another. Fighting foxes also stand on their hind legs, placing their forepaws on each other's shoulders and screaming with open mouths. These pushing, screaming matches may last 15 minutes, until one of the foxes gives up and skulks away. This ritualized combat allows the foxes to establish territory, but is a lot less risky then actual bloodletting. Listen also for a barking "wo-wo-wo" issued by the male when traveling and staking out his territory in late winter. Mates will trade softer yaps to keep in contact with one another when traveling.

Loggerhead

At one time, certain Atlantic and Gulf coast beaches between New Jersey and Texas were scenes of massive egg-laying rituals. Huge loggerhead turtles, weighing as much as half a ton, would lumber onto beaches by the hundreds, each digging their pear-shaped egg chambers and depositing up to 125 eggs at a time. Today, these large spectacles occur only on remote island beaches. You can still see loggerheads nesting on our popular beaches, but not as abundantly as they once did. There are several factors that combined to discourage them.

Shrimping boats off our shores once tangled many a turtle in their trawls. Those turtles that managed to reach the beaches found dangers that evolution had not prepared them for. In many areas, tourists photographed the egg-laying amid bright lights, and merchants collected the eggs for morning market. In resort towns, beach cleaning machines trampled the delicate nests nightly, while beach dredgers buried them under layers of pumped sand. Today, through the efforts of conservationists, the few turtles that still use our shores are largely protected from such horrors.

When the young turtles hatch and scratch out of their underground nests, they are possessed by what has been called "travel frenzy." (Even when hatched indoors, baby turtles will swim against the side of tubs for hours on end.) They are genetically programmed to get to the sea as soon as possible to avoid the beaks, claws, and teeth of land predators. Millions of years on dark beaches taught them to head to the most brightly lit object they could see—the ocean. These days, floodlit condominums are far brighter than the sea, leading thousands of baby turtles to highways, back porches, and parking lots.

Those few that manage to head in the right direction swim straight out for days, nourished by a yolk sac that they are born with. For many years, scientists could not figure out how the baby turtles were finding enough to eat in the open sea, where floating food can be scattered over vast distances. How did these tiny creatures survive once their "packed lunches" were exhausted?

By interviewing deep-sea anglers, the scientists began to gather clues. Anglers often saw tiny turtles in the floating mats of sargasso weed that form huge driftlines hundreds of miles off our coast. These mats form at the junction of two different bodies or currents of water. Where the bodies collide, a sinking or downwelling occurs, and this draws in all floating objects from miles around. Plankton, fish, and other organisms crowd together in the surface layers of this "front," providing a stable feast for the tiny turtles, even where sargasso is not available. Something else collects at these driftlines, however, causing biologists deep concern. Bobbing along with the turtles for miles and miles is a slick of styrofoam cups, plastic trash bags, bottles, and other artifacts of our "disposable" society.

Look for loggerheads—coming ashore at night to lay eggs, once or twice a year. They may also be seen swimming in bays and other inshore waters. They row with their front flippers in unison, achieving a kind of "aquatic flying" at speeds of 18.6 miles per hour, as fast as humans can run.

Shell length: 31–48 inches.

Don't disturb nests—or nesting females! The process of laying 100 or more eggs can take up to a half hour. The female drops each egg onto her hind flipper, and then gently lowers it into the nest. For years, scientists have been giving some turtles a "helping hand" by collecting eggs and incubating them at uniform temperatures. Recently, they realized that cool nesting temperatures (below 82.4 degrees F) produce all males, and warm nests (above 89.6 F) produce all females. Mother loggerheads, light-years ahead of modern science, have always spread their eggs around in the nest to ensure variable temperatures and, thus, a good mix of males and females.

Listen for—the hissing of an enraged female. This means you are too close for her comfort. If you try to move her at this point, you're likely to be slashed by her shell-sharp flippers.

SIX-LINED RACERUNNER

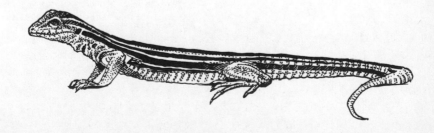

 SHORT-EARED OWL  NORTHERN HARRIER

SNOWY EGRET

CLAPPER RAIL

MARSH RICE RAT

Saltmarsh Cordgrass

Glasswort

Sea Lavender

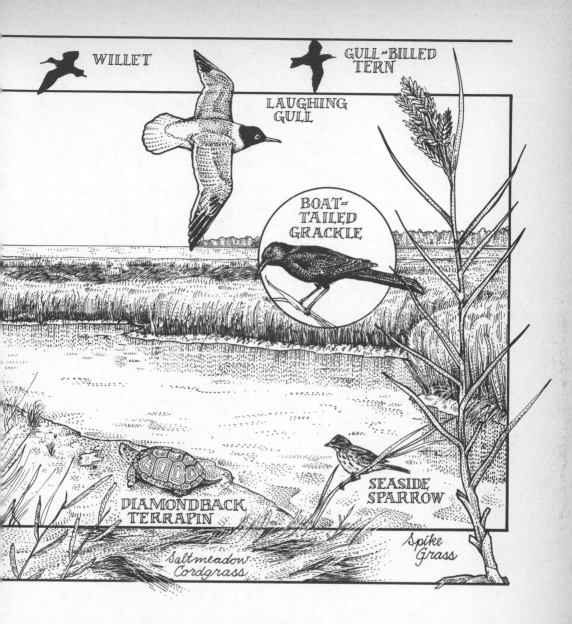

WILLET

GULL-BILLED TERN

LAUGHING GULL

BOAT-TAILED GRACKLE

DIAMONDBACK TERRAPIN

SEASIDE SPARROW

Saltmeadow Cordgrass

Spike Grass

Salt Marsh

WHERE TO SEE THIS HABITAT:

Connecticut: Salt Meadow National Wildlife Refuge

Delaware: Bombay Hook and Prime Hook national wildlife refuges

Florida: Chassahowitzka, Merritt Island, St. Marks, and St. Vincent national wildlife refuges; Gulf Islands National Seashore

Louisiana: Sabine National Wildlife Refuge

Maine: Rachel Carson National Wildlife Refuge

Maryland: Assateague Islands National Seashore; Blackwater National Wildlife Refuge

Massachusetts: Cape Cod National Seashore; Parker River National Wildlife Refuge

New Jersey: Barnegat and Brigantine national wildlife refuges

North Carolina: Alligator River and Pea Island national wildlife refuges; Cape Hatteras and Cape Lookout national seashores

South Carolina: Cape Romain National Wildlife Refuge

Texas: Aransas National Wildlife Refuge

Virginia: Back Bay and Chincoteague national wildlife refuges

Salt Marsh

BEGINNINGS

Salt marshes fill the gap between the salty, wave tossed ocean and the quiet, fresher waters inland. They are a familiar sight in the sheltered lagoons behind barrier islands or near estuaries where rivers flow into the sea. Sediment is washed into these holding tanks by sea tides or rivers and settles to form a muddy or sandy floor.

In the case of estuaries, the floor can build up quickly. Some rivers of the mid-Atlantic carry a million tons of sediment a year to their mouth, and in fierce storms, many carry that much in a day. When the river slows, it drops the sediment in a wide fan. Likewise, when incoming ocean tides reach the quiet waters behind barriers, they too drop fine suspended particles. Thus, the sand or mud flat gradually builds up and spreads out.

During part of the day, the flat is covered by water (look for gulls standing or moving about on these submerged flats, as if they are walking on water). When the tide drops, the flat is exposed to the open air. The remains of algae and other marine organisms begin to decay in the sun, fertilizing the flat and making it ripe for a special class of plants called "halophytes" that can tolerate tidal flooding, waterlogged soil, and a highly salty water source. The first halophyte to colonize the flat and transform it into a marsh is saltmarsh cordgrass.

You'll find the tallest specimens of saltmarsh cordgrass growing along the bay's edge (the "low marsh") and along the tidal creeks that braid their way through the marsh. Here, the pulse of tides flushes away debris from the plant's base and brings in nutrients and oxygen that stimulate growth. Behind these 6-foot blades, a shorter growth form of the same species grows to just 1½ feet tall.

Farther back from the incoming tides, in the "high marsh" zone, a different *Spartina* species called saltmeadow cordgrass forms a low, dense carpet. You can recognize it by its tendency to lay flat in swirled clumps called "cowlicks." Unlike the front-line cordgrass that is constantly cleansed by the tides, the remains of dead saltmeadow cordgrass do not get washed out to sea. Last year's growth remains like a mulch at the base of the current crop, keeping the ground moist and providing protected runways for many small rodents.

Shallow dips in the marsh often fill with water when tides are extremely high. When the tide falls, the water stranded in these pools may sink into the soil or evaporate, leaving a crystalline coating of salt on the soil. These depressions, called salt pans, are characterized by concentric rings of special vegetation that can tolerate these highly salty conditions. The fleshy-stemmed glassworts are the most prominent, especially in winter, when they turn bright red. Also look for widgeon grass growing in more permanent pools.

Farther up, where only the highest tides lick, black grass (actually a rush) forms the official inland boundary of the marsh. Its black fruit darkens the border of the marsh throughout summer and fall. Farther back still is a zone affected only by a spray of salt. Flowering plants such as swamp rose mallow, salt-marsh pink, marsh thistle, and eastern bacharris lend splashes of color to the scene. Beyond this (on dry land), black, northern red, and "scrub" oaks can get established, along with pitch pine, beach plum, and bayberries.

COPING WITH CHANGE

The dominant theme in all salt marsh life is the regular waning and waxing of the tides that alternately submerge or expose the moist soil. "Spring" tides occur twice a month, when the earth, moon, and sun are all in a line. At this time, water seems to spring from the earth (hence the name) as the tides cover even the upper marsh. The inland edge of the marsh is marked by how far up these spring tides come. Throughout the month, two high tides and two low tides occur every day. All marsh life is adapted to feed, move, rest, and nest in rhythm with these tides.

The air-breathing coffee bean snail, for instance, climbs the stem of the cordgrass twice a day, staying just ahead of the rising tide. Birds that dine on the rising and falling snails use the shell to help grind up food in their stomach. Flying insects that are in the "grounded" stage between nymph and adult must also climb up and down the stalks to avoid the high water. This gives insect-eating birds such as wrens and swallows a convenient buffet during high tide.

The flip side of this flooding is the phenomenon of dry-down, which occurs when the tide goes out. Suddenly, animals that have been bathed in 50-degree water may have to survive temperatures of 90 degrees on the sun-baked mud flats. They might also experience changes in the amount of salt in the water. A major storm can bring in large volumes of fresh river water in a matter of hours. In other parts of the marsh, conditions may remain extremely salty. Those depressions farthest from the sea collect water only during very high tides, and, as the pools dry down, the remaining water becomes saltier and saltier.

Marsh animals must somehow get rid of this salt before it builds up in their bodies and poisons them. Birds have special nasal glands through which they "blow brine." Salty drops flow down grooves to the end of

CHARACTERISTIC PLANTS:

Low Marsh:
rockweeds
saltmarsh cordgrass
   (tall and short
   growth forms)

High Marsh:
black grass
black needlerush
   (south)
marsh elder
marsh orach
salt marsh arrow
   grass
salt marsh aster
saltmarsh bulrush
saltmeadow cordgrass
sea blites
sea lavender
seashore alkali grass
seaside gerardia
seaside goldenrod
spike grass

Salt Pans:
blue-green algae
glassworts
sea milkwort
seaside gerardia
seaside plantain

Salt Pools:
widgeon grass

Inland Edge:
Trees and Shrubs:
American holly
beach plum
common winterberry
eastern bacharris
inkberry
oaks: black, red, and
   "scrub"
sweet gale (north)

Herbaceous Plants:
hedge bindweed
marsh elder
marsh thistle
poison-ivy
red fescue
reeds
salt-marsh pink
seashore mallow
slough grass
swamp rose mallow
switch grass
wood sage
   (germander)

Sea Lavender

their beaks, and are then whisked away in the characteristic "headshake." Turtles "cry" out the salt through special tear glands.

Even though the water is salty, there is always a threat of freezing over in northern marshes. Small fish and other marine life usually burrow beneath the mud before the water reaches the freezing point. Others remain active under the lowering ceiling of ice. If the freeze lasts for several weeks, these organisms begin to feel the pinch of reduced oxygen supplies. Only the healthiest and most tolerant will survive.

When the frozen ice slabs finally break up, they move like bulldozers across the marsh, moving great slabs of marsh peat and shearing plants down to stubble. All is not lost, however, because the roots of these plants remain alive. In the spring, they send forth new growth nourished by the mulch of sheared plant parts. If one of the sheared fragments lands on a fertile mud flat, it can even start to take root! The same plant can multiply by sending out underground stems that emerge as new plants on the surface.

WHAT GOOD IS A SALT MARSH?

Despite the challenges of salt marsh living, many creatures (including us) depend heavily on the services the salt marsh performs. It's a fish nursery, a wave buffer, a water purifier, an oxygen pump, and a food pantry to a menagerie of wildlife. Perhaps the best way to appreciate these services is to imagine a world without them.

In a world without salt marshes, there would be no storage tanks for flood waters, and less of a buffer between the mainland and violent ocean waves. Gone too would be the water-purifying capabilities of the marsh sediment—its ability to move compounds such as copper out of a solution when they reach toxic levels, and then release them to the water when they are in short supply.

Salt marshes produce 10 tons of organic matter per acre per year, which is twice as productive as most of our farms. Without these "bread baskets of the coast," hundreds of thousands of waterfowl would have no place to fuel up during migration. Likewise, the floating food that salt marshes "export" to surrounding bays would be sorely missed by the millions of living creatures that depend on it.

Salt marshes are also excellent nurseries. The southeastern coastal marshes alone produce an estimated 800,000 ducklings annually. More than three-fourths of all the shellfish and seafood we harvest spend their early lives in a salt marsh. These spawning and rearing areas are equally important to other organisms. Per acre of lost marsh, we'd lose one million fiddler crabs, thousands of ribbed mussels, and untold numbers of invertebrate species such as insects. The food chains that are built on the backs of these creatures would quickly unravel, affecting whole populations both inside and outside the marsh.

WHAT'S IN IT FOR WILDLIFE?

Much of the wildlife activity in the marsh takes place in and around the tidal creeks. Fresh food is brought in twice daily, and the tall saltmarsh cordgrass along the banks provides ample shelter for wary birds like rails. Hoards of fiddler crabs scrabble about on the banks, providing a staple entree for many marsh animals, including wading birds, shorebirds, diamondback terrapins, and raccoons. Long-legged egrets and herons stand ankle deep in the water, waiting for dinner to swim by. Muskrats often bring mussels up on the banks to eat before returning to their lodges or bank burrows. Minks prowl the banks at night, ducking in occasionally for a fish or muskrat meal.

Farther back from the creeks, waterfowl find the energy they need for their migratory flights in marshy pools and stands of cordgrass. Spike grasses and bulrushes are important seed sources for dabbling ducks, scaups, snow and Canada geese, American coots, and rails. Muskrats eat the entire rush plant. Spike grass is eaten by Canada geese, northern shovelers, and blue-winged teals. Seeds of cordgrasses are important to American black ducks, seaside sparrows, and sharp-tailed sparrows. Underground stems (rhizomes) of cordgrasses are heavily consumed by Canada geese and tundra swans in winter, and by snow geese during spring migration. Look for empty areas called "eat outs," where most of the cordgrass has been removed.

Widgeon grass, a submerged plant that grows in marshland pools, is particularly valuable because all of its parts are edible; it constitutes a large part of the diet of Canada geese, brants, coots, scaups, and many dabbling ducks. The fleshy roots of sago pondweed, also growing in pools, make up half the diet of canvasbacks and are also enjoyed by a variety of other ducks, swans, and geese. Sago seeds are eaten by shore and marsh birds, while the greenery is relished by muskrats.

The high marsh, up above the regular inundation of tides, may be dry enough to provide ground nesting for some of the shorebirds, such as willets, that you see in the sandy beach habitat. Meadow voles race along the ground here, trying to stay secreted from the eyes of aerial hunting birds such as northern harriers and short-eared owls. Even higher up, the shrubby transition plants attract swarms of insects and provide food and nesting sites for many birds.

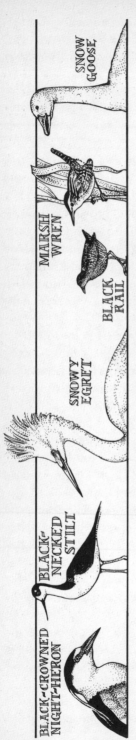

BLACK-CROWNED NIGHT-HERON · BLACK-NECKED STILT · SNOWY EGRET · MARSH WREN · BLACK RAIL · SNOW GOOSE

WILDLIFE LOCATOR CHART—SALT MARSH

	Feeds from Air	Feeds on Ground	Feeds While Standing in Water (Wades)	Feeds from Surface of Water (Dives or Dabbles)	Feeds Underwater (Swims)
Nests in Tree Canopy		Cattle Egret Raccoon	Snowy Egret Green-backed Heron Black-crowned Night-heron Yellow-crowned Night-heron Glossy Ibis		
Nests on Ground	Northern Harrier Short-eared Owl	Black Rail Clapper Rail Willet Laughing Gull Sharp-tailed Sparrow Seaside Sparrow	Greater Yellowlegs Lesser Yellowlegs	Snow Goose* Brant* Canada Goose* American Black Duck Mallard* Red-breasted Merganser (*also feeds on ground)	Atlantic Salt Marsh Snake Carolina Salt Marsh Snake
Nests Beneath Ground or Debris		Northern Short-tailed Shrew Least Shrew Marsh Rabbit Marsh Rice Rat Meadow Vole			Diamondback Terrapin Mink
Nests in Vegetation or Mound Above Water	Forster's Tern	Marsh Wren Boat-tailed Grackle (also nests in shrubs)	American Bittern Black-necked Stilt	Canvasback American Coot	Muskrat

NOTE: *Some animals that feed in salt marshes may nest elsewhere.*

Clapper Rail

If the salt marsh had an orchestra, this bird would be its lead instrument. The infamous "voice of the marsh" sounds like old-fashioned clappers, and any loud noise, such as an airplane or your laughter, may trigger a "clapping" thoughout the marsh. The rails need this distinctive vocal signature because they can't see each other in the dense jungle of grass blades. Without a way to keep in contact, the vegetation that hides them so well from predators would suddenly become a liability.

Other adaptations to their habitat are strong, muscled legs and feet that are specially built for walking. Three toes point forward, and one raised toe points backward, acting as a brace. Their bodies are deep but narrow (the inspiration for the phrase "thin as a rail") enabling them to slip between tightly spaced stalks. The short, rounded wings add very little bulk, but perform admirably when the rail is migrating or flushing from its hiding place.

Rails are also well adapted to change. Although the salt marsh is lavishly appointed with edible plants, animals, and water, its tides make it somewhat unpredictable. Nesting, for instance, takes some forethought. Clapper rails place their nests high above normal tides on a woven platform in the cordgrass. Sometimes, despite their planning, a flood tide may sweep into the creeks and rise dangerously close to the eggs.

When it does, the clappers go into high gear. They rush around, nearly tipping over backward with the exertion of tugging grasses out of the ground. They use these grasses to jack up the nest, often saving the eggs just in the nick of time. During peak tides, clappers show themselves to be surprisingly good swimmers, despite the fact that their feet are not webbed. When water covers their creekside cupboards, they swim to higher parts of the marsh where food is still accessible.

Look for clapper rails—hiding in the tall cordgrass along tidal creeks or searching for food on the banks. They eat fiddler crabs, mollusks, worms, fish, aquatic insects, and other marine animals. Watch while they declaw a fiddler crab—grasping the base of the large claw with their beak, they vigorously shake their head until the claw flies one way and the body another. Rails are usually secretive, but may be forced into view by high tides. At these times, look for them swimming across marsh creeks, crossing marsh roads, or floating on boards. At low tide, they sometimes wander out from the marsh edge to bathe in shallows or forage on mud banks. True to their nickname, "marsh hens" bob their head and twitch their tail as they walk. When they fly, they stay low and dangle their legs.

Length: 14–16 inches.

Look for nests—on the ground in 3- to 4-foot-high saltmarsh cordgrass. The 8- to 10-inch-wide saucer or bowl of dead marsh grasses is set up high on a grass clump, holding eggs about 1 foot above normal high tide. Some nests are domed over with interlocked green blades, rising another foot above the nest. This awning protects the eggs from sunlight and predators.

Look for runways—beaten-down trails in the grass leading to and from the nest.

Look for pellets—small clumps of indigestible material (fish bones, crab shells, etc.) that the rails cough up. Often feeding debris and tracks are nearby.

Look for tracks—chickenlike marks on the muddy shores of creeks, splattered with white droppings the size of a half-dollar.

Listen for—a potpourri of sounds—clacks, grunts, groans, and shrieks. The most well-known call, given just after dawn, shortly before dusk, and more often in the breeding season, is a hoarse, chattering "kek-kek-kek-kek-kek-kek." A surprised group of these birds sound like guinea fowls, giving guttural "rack-k-k-rack-k-k-k" calls that may go on for several minutes.

Marsh Rice Rat

Most people don't think of rats as being particularly clean animals, but in fact, marsh rice rats are downright fastidious about their personal grooming. One early biologist said he'd never seen a small animal "so solicitous of its toilet." This thorough grooming may be a way for rice rats to maintain the water-repellent quality of their fur.

Marsh rice rats swim underwater with ease, reaching down to snip the tender parts of aquatic plants. They also eat crabs, fruits, the eggs of marsh wrens, muskrat carcasses, mice, insects, snails, and an underground fungus called *Endogone*. After a particularly heated fight between two marsh rice rats competing for the same space or mate, the victor may really spice up its diet by eating the vanquished!

Rice rats have a great capacity to reproduce. Females are sexually mature at 4 weeks old, and can become pregnant again a mere 10 hours after giving birth to a litter. Their lives are usually cut short before they can reach the 7 litters/year mark that they are capable of, however. Most live only long enough to have 3–4 litters of 1–7 young—still a sizable legacy. For predators such as northern harriers, barn and barred owls, cottonmouths, raccoons, red foxes, and minks, the more rice rats the merrier.

Look for marsh rice rats—creeping in the cordgrass or swimming in tidal creeks and pools. They may be active at any time, but are most active at night. Be very quiet when stalking rice rats; the slightest noise in their territory will send them scurrying out of sight.

Length: Head and body, 4³/₄–5¹/₅ inches; tail, 4¹/₃–7¹/₅ inches.

Look for feeding platforms—bent-over stalks of cordgrass, covered with the remains of crabs.

Look for runways—at the base of marsh plants where rice rats habitually travel.

Look for nests—well-concealed, woven balls of grass, 12–18 inches in diameter, in slight depressions on high ground or suspended from vegetation. In areas subject to frequent flooding, nests may be as high as 3 feet above the ground. In drier areas, the rats may move into a ground burrow.

Look for tracks—in soft mud or dust. The hindprint (⅜ inch) has 5 toes, but the foreprint, which is smaller, has only 4 toes.

Diamondback Terrapin

Floating straight up and down, with only its nostrils piercing the surface, this turtle hunts in the tidal creeks and sloughs of the salt marsh. It moves without a ripple, sneaking up on snails and clams, then grinding them between powerful jaws.

For many years, the diamondback terrapin was hunted for its delicate meat. In the Chesapeake Bay alone, 45,000 turtles a year wound up in the soup terrines of area restaurants. Today, thanks to protective legislation and reduced demand, diamondbacks have rebounded in many areas.

The turtles take great pains to protect themselves during egg laying, when they are most vulnerable to predators. The females wait until high tide, then climb up onto land to dig their nest pit. By choosing a spot above the highest tide, they make sure their eggs won't be swamped. In addition, the high water floats them close to the spot, so they don't have to travel very far overland. Their nests are usually located on gentle, stable slopes with just the right amount of vegetation—enough to prevent erosion (which would uncover the eggs), but not enough to clog the soil with roots that would be hard to dig through.

Despite the turtle's precautions, predators such as foxes and crows are bound to find and dig up a large percentage of the eggs. Laughing gulls may even perch on the edge of the nest, feasting on the eggs as soon as they are laid. If disturbed when laying, a female will wait a few hours, then move to another nest to try again. Over a year, she will lay up to 35 eggs, 4–12 at a time.

Look for diamondback terrapins—basking on mud flats or prowling grassy lowlands during low tide in search of insects. They drift in creeks with only the tip of their snout exposed.

Shell length: Males, 4–5½ inches; females, 6–9⅜ inches.

Don't disturb nests—triangular cavities, 4–8 inches deep, dug at the sandy edge of marshes and dunes.

Black-mangrove

SWAMP RABBIT

ROSEATE SPOONBILL

MUDSKIPPER

CROWN CONCH

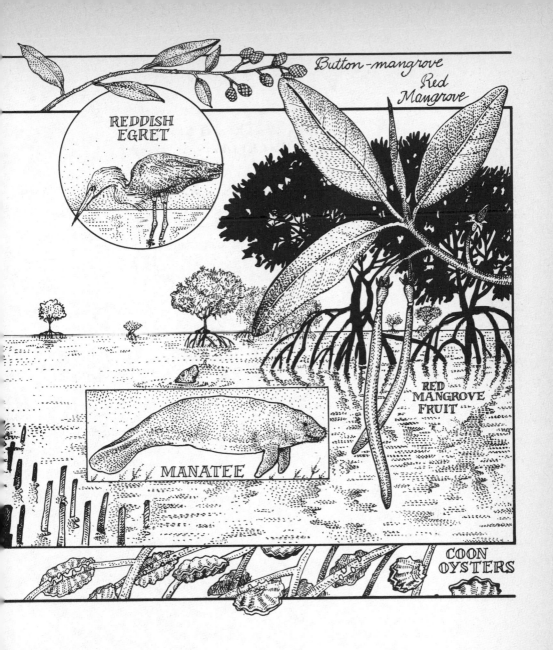

Button-mangrove

Red Mangrove

REDDISH EGRET

RED MANGROVE FRUIT

MANATEE

COON OYSTERS

Mangrove Forest

WHERE TO SEE THIS HABITAT:

Florida: Biscayne and Everglades national parks; Chassahowitzka, Great White Heron, J. N. "Ding" Darling, Florida Keys, and Merritt Island national wildlife refuges

Mangrove Forest

BEGINNINGS

Millions of years ago, the first green plant left the sea to begin its career on land. Since then, countless varieties of land plants have evolved, including one called the red mangrove that is busy working its way *back* to the sea. In the process, it's keeping mapmakers busy by reshaping the southern margin of our continent.

Rather than finding suitable land and invading it, the red mangrove manufacturers land where there was none before. At first, it has very little company, because most plants can't tolerate the stinging saltiness or the powerful wave action at the land's edge.

Part of their pioneering genius is the way mangroves distribute their offspring. Instead of dropping seeds to the ground like other trees, the mangrove's seed develops while it is still attached to the tree. The cigar-shaped seedling grows 10 inches long before it drops off. If it falls while the tide is out, the pointed root end will spear the soft mud at the mangrove's base and begin to drive home its anchoring roots within hours.

If the tide is full, the seedling will land in water and begin its journey away from the parent plant, a captive of tides and waves for weeks or months at a time. At first, it floats on its side, keeping its bud cool while exposing its green cells to the sun so it can make food. When the tiny future tree begins to grow, its center of gravity changes and the root end sinks downward, tipping the seedling into a vertical position. Eventually it will nudge up against a spit of land and become embedded. With each rise and fall of the tide, the seedling is pushed deeper into the sediments, until it can withstand the motion without pulling out. In a phenomenal spurt of growth, its roots arch out and downward from its stem, forming a circle of proplike projections that absorb nutrients and oxygen. As the tree grows, its roots arch farther and farther out, forming a wide horizontal mat that sits atop the mud and helps keep the mangrove from tipping in tropical storms.

This tangle of roots acts like a sieve, slowing the seawater down and straining sediments from it. Particle by particle, sand, clay, and silt begin to pile up around the roots, along with bits of coral, shells, driftwood, seaweed, sponges, etc. In this way, the mangrove builds a shoal of land on which other mangroves can get started. Within several decades, a forest is erected, substantial enough to withstand the pounding surf and storm-tossed tides.

As the surface rises and becomes more landlike, it becomes less suitable for red mangroves. They advance farther into the sea, leaving behind rich, organic soils that are better suited to other kinds of trees. Black-mangroves fill in behind the pioneering reds, followed by white-mangroves, button-mangroves, and tropical hardwoods.

NOT A DROP TO DRINK—LIFE IN SALT WATER

Humans have been busy for centuries trying to find an economical way to desalinate water, a trick that mangroves have already mastered. Some

CHARACTERISTIC PLANTS:

Trees:	Patches of Tropical Forest:	Herbaceous Plants:
black-mangrove	Bahama lysiloma	cattails
button-mangrove	false-mastic	glassworts
cabbage palmetto	Florida fishpoison-tree	sawgrass
red mangrove	Florida nectandra	sea-grape
white-mangrove	Florida strangler fig	sedges
	gumbo-limbo	
	inkwood	
	milkbark	
	paradise-tree	
	sweetbay	
	West Indies mahogany	
	willow bustic	
	wingleaf soapberry	

species have walls around each root cell that act as ultrafilters, letting in mostly fresh water. Traces of salt that sneak in are stored in special leaves that are periodically shed. Others, such as black-mangroves, tolerate high amounts of salt water in their tissues, finally expelling it through unique salt-secreting glands.

The fresh water that mangroves "capture" is understandably precious. To prevent water vapor from escaping through the leaves, tiny surface pores called stomata close down occasionally. In addition, the leaves themselves are succulent (fleshy) so the trees can store water in them for later use. Needless to say, the unique adaptations of mangroves have earned them a habitat of their own, with few competitors to hamper them.

BREATHING IN MUD

In the waterlogged mud of the swamp, water takes up space that would normally be filled with air. This makes the soil very low in oxygen—yet another challenge for the mangroves. By looking at the different kinds of roots they grow, you can learn to identify different species of mangroves, and know something about the land they are sitting on.

Red mangroves, which live in the wettest and least stable environments, have flying buttress type roots that keep them from tipping over. The surface of the roots is covered with tiny, air-breathing openings called lenticels. Inside, extra-large air tubes shuttle this oxygen to the rest of the plant. Black-mangroves, which live farther from the edge, don't need the elaborate arches for support, but still need aerial breathers. They grow a garden of vertical stalks that look like spikes, also laden with lenticels. White-mangroves grow even farther back on soil that is by now somewhat aerated. They therefore don't have aerial roots, depending instead on tiny root hairs just under the surface of the ground.

WHAT'S IN IT FOR WILDLIFE?

Along the storm-driven, salt-scoured coast, mangroves offer a relatively safe and fruitful haven for many kinds of wildlife, including a good number of tropical species. Many species of insects, waterbirds, and lizards have floated or flown to these forests from their ancestral home in the West Indies. The mixture of temperate species feeding on tropical ones is unique indeed, and just another reason to visit this exciting habitat.

The best way to see the various habitats within the mangrove forest is to travel the winding waterways by boat. Start by examining the roots that rise up like bristles or arch down like buttresses. Tides swirl around these roots, bringing in a twice-daily supply of tiny plants and animals to feed the young shellfish, shrimp, crabs, and fish that lurk in the tangle. Clinging to the prop roots are oysters, sponges, sea squirts, hydroids, sea anemones, and crustaceans. At night, when the tide is out, raccoons creep down to the root line to feast on the moist meat of the oysters. The beautiful crown conch feeds on them too.

Rain-filled holes in the roots harbor wriggling mosquito and midge larvae that attract birds. If you're lucky, you may see a fish called the mudskipper climbing on the roots, using its tail and fins as a makeshift set of legs. You can anticipate the tides by looking for the mangrove snail, which climbs the mangrove's trunk each day just before the tides to get beyond the reach of water-bound predators such as crabs and fish.

The protected pools and channels that snake through the forest are nurseries for fish and shellfish, refuges for American alligators, and feeding grounds for nesting birds. The tidal water that flows in these channels becomes enriched with organic matter—bits of fallen leaves and branches that are covered with tiny decay organisms. This stew is then flushed out to surrounding bays on the outgoing tide. Each year, nearly 4 tons of this material is "exported" from every acre of mangroves, providing food for untold numbers of marine organisms.

As you drift along the channels, you may hear what sounds like rain falling from a clear blue sky. Look up carefully, and you'll find that the "shower" is actually the guano of hundreds of nesting waterbirds, including brown pelicans, wood storks, egrets, roseate spoonbills, and herons. In the mangroves, these birds find not only solid nest platforms above a year-round food supply, but also relative safety from land predators.

Ironically, the birds that are most dependent on these rookery sites often wind up destroying them. The guano you heard pelts down in a steady rain year after year, burning the exposed roots and trunks with its acid. Eventually, the scorched trees die, creating a ghost forest of bleached white skeletons. Storms and tides eventually topple the trees and wash them out to sea, leaving a bare sand spit. Before long, however, the cycle is destined to begin again. All it takes is one small, cigar-shaped "twig" nudging against the shore.

Roseate Spoonbill

Spoonbills seem to "see" better with their bills. They fish by sweeping their spatula-shaped bills from side to side in shallow water. Eventually, a living animal may bump up against the slightly agape bill, stimulating sensitive nerve endings. Before an eye can blink, the roseate's bill snaps shut on the item and swallows it down.

WILDLIFE LOCATOR CHART—MANGROVE FOREST

Illustrations: FLORIDA REDBELLY TURTLE, BROWN PELICAN, SOUTHEASTERN FIVE-LINED SKINK, GREEN TREEFROG, FLORIDA COTTONMOUTH, FISH CROW

	Feeds from Air	Feeds in Upper Canopy	Feeds in Lower Canopy	Feeds on Ground	Feeds While Standing in Water (Wades)	Feeds Underwater (Swims)
Nests in Tree Canopy	Brown Pelican Magnificent Frigatebird Short-tailed Hawk Gray Kingbird	Black-whiskered Vireo	Mangrove Cuckoo	Cattle Egret Fish Crow Raccoon (nests in trunk)	Snowy Egret Tricolored Heron Reddish Egret Green-backed Heron Yellow-crowned Night-Heron White Ibis Roseate Spoonbill Wood Stork	
Nests on Ground			Green Anole Yellow Rat Snake	Clapper Rail		Florida Cottonmouth Mangrove Salt Marsh Snake
Nests Beneath Ground or Debris			Swamp Rabbit Southeastern Five-lined Skink			River Otter Diamondback Terrapin Florida Redbelly Turtle American Alligator
Nests in Water			Green Treefrog			Manatee

81

Feeding by touch comes in handy when water is turbulent, muddy, or thick with vegetation. Even in clear water where they can see their prey, spoonbills still prefer to bill-sweep for crustaceans, mollusks, slugs, and aquatic insects.

Roseates are wonderfully colorful, with pink coats (adults only—immatures are white); white necks streaked with red; green, featherless heads; and red feet and legs. Seeing a flock of them undulating like a pink streamer in the sky is a real treat. You may also see them congregating in mangrove branches for nesting.

One of the advantages of colony living is security; because many eyes are on the lookout, predators are usually spotted well in advance. Even when predators do attack, most of the birds can afford to relax. With so many prey to choose from, the statistical chance of any one bird or its young being the one eaten are slim.

Despite their security systems, spoonbills were almost hunted to extinction at one time, but not by predators. Plumage hunters shot thousands of these birds so that their feathers could be made into hats. In 1939, fewer than 30 pairs of spoonbills were reportedly alive in Florida. Today, under strict protection, that figure has thankfully risen to about 900–1,000 nesting pairs.

Look for roseate spoonbills—foraging in shallow water, roosting in branches, or flying in wedge-shaped or long, diagonal formations. They fly with their bills straight out and often glide between flaps.

Length: 32 inches.

Look for nests—in dense thickets of small, leafy trees or bushes along the coast, usually on islands of mangroves. Nests are bulky stick structures within 30 feet of the ground, usually 5–15 feet up. They are often in nesting rookeries shared by herons, ibises, and other waterbirds.

Listen for—a low croak or cluck.

Raccoon

The Algonquin Indian name for raccoon means "he who scratches with his hands." The raccoon's "hands" are as sensitive as our own and as facile as a monkey's. Their paws double as eyes when raccoons creep down to the water at nightfall.

Here they wait for the changing of the guard as daytime animals retreat and nighttime animals emerge for a night of foraging. With eyes diverted in a far-off look of concentration, the raccoon "reads" the bottom of the pool, sweeping circles with its palms and poking fingers into crannies and crevices. When it "spots" a live meal, or even the vibration from one, the raccoon jerks and lunges, plucking the creature from its hideout in an instant.

The stories about raccoons washing their food seem to be mythical. Raccoons are known to douse some food items, but they will eat prey whether it is dirty or not. Water does seem to soften the extra-sensitive skin on their paws, however, and may make them better dabblers.

Raccoons are feeding opportunists, eating everything they can get their paws on, from algae to garbage. Their ability to find a variety of food stems from their ability to solve problems and learn. A raccoon learns much of what it knows from its mother, but continues to master and remember new tricks throughout its life. Anyone who's ever matched wits with a raccoon can vouch for its abilities. One homeowner was advised to light a fire to smoke out the raccoons living in her chimney. "We tried that," she explained. "But they climbed down, shut the flue, and smoked us out!"

Look for raccoons—at night, hunting in shallow pools, turning over rocks, digging into rotten logs, or ambling up a tree. Their ideal habitat has at least one large, 50+ year old den tree every 15–20 acres. Yearlings disperse in the spring to claim their own habitats, walking as much as 6 miles a night. Raccoons' coats are two-toned, dark above and light below. This "countershading" helps soften shadows beneath them so that predators have a harder time distinguishing them as three-dimensional objects. You can spot them in your headlights by the orange-red glow of their eyes.

Length: Head and body, 18–28 inches; tail, 8–12 inches.

Look for dens—in cavities 10–60 feet up in trees. A typical den is 26 feet up and has a horizontal, elliptical opening measuring 6 inches by 4 inches and facing south. Look for raccoon hairs stuck in the entrance and on the trunk leading up. Also look for droppings on the ground below. At breeding time, males travel from den tree to den tree to find a willing mate; they may travel 8 miles a night. Dens may also be under tree roots or in woodchuck burrows.

Look for basking places—where they drape themselves during the day to feel the sun. Look in the crotches of tree branches, atop a muskrat home or squirrel nest, or on a hummock in a sunny marsh.

Look for scat stations—piles of droppings (crumbly, ¾ inch in diameter with flat ends, containing bits of insects or shells) atop a limb, rock, or tangle of woody debris along the bank. Family groups traveling together in late summer through winter will use the same scat station, choosing a spot that other raccoons will easily notice.

Look for claw marks on trees—left on smooth bark when a climbing raccoon slips. The 5-claw pattern is about 2½ inches wide.

Look for tracks—like small human hands, with 5 toes, 2½–4½ inches long, most commonly on muddy shores. Raccoons "pace" when they walk; both left feet are moved and then both right feet are moved. This leaves paired prints, with a hindpaw next to a forepaw. When the trail you are following disappears into the water, try looking farther down the bank where the raccoon might have crawled out again.

Listen for—purrs of contentment, trills and chirrs, banshee wails when fighting, piercing alarm screams, low warning grunts and loud growls. The young whimper like human infants when hungry or abandoned. Some people say they sound like treefrogs. You can buy a whistlelike device called a "coon talker" that imitates these sounds and may bring a curious raccoon into view.

Mangrove Salt Marsh Snake

It's a scene that is repeated in every Hollywood adventure film set in the swamps. The boat drifts slowly under overhanging branches, and the camera zooms to a large, ropy snake slipping off and gliding into the water just in front of the boat. Despite the ominous effect, you have no reason to be afraid.

Mangrove salt marsh snakes are not poisonous and are genuinely interested in getting away from you. Unfortunately, many a salt marsh snake loses its life because people mistake the innocent snake for the truly venomous Florida cottonmouth. Here are two quick ways you can tell these snakes apart: (1) a cottonmouth beats a slow, dignified retreat, whereas a salt marsh snake really *moves,* and (2) when cornered, a cottonmouth opens its mouth wide and you'll be able to see its cotton-white lining.

Salt marsh snakes are killed for another "crime" they don't commit. Some anglers believe that these water snakes kill the game fish they are after, when, in fact, salt marsh snakes are not fast enough to catch these fish. Instead, they actually bolster game fish population by weeding out weak, slow fish and thus checking the spread of fish diseases. In addition, they provide thousands of baby snakes for the fish to eat.

When snakes bask in the sun in front of your boat, they are not simply waiting to scare you. They are, in fact, keeping themselves alive. Snakes, unlike mammals or birds, have no insulating layer of fat to keep in the heat they have absorbed. Nor do they have sweat glands to help them cool themselves. Instead, they must move to areas of sun or shade in order to bring their body temperature within 70–98 degrees F. If they get colder than this, they will be too sluggish to move, and if they get too warm, some proteins in their tissues will undergo irreversible and fatal changes.

The hypothalamus in the brain acts like a thermostat that tells the snakes when to change their position. Also, small circular pits on their back, flanks, and tail are packed with bundles of nerve fibers that can detect even slight variations in temperature. The skin above these pits is thinner than in other parts of the body. After eating, snakes often select places with higher-than-normal temperatures to help them digest.

Look for mangrove salt marsh snakes—basking on mangrove roots or branches, or in the water, searching for frogs, tadpoles, and fish. In spring and early summer, when temperatures are still moderate, snakes are likely to be found out sunning. In the heat of the summer, they switch their activity period to nights, becoming especially active after heavy rains when frogs are moving around. In cool weather, look for salt marsh snakes under leaf litter. When threatened, they flatten their bodies, strike repeatedly with tiny teeth (no venom), and discharge a foul-smelling musk. If you come across a roiling tangle of snakes, it may be several males trying to mate with one female.

Length: 16–62½ inches.

Look for young—they give birth to live young.

MANGROVE CUCKOO

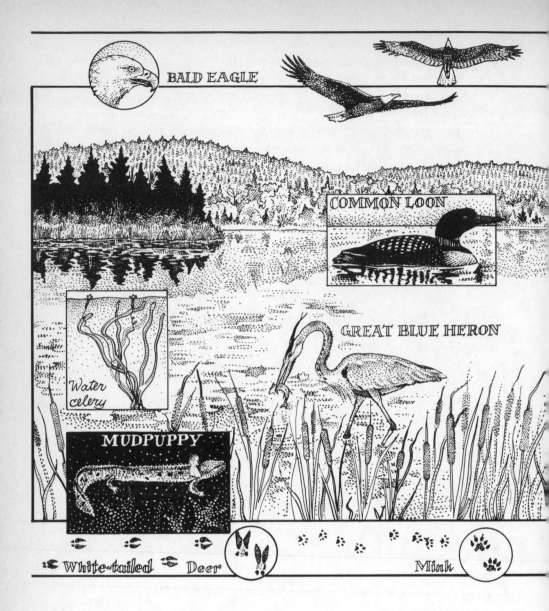

BALD EAGLE

COMMON LOON

GREAT BLUE HERON

Water celery

MUDPUPPY

White-tailed Deer

Mink

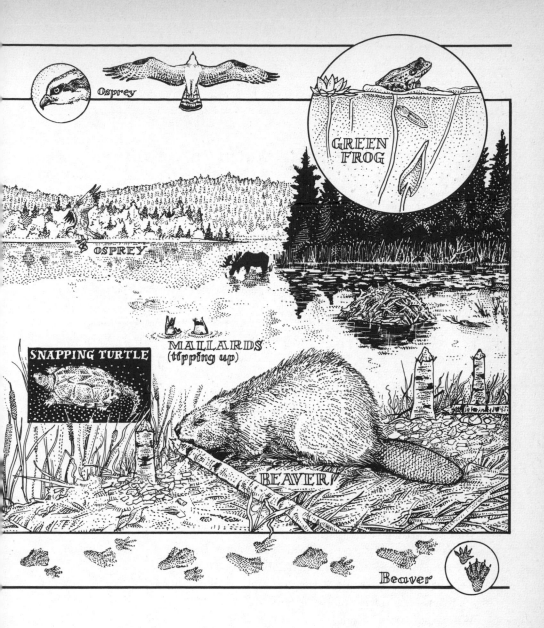

Osprey

GREEN FROG

OSPREY

MALLARDS
(tipping up)

SNAPPING TURTLE

BEAVER

Beaver

Lake and Pond

WHERE TO SEE THIS HABITAT:

Lakes and ponds are common throughout the East. This is just a sampling; there are many more.
Arkansas: Big Lake and White River national wildlife refuges
Indiana: Indiana Dunes National Lakeshore
Iowa: DeSoto National Wildlife Refuge
Louisiana: Lacassine and Sabine national wildlife refuges

Maryland: Blackwater National Wildlife Refuge

Michigan: Ottawa National Forest; Pictured Rocks and Sleeping Bear Dunes national lakeshores; Seney National Wildlife Refuge

Minnesota: Agassiz, Rice Lake, and Tamarac national wildlife refuges; Voyageurs National Park; Chippewa and Superior national forests; Minnesota Wetlands Complex

Mississippi: Noxubee National Wildlife Refuge

Missouri: Swan Lake National Wildlife Refuge

New York: Iroquois National Wildlife Refuge

North Carolina: Mattamuskeet National Wildlife Refuge

South Carolina: Santee National Wildlife Refuge

Tennessee: Tennessee and Reelfoot national wildlife refuges

Vermont: Missisquoi National Wildlife Refuge

Wisconsin: Apostle Islands National Lakeshore

Lake and Pond

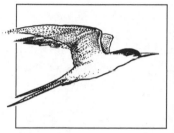

BEGINNINGS

From his summit atop Maine's Mount Katah-
din, Thoreau said New England looked as
though a giant had shattered a huge mirror and
flung the glittering fragments across the landscape. The giant he spoke of was a two-mile-
high glacier that melted a mere 12,000 years ago, leaving countless lakes
and ponds in its passing.

"Kettle" lakes were formed when chunks of ice buried in the rocky
margin of the glacier finally melted. Other lakes formed when rivers backed
up behind piles of glacial debris. Still others filled into shallow "thumb-
prints" where the land had sagged under the glacier's great weight. Today,
the great lake builders of the northern U.S. are not glaciers but beavers,
which flood lands to create a habitat for themselves.

Farther south, lakes were formed in a variety of other ways. Although
the land was never scoured by glaciers, it was periodically covered by
seawater as ocean levels rose and fell. The largest lakes in the South are
leftovers from the draining of these ancient seas. The sea floor was layered
with shells and skeletons, now compacted into the limestone that underlies
much of the South. Some lakes are formed when this limestone dissolves,
leaving a "sink hole."

Other than these, most southern lakes are associated with large rivers.
Sometimes they occupy hollows in a river floodplain, or are backed up
behind the natural levees that flank many stretches of river channel. Oxbow
lakes are formed when high water causes a meandering river to take a
more direct route, thus cutting off a C-shaped bend of still water.

However they originate, lakes and ponds are a short-lived phenomenon.
Many ponds are merely lakes in their old age, growing smaller and shallower
as the collar of vegetation around their shores tightens.

If you could film the life of a lake, then play it at high speed, you'd see the lake shrink before your eyes. First, the vegetation on its edges would march closer to the center. Silt would collect around the roots, and layers of decaying plants would build up, making the edges shallower and shallower. The outlet stream might eventually erode a notch below the level of the lake and suddenly drain much of its water. Plants could then take root all the way across the lake. As they built up the bottom and gave up their water to the air, the land beneath them would grow drier and drier— so dry in fact, that other plants better suited to land would begin to replace the water plants. If you could watch long enough, you might see the lake become a pond, a marsh, a rippling meadow, a shrub swamp, and eventually a forest rising where the waves once rolled.

Lakes, because of their sheer size and depth, may take a geologic age to be reduced to ponds. But a pond, being shallow to begin with, may change in as little as a century's time. This "schedule" is far from fixed, however; the successional clock can be set back by fire, by floods, or even by a beaver family deciding to take up residence.

HOW IS A LAKE LIKE A FOREST?

To help visualize the layers of life in the open water of a lake, try imagining a tall, dark forest from treetops to roots. Instead of having leaves to intercept the sunlight in the upper layers, the lake has green plants called algae. These provide food for larger organisms such as fish. When plants and animals in the upper layers die, they filter down to the lake floor, just like leaves and twigs fall from trees to carpet the forest floor. A world of burrowing and grazing organisms live in the depths, feeding on the subsidies that filter down to them from above.

A thin film of water molecules caps the top surface, forming an elastic skin that is firm enough for some life to skate on, run on, land on, and float on. Just underneath, a whole world of insects, snails, and microscopic organisms hang upside down from this ceiling.

In addition to top-to-bottom zones, there are horizontal zones in a lake as well. Pretend you are in a canoe traveling from the open center toward the shore. Deep beneath your keel, there is a cold dark zone beyond the reach of the sun's rays, where no plants can grow. Above this, in the lighted layers, the water teems with tiny green plants, just one cell wide. As you head toward shore, the bottom slopes upward. Your paddle begins to snag on submerged plants, rooted in the bottom but reaching toward the lighted layers near the top. Their fine, segmented leaves are designed to expose as much photosynthesizing surface as possible.

The zone nearest the shore will look different, depending on how deep the lake or pond is, how large it is, and how exposed its beaches are. Windward beaches, especially on large lakes, may be scoured clean by white-capped waves. Fewer plants grow here, and the beaches are often made up of gravel, cobbles, or rocks. Where shorelines are protected from waves, however, a marshy plant community crowds the shallows and scrapes the bow of your boat. Floating-leaved plants such as water lilies sink their roots into the mud, and sail their leaves atop the water. Closer to shore, emergent plants such as cattails and bulrushes extend their vertical stalks above the water. Around the edges of the lake or pond, swampy plants and bushes able to tolerate "wet feet" form a transition zone from water to land.

A LOWERING CEILING OF ICE

The summer lake or pond, with its profusion of plant life, is a very different place come winter. A lid of ice caps the water, and as it gets colder, it contracts, shrinking toward the center. The water between the ice and the

---

CHARACTERISTIC PLANTS:

Protected Shores (i.e., Bays):

Emergents:
arrowhead
blue flag
bulrushes
bur reed
catttails
featherfoil
golden club
pickerelweed
purple loosestrife
sedges
sweetflag
water plantain
water smartweed

Floating-leaved:
duckweeds
fragrant water lily
water hyacinth (south)
water shamrock
water shield
yellow pond lily

Submergents:
bladderworts
hornwort
pondweeds
quillwort
stoneworts
water celery
water milfoils
yellow water
  buttercup

Exposed Shore:
On Sand:
black grass
common pipewort
rushes
silverweed
three-way sedge

On Gravel:
horsetails
lichens

---

shore now freezes, and that contracts slightly too, with the unnerving booming that ice cracking brings. When warm temperatures thaw this tightly compacted ice, it expands, jamming up against the shoreline, sculpting off ragged edges and sending a bulwark as high as 10 feet up the shore. Like a potter working clay, the ice gradually smoothes the irregularities of the shoreline, working it year after year into a rounded shape.

Plants that could be sheared by this action are spending the winter protected in a variety of ingenious ways. Duckweed, the smallest flowering plant (the size of a match head), manufactures an excess of starch toward the end of the summer, making it heavy enough to sink to the bottom. During the winter, it slowly uses up its supply so that, come spring, it's light enough to bob back up to the surface again. Cattails store starch in tubers under the mud in autumn. Their old, dead stalks are hollow and act like snorkels to bring air down to the living roots. Other plants, such as pondweeds, pack starches in fleshy roots before the winter. When spring comes, they tap these reserves for their first big spurt of growth.

Wildlife is also keeping itself alive beneath the ice. Muskrats and beavers are huddled in the dry, upper part of their lodge that extends above the ice. They descend occasionally to snack from their underwater hoards of food. Hibernating turtles and frogs are under the mud, breathing through their skin or through mucous membranes lining their mouth. (Turtles can also use blood-filled tissues in their anus to filter oxygen out of the muddy water.) These hibernators are operating at a slower pace, with heartbeats and temperatures lowered so as not to use up too much energy.

MAP TURTLE

As the winter drags on, the finite supply of oxygen under the ice begins to get used up. If the freeze lasts too long, gasping fish begin to crowd at cracks in the ice, and muskrats must stagger onto the surface looking for food. Land predators such as minks and hawks find a feast of "easy pickings" at this time, proving that one species' disaster may be another's blessing.

WHAT'S IN IT FOR WILDLIFE?

Lakes and ponds are a welcome oasis in any landscape, supplying drinking water, food, a breeding place, an underwater escape, and even a respite from insects. Besides the dozens of permanent residents, many animals from other habitats visit lakes and ponds regularly.

In the spring, moose and deer often wade shoulder deep into ponds to feast on the sodium-rich aquatic plants. After a winter of eating woody browse, they are literally starved for salt. Also in the spring, frogs and salamanders crowd into ponds for their annual jamboree of mating. Waterfowl migrating back to their northern breeding grounds land by the thousands on lakes and ponds, hungrily dabbling and diving for food.

In large lakes, common loons set up breeding territories, calling to each other with an eerily beautiful music. These large birds use the open water, along with mergansers and cormorants, to dive after fish. Above them, bald eagles and ospreys dive like winged rockets from the clouds, emerging from the spray with fighting fish between their talons.

Along the shallower edges of the lake or pond, the summer brings a rich profusion of plants. Tadpoles scrape the algal coatings off the stems, and adult frogs climb atop water lily pads to bask in the sun. Water snakes and turtles prowl with their eyes above the water, hunting down slippery prey. Mudpuppies, hellbenders, and sirens creep along the bottom. Chickenlike birds called common moorhens walk with their widespread toes along the tops of water lily pads, while American coots turn the leaves over in search of insect prey. Ducks teach their young to tip-end for food in the plant-choked shallows, and long-legged waders stand statue-still, waiting for hapless minnows to school within striking distance.

Great Blue Heron

You're casting into the shallows, letting your boat drift closer and closer to shore. Finally, you notice a 4-foot-tall wading bird larger than life in front of you. You needn't chide yourself for overlooking the huge heron; its frozen stance and gray-blue coloring have done exactly what they are designed to do. Now, deciding you are too close, the heron stretches out its long neck, crouches down on stiltlike legs, and hesitates for a split second before springing into the air. As its enormous wings unfurl, it looks almost prehistoric, like a bird that would land on a dinosaur's back.

Your lucky fishing spot may also be the heron's favorite, but the tools the great blue comes equipped with far surpass even your best rig. Sticklike legs hoist it up above the shallows, while telescopic eyes register movement even in the deepest shadow. Herons use a wade-and-wait method of fishing, folding their sinuous neck in a flattened "S" curve while letting a school

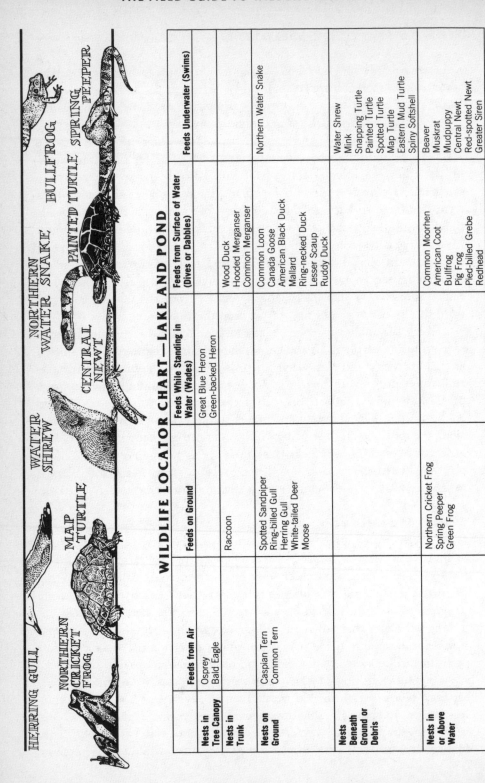

WILDLIFE LOCATOR CHART—LAKE AND POND

	Feeds from Air	Feeds on Ground	Feeds While Standing in Water (Wades)	Feeds from Surface of Water (Dives or Dabbles)	Feeds Underwater (Swims)
Nests in Tree Canopy	Osprey Bald Eagle		Great Blue Heron Green-backed Heron		
Nests in Trunk		Raccoon		Wood Duck Hooded Merganser Common Merganser	
Nests on Ground	Caspian Tern Common Tern	Spotted Sandpiper Ring-billed Gull Herring Gull White-tailed Deer Moose		Common Loon Canada Goose American Black Duck Mallard Ring-necked Duck Lesser Scaup Ruddy Duck	Northern Water Snake
Nests Beneath Ground or Debris					Water Shrew Mink Snapping Turtle Painted Turtle Spotted Turtle Map Turtle Eastern Mud Turtle Spiny Softshell
Nests in or Above Water		Northern Cricket Frog Spring Peeper Green Frog		Common Moorhen American Coot Bullfrog Pig Frog Pied-billed Grebe Redhead	Beaver Muskrat Mudpuppy Central Newt Red-spotted Newt Greater Siren

HERRING GULL
NORTHERN CRICKET FROG
MAP TURTLE
WATER SHREW
NORTHERN WATER SNAKE
CENTRAL NEWT
PAINTED TURTLE
BULLFROG
SPRING PEEPER

of fish come to them. When the fish realize the shadow is alive, they veer away instinctively, but it is too late. The great neck uncoils like a striking snake, driving the dagger bill down to snap shut on the last of the school. With a leisurely toss, the heron flips the fish up, then ducks under to swallow it down.

It's hard to believe that the stately, graceful figure you are watching was once a half-feathered, gangly juvenile awkwardly fighting for balance on a limb. Heron young are raised in high-rise nests, in a colony that may include several hundred other wading birds. Before the young can fly, they have practice lessons at dizzying heights, opening and closing their wings to build up their flight muscles. Many young fall off their practice platforms, or are pushed out of the nest by more aggressive siblings. If the fall doesn't kill them, the foxes, raccoons, and turkey vultures that regularly dine beneath the nests will. Adult herons seem to plan for this casualty—they lay 5 or 6 eggs, usually managing to raise at least 2 or 3.

To find a heron rookery, look in the sky. Like airplanes queuing at an airport, you'll begin to notice the "blue bombers" flying to and from the rookery every few minutes. They are flying out for baby food, which might be more plentiful in outlying areas. As you get closer to the rookery, you'll hear a deafening rabble of sound—squawks, screeches, and croaks— heightened every time a new bird flies in. Closer still, the stench of rotting fish, nestlings, and quarts of excrement heaved over the sides of the nest will overwhelm you. If you dare to stand beneath a nest tree, be sure you're wearing a hat. Agitated young tend to defecate or regurgitate their last meal on intruders! It's a clever defense, but unfortunately it tends to ruin the neighborhood. After being pelted with a steady rain of these caustic droppings for years, the nest trees lose their bark and die. Eventually, herons must find a new place to nest.

Look for great blue herons—fishing at the shallow edges of lakes, ponds, or rivers, especially at dusk and dawn. They fly with slow, steady wingbeats, their neck doubled in an "S." If you disturb the herons, leave and come back later. They are likely to circle around and come back to the spot when they find you gone.

Size: Height, 4 feet (including head and neck); wingspan, 6 feet.

Look for nests—in colonies of as many as 1,000 nests, but the average is 50. Nests are bulky structures of intertwined sticks built as high as 130 feet from the ground. Each tree may have several nests at different levels belonging to other herons, egrets, ibises, or cormorants. Biologists believe the birds nest together for protection from predators and perhaps to share information about fruitful food sources. When a parent arrives at the nest, the young grab its bill to induce it to regurgitate the food to them. Watch nests from a distance; a close encounter with humans can cause parents to abandon the nest or cause young to jump ship before they are ready to survive on their own.

Listen for—a gooselike "onk," croaks, or squawks. The young can sound like barking puppies or squealing pigs.

Beaver

According to an American Indian belief, giant beavers fetched the mud with which the earth was built. It's not so outlandish an idea when you consider that beavers, in all their forms, have lived on this continent for a million years—long enough to have modified every watershed in North America. In fact, we owe much of our tillable land to their efforts. Dig down in any farmer's field and you're likely to find silt that long ago accumulated in the stillness of an ancient beaver pond.

When a stream is broken by a series of beaver dams, it spreads over its banks and becomes a necklace of ponds and marshes. The swift water slows enough to support plants and attract insects. In turn, these insects attract aquatic organisms and their predators. The lodges, dams, and canals that beavers construct create new travel lanes or nests for many creatures.

It's not a civic conscience that prompts beavers to do their good works, however. In building dams, they are solving a basic problem of their own; the stream is too shallow and narrow to hide them from the eyes of predators. By spreading the stream into a pond, beavers gain a protective moat for their lodge, as well as a safe travel lane to and from their feeding grounds on the shore.

Beavers cut trees down to get at the succulent leaves, twigs, and bark in the canopy (a novel approach to browsing). It takes a beaver less than 10 minutes to fell a 3-inch-diameter tree, but they've been known to labor for hours over record 60-inchers. Contrary to popular opinion, they don't direct the fall of their trees. Most trees fall toward the water simply because they are lopsided—they have more branches on the side that was near the open water and sun.

By removing the shoreline trees, beavers let in a flood of sunlight that encourages more palatable shrubs and saplings such as aspens, birches, and willows (which are, of course, the beaver's favorites). By removing overstory competitors, the beavers also make way for trees that have been waiting in the understory. By releasing them for growth, beavers actually accelerate the "aging" process of a forest around the edges of their pond.

When food supplies around the pond run out, beavers move on, leaving dams that become leakier every year. Eventually the pond drains and the marsh becomes a meadow, a shrub swamp, then finally a forest with its roots in rich beaver soil. Few other mammals, beside humans and perhaps elephants, can so drastically change their habitat to suit their needs.

Look for beavers—paddling from their lodge every day about the same time (dusk). They work mostly at night, but also during the day in the fall when they are laying in a store of winter food. A family of 9 beavers may need as much as a ton of bark to survive the winter. It's easy to tell beavers from muskrats; beavers weigh 45–60 pounds, while muskrats weigh 2–4, and beavers' tails don't show when swimming. Like muskrats, beavers have a complete array of adaptations for water life: a wet suit of waterproof fur, webbed feet to propel them, furry lips that seal watertight behind their chopping teeth, flap valves on their nostrils and ears, transparent eyelids for "goggles," a body that can tolerate high levels of carbon dioxide, and a special air passage that is separate from the larynx so they can breath while toting branches in the water.

Length: Head and body, 25–30 inches; tail, 9–10 inches.

Look for lodges—large domes of branches smeared with mud, 5–6 feet above water level, and 12–14 feet wide. They may be built along a bank or in the pond itself. Beavers pile branches together, then swim up under the pile to hollow out a dry center for raising young. The apex of the lodge is loosely constructed to let air in and humid vapor out; in the winter, beaver breath looks like smoke coming from the lodge "chimney." The mud on the outside of the lodge freezes solid to keep predators from clawing their way in. In the summer, look for northern harriers or Canada geese nesting atop the lodges.

Look for dams—2 to 10 feet high, and up to 2,000 feet long. A pair of beavers can build a 2-foot-high, 12-foot-long dam in two nights. They begin by piling brush and tree limbs in the stream and cementing them together with mud, leaves, and rocks. Long poles are dragged over the dam and left on a slant, with their upper end perched on the dam and their lower end anchored in the mud on the downstream side. These buttresses, plastered in place by more debris, help to hold back the weight of the dammed water. Dams are not completely watertight; beavers allow some water to percolate through as a way to ease the pressure. A serious break will bring them running to repair it, however. Researchers believe it's the sound of running water that they respond to; captive beavers can be induced to start damming by running water into a bathtub! Many other animals use beaver dams to cross the stream (look for their scat).

Look for canals—winding from the pond up into the forest. Canals carry the beavers to a whole new set of food resources, and allow them to float the logs back to the pond. Hauling these logs overland would be too energy-expensive and risky.

Look for gnaw marks—in a circular pattern around trunks. Stumps are pointed and scarred with broad tooth marks. Some marks may be higher up, indicating that the work was done during winter, when the beaver was standing on snow. Branches used to build lodges will often have the bark peeled off.

Look for "mud pies"—mounds of mud marked with drops of castoreum, a musk that beavers use to communicate their presence to other animals. There are 50 different volatile substances in castoreum, and every beaver has a unique odor signature. Humans use castoreum in perfumes—also to leave memorable messages. There may be between 40 and 120 of these mounds within the home range of a beaver family.

Look for tracks—splay-toed, 3 inches long, sometimes with only three or four toes printing. The webbed hindprints are 5 inches wide, twice as wide as the foreprints. Often, the prints will be obliterated by the drag mark of the flat tail.

Listen for—the resounding slap of a beaver's tail on the water, telegraphing "danger" to the rest of the beaver family. By protecting its relatives, the tail-slapper also protects some of its own genes, even though it risks giving away its own location. If you're close enough, you can easily hear the cries and whimpers of hungry, begging beaver kits in the lodge. Angry beavers blow through their nostrils.

Snapping Turtle

The snapping turtle has a reputation for being nasty. In reality, however, these turtles would rather swim away than fight. As long as they are underwater, their cryptic coloration, stalking prowess, and escape reflexes serve them well. It's only when they venture onto land that a Jekyll-and-Hyde transformation takes place.

Snappers resort to land only to lay eggs or to find a new home if their ponds have dried up. They naturally lunge when they feel threatened, snapping viciously with their sharp, hooked jaws. Once a turtle seizes its attacker, it holds on with bulldog tenacity, often releasing only when the muscles are cut.

Despite their protective efforts at egg-laying time, more than half of the nests will be destroyed by mammal predators such as skunks, raccoons, and foxes. Each female snapper lays up to 1,000 eggs in her lifetime, supplying food for many a pond visitor over the years. Hatchling turtles are another important source of food for herons, bitterns, crows, hawks, bullfrogs, large fish, and snakes.

Once they become too large to tangle with, the snappers become successful predators in their own right. They use their algae-covered shells and muddy coloring to remain incognito while waiting for fish, crayfish, or other aquatic creatures to wander by. Or they may sneak up on unsuspecting prey like a cat stalking a mouse. As they approach, they raise their hindquarters and lower their front legs, building the leverage they'll need for a lunge. Their head is withdrawn into their shell until the prey is within striking distance. Finally, in one swift movement, they dart their neck and open mouth forward, creating a suction that vacuums up everything in its path—water and plants as well as the prey item.

Because of the way they're built, snappers can't change their direction once they make their move. This hasn't hurt them in the quest for crayfish, however, because crayfish instinctively back up when attacked. Fish, which shift quickly to the side, are harder for snappers to catch.

Look for snapping turtles—resting or crawling on the muddy bottoms of ponds, lakes, and rivers. You may also see the ridged top of their shell above the water, doing a convincing imitation of a slime-covered rock. They prefer water that is shallow enough so that they can extend their neck and poke their nostrils into the air for breathing. To smell underwater, they inhale water through these nostrils and pump it out via their mouth. By analyzing the odor-causing particles, they can identify food and other turtles in the water. Smell may also help them navigate when moving overland to ponds. Look for females laying eggs on shores in June.

Shell length: 8–18½ inches.

Don't disturb nests—dug into the sides of banks, on sandy or gravelly shores, or even along roadbeds far from water—wherever there is loose soil and enough sun to keep the eggs warm. The female digs the 6-inch-by-6-inch cavity with her hind legs and deposits 20–40 eggs that look like small Ping-Pong balls (1⅛ inches wide). She then covers them with about 3 inches of soil and tamps this lid down with her body. The young either emerge in late summer or spend winter in the nest and emerge the next spring. If you find a dug-up nest strewn with broken shells, look for the prints of the culprit.

In the winter—snappers burrow into the muddy bottom of ponds, beneath logs or plant debris, in holes on the banks, or even in abandoned muskrat houses. When hibernating on the pond bottom, they breathe through membranes in their throat or through anal sacs that are filled with capillaries just like gills. On land, it's important for turtles to find a place beneath the frost line since their bodies will essentially take on the temperature of their den. They may become active in the winter, and you may see them swimming under the ice.

Listen for—the hiss of an enraged female disturbed (hopefully not by you) while laying eggs. Her "hiss" is actually a rapid exhale as she pulls her head and neck in. Snapping turtles have smaller undershells than most other turtles. This allows them to keep their mouth wide open when their head is pulled in—making it tough for enemies to get a handle on them.

Speckled Alder

Sandbar Willow

DEER

BEAR

GREEN-BACKED HERON

BELTED KINGFISHER

Swamp Horsetail

HELLBENDER

Bur Reed

Watercress

MOOSE

Pussy Willow

MINK

Jewelweed

RACCOON

BANK SWALLOW

RIVER OTTER

NORTHERN WATER SNAKE

EASTERN SPINY SOFTSHELL

Pondweed

River and Stream

WHERE TO SEE THIS HABITAT:

Rivers and streams are common throughout the East. This is just a sampling; there are many more.

Arkansas: Buffalo National River; Holla Bend and White River national wildlife refuges

Florida: Lake Woodruff National Wildlife Refuge; Oklawaha Wild and Scenic River

Georgia: Chattahoochee River National Recreation Area

Illinois: Mark Twain National Wildlife Refuge; Shawnee National Forest

Kentucky: Daniel Boone National Forest

Michigan: Huron National Forest; Shiawassee National Wildlife Refuge

Missouri: Ozark National Scenic Riverway; Eleven Point Wild and Scenic River

Pennsylvania: Delaware Water Gap National Recreation Area

South Carolina: Chattooga Wild and Scenic River

Tennessee: Big South Fork National River

Vermont: Missisquoi National Wildlife Refuge

Virginia: Presquile National Wildlife Refuge

West Virginia: New River Gorge National River

Wisconsin: Lower St. Croix and St. Croix national scenic riverways; Chequamegon National Forest

River and Stream

BEGINNINGS

When you move inland away from the influence of tides, topography begins to dictate whether water will be still or moving. Gravity directs the show, bringing water from higher lands to lower ones. A stream begins when water in an upland basin overflows its banks and begins to trickle downhill. As it flows, it cuts a channel, tearing rocks and vegetation loose from the banks and grinding pebbles into fine particles. These are used like sandpaper to deepen the streambed even further. Along the way, smaller streams flow into the river, adding their cargo of silt, nutrients, and fragments of plants and animals. As the river increases in volume, it flows faster and with greater force. Doubling the speed of a river (during a storm for instance) increases its rock-toting force by 64 times!

The ultimate destination of most rivers is the sea. When viewed from above, the trelliswork of eastern rivers looks like the circulatory system of the land, carrying millions of tons of topsoil to the sea each day. In a year, 1 foot of the United States is eroded through this system, but we don't notice it because the forces of gradual uplift are also at work.

Steeper landscapes (those "recently" uplifted) have faster flowing, more erosive rivers. You can tell a young river by its V-shaped valley, its rapids and falls, and its rocky or gravelly bed. The vegetation clinging to the steep ravine walls will have a northern character because of the deep shade and cool air around the stream. You'll find eastern hemlock, yellow birch, sugar maple, American beech, witch-hazel, wood-sorrel, foamflower, and ferns. As the river becomes older, its sides erode into gentler slopes, and the valley is widened into a U instead of a V. Now the two sides of the valley have different kinds of forests, depending on how much sun they receive during the day. Shaded, north-facing slopes remain northern in character, while sun-baked south-facing slopes sport oaks, hickories, or eastern redcedars.

Smaller plants are mostly grasses, lowbush blueberry, and sweet-fern. (Large floodplain rivers have their own set of habitat characteristics. See description on pages 175 and 187.)

A QUESTION OF CURRENT

As you walk along the river, notice how life within the water and along the banks changes. The vegetation, just as in land habitats, is "zoned," not by soil or moisture content, but by the phenomenon called current.

Current is an inescapable fact of life in a river. It can be a blessing, in that it carries food to downstream organisms and mixes oxygen into the water with each wave crest. On the other hand, it can be a challenge, constantly abrading the bed and prying loose what is not anchored in place. River creatures are outfitted in a variety of ways to deal with the force and friction of moving water.

Some adapt by simply avoiding the current—living in eddies behind rocks or burrowing into the streambed. Others use the current to help them snag a passing meal or to keep them in place against the upstream side of rocks. On the top of rocks, there is a thin layer of friction that slows the current so that insects with flat bodies can hold on.

Also growing on the tops of rocks are colonies of slimy algae, familiar to anyone who has tried to rock-hop across a stream. The algae you dislodge when you slip is quickly replaced. As an adaptation to fast-current life, stream algae reproduce new generations faster than any other kind of algae. Larger stream plants adapt to frequent tearing by regenerating whole plants from the broken fragments. Many stream plants, like watercress and water hypnum, are sleek and flexible so they have less drag in the water. Others, like cushion moss, are rounded so that water finds the fastest way around them.

WHEN THINGS SLOW DOWN

Once the river drops into lower, flatter terrain, it usually widens, and the current begins to slow. The water is now able to drop some of the sediment it has been carrying for miles. This soft muddy ooze creates a perfect home for burrowing worms and mussels. Along the quiet edges and backbays, pond plants can also get their footing in the ooze. These plants offer many surfaces for algae to grow on, thus providing a food source for nibbling tadpoles and a good fishing ground for tadpole eaters such as turtles and egrets. The forest of stems slows the water even more, prompting it to drop more sediment in these marshy areas.

Other still-water organisms such as frogs find likely breeding grounds here and plenty of wet-footed greenery where they can hide their eggs. Waterbirds stalk the margin, hunting for schools of young fish that swirl in the shadows. Migrants fly in, attracted by the best of both worlds—both open water and marsh.

The tradeoff in these relaxed waters is that oxygen is not as plentiful as it was in the riffles and rapids. The water, which is shallower and more exposed to the sun, tends to be warmer. Fish like trout and whitehead that may have thrived in the cold, aerated upper streams are replaced by carp and catfish in the lower.

CHARACTERISTIC PLANTS:

In Fast Water:
filamentous algae
stoneworts
water hypnum

In Slow-Moving Water:
arrow arum
arrowheads
bur reed
duckweeds
horsetails
pondweed
riverweeds
rushes
watercress
water hyacinth
water willow
wild rice
yellow pond lily
yellow water
   buttercup

Shoreline:
Trees and Shrubs:
arrowwood
black ash
eastern hemlock
highbush blueberry
pussy willow
red maple
sandbar willow
speckled alder
spicebush
sweetgum
white ash
witch-hazel

Herbaceous Plants:
cardinal flower
cinnamon fern
false hellebore (Indian
   poke)
Indian cucumber root
jewelweed
marsh marigold
   (cowslip)
monkey flower
reed canary grass
rice cut grass
royal fern
spineleaf moss
tall meadow rue
true forget-me-not
turtlehead
wood nettle
yellow flag

This slow, idyllic backwater can roar with snowmelt in the spring, or slow to a trickle in a drought, reminding us that this is a river, one of the most changeable and challenging habitats of all. Whatever enters the stream must eventually change it as well. Agricultural runoff, sewage, heat discharge, acidic snowmelt, or chemical dumping can make the river unlivable for all but the most tolerant residents.

WHAT'S IN IT FOR WILDLIFE?

Rivers are one long "edge" habitat—the interface between land and water. True to their edge status, they offer wildlife the bounties of both water and land. Unlike other freshwater habitats that have limited, circular shorelines, the river's edge goes on for miles and miles. Often, it is the only continuous, wild vegetation remaining in farmlands or suburbia, and thus, the only safe highway for wildlife to travel.

In addition to cover, these corridors provide easy access to drinking water, protected sites for dens and nests, and a sunny spot for berries and other fruit-producing shrubs to grow. The muddy banks are great places to look for the tracks of upland mammals that visit the river throughout the day. Deer, bear, and moose, for instance, will come to drink the cool water and dine on aquatic plants. Minks and raccoons come down at night to hunt for crayfish and turtle eggs.

Besides visitors from terrestrial habitats, there are some species that spend almost all their time in or near rivers. Giant salamanders called hellbenders can be found prowling the bottom of southern streams, looking for worms. Water shrews ply the banks, diving in every now and then wrapped in silvery "suits" of air bubbles. Belted kingfishers find high sandy banks in which to dig their nests, and a long run of river in which to find fish. River otters slide down the banks and dive for fish in the moving water of streams. Beavers seeking to dam the stream may cut aspen along the shore.

The water itself is alive with fish, crustaceans, insects, plants, and an assortment of amphibians and reptiles. It is also a conveyor belt for food, decaying matter, and even plant seeds from farther upstream. In their larval stage, a great many insects wriggle at the bottom of rivers and streams. When they rise to the surface to mature and fly away ("hatch"), they are snapped up not only by trout, but also by frogs, kingfishers, swallows, and bats. In slower parts, a pondlike environment offers a jungle of underwater cover, hiding places for secretive birds, perching places for songsters, and safe spots for frogs to lay eggs. Many salamanders spend their early aquatic stages here as well.

Water also offers an inviolable retreat from many predators. As you approach a stream, listen for the loud plop of turtles sliding off logs and the quieter entry of the slippery otter.

Belted Kingfisher

Imagine diving headfirst into the water from a height of 50 feet and, at the precise moment, intersecting a fish that is desperately trying to evade you. Imagine repeating this every 20 minutes from 4 A.M. to 11 P.M. Parent kingfishers are on this schedule for weeks at a time until their young nestlings are old enough to fend for themselves. At first, the fledgling birds are not particularly eager to dive for their own food. It is only after the parents stop bringing handouts that they become interested in the river. To inspire that first headlong dive, parents will stun a fish and let it float beneath the hungry nestlings. Eventually, they get the idea, and are soon plunging after fish of their own.

Their oversized head and neck are built to absorb the shock, and their spearlike bill is designed to get a grip on slippery prey. Kingfishers usually retire to a tree to eat, first whacking the fish on a branch, then tossing it up in the air to catch. When the fish is too long to swallow, the kingfisher simply waits, fishtail dangling from its bill, until its stomach juices reduce the prey to size.

Their bills also come in handy when digging their 3- to 7-foot-long tunnel in the side of a cutaway bank. Kingfishers are enthusiastic diggers, kicking a flying fountain of sand behind them as they work. At the end of the upward-sloping tunnel, they carve a flattened sphere for a nest. Unlike their neighbors the bank swallows, which hang their hind end out of the holes to defecate, kingfisher young spray their excrement all over the nest. To their credit, however, they do rap the walls with their beaks, loosening dirt that soon covers the wastes. By the time this rising floor begins to crowd them, they are ready for their first flight.

Look for kingfishers—plying the air above a stretch of river territory that may be 500 yards long, or up to 5,000 during breeding season. In spring, when they are stringing "territorial fences," they make up to 90 circuits a day around the edges of their range, broadcasting their claim with loud calls. Watch when an intruding kingfisher enters the area; you'll see two blue forms darting past, one "escorting" the other out of his territory. You can gauge for yourself how long the owner's territory is by watching as it flies up ahead of your canoe. Eventually, it will reach the end of its territory, and come circling back for another pass. For fishing, kingfishers prefer shallow borders and water that is clear enough to see beneath the surface.

Length: 13 inches.

SPOTTED SANDPIPER • BLACK PHOEBE • LOUISIANA WATERTHRUSH • NORTHERN ROUGH-WINGED SWALLOW • HOODED MERGANSER

WILDLIFE LOCATOR CHART—RIVER AND STREAM

	Feeds from Air	Feeds on Ground	Feeds While Standing in Water (Wades)	Feeds from Surface of Water (Dives or Dips)	Feeds Underwater (Swims)
Nests in Tree Canopy	Osprey Silver-haired Bat		Great Blue Heron Green-backed Heron		Northern Water Snake Queen Snake
Nests in Trunk		Raccoon		Wood Duck Hooded Merganser	
Nests on Ground		Spotted Sandpiper White-tailed Deer		Eastern Ribbon Snake	
Nests Beneath Ground or Debris	Belted Kingfisher Black Pheobe (ledge nest) Northern Rough-winged Swallow Bank Swallow Indiana Myotis (nests in caves)	Northern Waterthrush Louisiana Waterthrush Black Bear Least Weasel			Water Shrew Beaver Mink River Otter Snapping Turtle Painted Turtle Spotted Turtle Wood Turtle Map Turtle River Cooter Slider Stinkpot Spiny Softshell
Nests in Water		Northern Cricket Frog		Bullfrog River Frog	Hellbender Spring Salamander Alabama Waterdog Mudpuppy Dwarf Waterdog Red-spotted Newt Northern Red Salamander

Look for perches—dead branches hanging out over water, where kingfishers take food to eat. Perches are usually within 100 feet of the nest, and there may be more than one in a territory.

Look for nest holes—3 to 4 inches in diameter, down about a foot from the top of a cutaway exposed bank, where the topsoil blends into sand. You can see two grooves at the bottom of the entrance hole where the kingfisher places its feet when leaving and entering. The nest tunnel slopes up to provide drainage and keep the nest dry. If there are no spider webs across the openings and a mound of fresh earth on the ground beneath them, the nests are probably active. Look for probe holes in the bank where kingfishers abandoned their first digging attempts. Other holes may lead to the nests of bank swallows or northern rough-winged swallows. Occasionally, nesting sites are inland, as much as a mile from water.

Listen for—a "k-k-k-k-k-" rattle that sounds like the clicking of a fishing reel. They give these calls when flying or when perched.

River Otter

After a flying leap, a wriggling otter bellyflops on the muddy bank and slides headfirst into a deep pool. Another follows, and another after that. As they scramble from the water, they seem to race each other back to the top of the bank. Nearby, an otter juggles pebbles on its paws, while another ferries a stick across the water on its nose. They romp. They cavort. They seem to play games. Even the most objective, emotionally detached biologist has to smile; otters look like they are just plain having fun.

Young otters at play are rehearsing behaviors that will one day determine their success. Their mock fights are mere previews of the real life-and-death contests of later life. Perhaps the pleasure that comes from play is nature's way of getting its pupils to practice their lessons.

Otters work as hard as they play. They have a fast metabolism that burns food quickly, so they must eat up to four times a day. In the water, otters swim along the surface until they spot a fish beneath them. They arch their back, dive, and by flexing their powerful body up and down, they swiftly overtake it. Sometimes they stay beneath a fish when chasing it, as if to follow its movements silhouetted against the surface light. They also nose along the muddy bottom for crayfish, frogs, and salamanders, feeling with their long whiskers, which are anchored in large nerve pads. On shore, they will raid bird, rabbit, and turtle nests, and even follow a muskrat into its burrow to kill it. They have been known to puncture a beaver dam, and then saunter in to collect the frogs and fish left stranded by the draining water.

Look for otters—fishing at the inflow and outflow of lakes, running rapids with their head up, eating fish on riverbanks, galloping along the shore, or swimming under the ice. They are active at any time of year, especially dawn to midmorning and again in the evening. They swim with the top of their head (where their eyes are) out of the water, trailing a "V" wake behind them. Sometimes the undulating movements of five or six otters "porpoising" one behind the other looks like a giant sea serpent.

Length: Head and body, 26–30 inches; tail, 12–17 inches.

Look for dens—under tree roots or rock ledges, in hollow logs, abandoned beaver or muskrat burrows, dense thickets along shore, or dug into the bank. They use an abovewater entrance in the summer, and an underwater one in the winter. Look for females teaching young to swim. The kits are reluctant at first, and must be ferried out to deep water on the mother's back.

Look for "haul-outs"—worn-down areas of shore where the otters habitually pull out of the water. Take one of the trails that leads away from these areas to find a patch (20 square feet) of disturbed vegetation where otters roll to dry themselves or to mark the ground with their scent.

Look for scent stations—any prominent object, such as a rock, stump, or even a tuft of grass that the otter has twisted together. They deposit droppings and scent on these spots as a way of marking the borders of their territory. Droppings are black, mucous-filled with shells or crayfish parts, and have a strong odor. The mucous is a protective coating in their intestines that prevents punctures by sharp fish bones.

Look for belly slides—on any grassy, muddy, or snow-covered hill. The slides may be as long as 25 feet, and may end in water or a snowbank. Otters will go out of their way to bodysurf a good hill.

Look for tracks—paired prints, 3¼ inches wide, with five splayed toes, especially noticeable in mud. The inner toe of the hind paw points out to one side.

In the snow—on level ground, look for dot-dash trails consisting of a few bounding leaps, a slide, and more bounding leaps. The 5- to 15-foot-long trough looks like it was made with a toy toboggan. Don't be surprised to find these trails far from water; otters travel as much as 3 miles overland to find new territory or fishing grounds.

Listen for—a deep "huh, huh, huh" repeated rapidly. Also chuckles, chirps, purring grunts, growls, hissing barks, and screams. A surfacing otter blows and sniffs loudly. Family members swimming together will exchange birdlike chirps.

Mudpuppy

Every year, biologists get calls from excited anglers who have caught what they believe must be a creature new to science. A foot-long "fish" with waving crimson gills, a long tail, and legs! Mudpuppies, however, are not fish at all. They belong to a class of giant salamanders, animals that were described in early texts as "looking more like bad dreams than animals." Unfortunately, ignorance and prejudice have led to the senseless killing of many of these harmless salamanders.

Mudpuppies spend most of their life hiding under rocks and crawling along the bottom of rivers searching for crustaceans, insects, fish, earthworms, and snails. Attracted to the lanterns of night anglers, they also occasionally reach for a baited hook. Those anglers who don't throw them back do the entire river community a disservice.

Mudpuppies provide food for many of our game fish. The salamander mussel is also dependent on the mudpuppy; it spends its entire life attached to the mudpuppy's gills and can live nowhere else. Rather than killing mudpuppies, we would be wise to consult them; they are excellent indicators of how healthy and clean our waters are. The waving crimson gills around the mudpuppy's neck change in size and condition depending on the amount of dissolved oxygen in their habitat. Small, contracted gills indicate a clean, cool waterway, while large, bushy, moving ones warn us of stagnation and pollution.

Look for mudpuppies—at the bottom of lakes and rivers, or moving among rocks below dams and bridges. They are active in all seasons, hunting in murky water during the day and in clear water at night. Look for large breeding congregations in October and early November. Their skin is not toxic like that of many amphibians, but it is very slimy. Captive mudpuppies reportedly "squirt out of your hand like a greasy hotdog."

Length: 8–17 inches.

Look for nests—cavities built in spring or early summer under rock slabs, in flowing water at least 3 feet deep. They prefer areas with weeds and rocks to provide cover. The female attaches as many as 180 pea-sized eggs to the ceiling of the cavity with individual stalks. She remains at the downstream-facing entrance to guard and aerate the eggs (fan water around them) for up to 2 months. Unlike many salamanders, mudpuppies don't metamorphose into land-dwelling creatures; they keep their gills throughout their long lives (as long as 20 years).

Water Hyacinth

Duckweed

Arrowhead

AMERICAN BITTERN

NORTHERN CRICKET FROG

Common Cattail

Pickerelweed

Fragrant Water Lily

RED-WINGED
BLACKBIRD

MUSKRAT

SPOTTED
TURTLE

MINK

GREATER
SIREN

Cattail Marsh

WHERE TO SEE THIS HABITAT:

Cattail marshes are common throughout the East. This is just a sampling; there are many more.

Florida: Lake Woodruff National Wildlife Refuge
Georgia (and South Carolina): Savannah National Wildlife Refuge
Iowa: Union Slough National Wildlife Refuge
Louisiana: Delta and Breton national wildlife refuges
Maine: Moosehorn National Wildlife Refuge
Massachusetts: Great Meadows National Wildlife Refuge
Michigan: Seney National Wildlife Refuge.
Minnesota: Agassiz, Minnesota Valley, Sherburne, and Tamarac national wildlife refuges; Minnesota Wetlands Complex
New Jersey: Great Swamp National Wildlife Refuge
New York: Montezuma National Wildlife Refuge
Ohio: Ottawa National Wildlife Refuge
Texas: Aransas National Wildlife Refuge
Wisconsin: Horicon and Necedah national wildlife refuges

Cattail Marsh

BEGINNINGS

Marshes can arise in any low spot that holds water long enough for soft-stemmed, water-loving plants to take root. (Soft-stemmed or "herbaceous" plants can be squashed between your fingers; they don't resist breaking the way woody plants do.) Marshes may appear in the backbay of a meandering river, on a dish of sands deposited by a glacier, on the edge of a lake that is silting in, or in the midst of a flooded sedge meadow. They may persist for generations, or they may disappear in just a few years.

Try watching your neighborhood marsh over the years. In a single summer, muskrats may cut out broad swaths of cattails for their food and lodges, transforming a weed-choked patch into an open pool. Over longer periods of time, the bottom of the marsh may build up as sediment flowing in from the uplands begins to settle around the "sieve" of stems. As plants and animals die and fall, they too add to the growing blanket. Eventually, the marsh becomes so shallow that the pools may dry completely, making life unbearable for the cattails, bulrushes, and water lilies.

As the marsh's muddy bottom steams and cracks in the sun, the stranded plants and animals will begin to decay. This is good news for the thousands of seeds that have been buried over the years. Nourished by a pulse of nutrients, a crewcut of green quickly covers the mud. Side by side, plants from the uplands and the lowlands compete for sun, space, nutrients, and water.

Sedges and grasses will make the strongest comeback at first, enjoying the relatively dry environment. If waters don't return, the marsh may become a sedge meadow or, in swampy areas, a sphagnum bog. If the skies open and the basin is reflooded, cattails and other water plants will once again have the upper hand.

THE NINE LIVES OF CATTAILS

The fuzzy brown punk of the cat-o'-nine-tails is the logo of the marsh. This seedhead may be packed with 250,000 seeds, each equipped with a fluffy parachute that catches the wind or floats atop the water. Seeds also stick to the fur, feathers, and muddy feet of wildlife, helping to start new cattail colonies wherever they fall off.

Any plant this successful doesn't depend solely on the whims of animals, waves, or wind to start its next generation, however. Cattails also "travel" by sending out a horizontal stem (called a rhizome) not far from the parent plant. This stem puts down roots and sends up shoots, creating an entirely new plant. Because it is still connected to the root system of the parent plant, however, the new sprout enjoys a subsidy that independent plants don't have.

CHARACTERISTIC PLANTS:

On the Shore:
jewelweed (spotted
    touch-me-not)
spotted joe-pye-weed
water willow

**Emergent Herbaceous
    Plants:**
Broadleaf:
alligator weed (south)
arrow arum
arrowhead
golden club
pickerelweed
purple loosestrife
water plantain

Narrowleaf:
bulrushes
bur reed
common cattail
grasses: blue-joint,
    giant reed, slough,
    maidencane
sedges
soft rush
southern blue flag
spike grass
sweetflag
wild rice

**Submerged Herba-
    ceous Plants:**
bladderworts
pondweeds
water celery
water milfoils
waterweed

**Floating-leaved Her-
    baceous Plants:**
floating hearts
water lilies: fragrant
    and yellow
water shamrock
water shield
yellow pond lily

**Free-floating Herba-
    ceous Plants:**
duckweed
water hyacinth

Cattails store nutrients in these fleshy rhizomes each autumn, before the upper stalks die. These storage pantries remain alive beneath the ice of a winter marsh, relying on dead, hollow stalks to "snorkel" air down to them. Their starches fuel early spring growth, sending new stalks skyward at an astonishing rate. Unless, of course, muskrats discover them first.

Muskrats are fond of rhizomes, and will dive deep to dig them up from the bottom. The rafts of floating plants you sometimes see in a marsh are the aftermath of this feeding. Luckily, the indomitable cattail uses even this uprooting to its advantage, floating to a new place and often taking root again.

Muskrat populations sometimes explode after a new flush of cattails appears, and they occasionally wind up eating themselves out of house and home. Under balanced conditions, however, muskrats' small-scale harvesting can actually improve the marsh and make it more attractive to migrating waterfowl. You can watch flocks on any autumn day, wheeling high over a marsh, then funneling down by the hundreds to rest on the muskrat-opened patches of water.

WHAT'S IN IT FOR WILDLIFE?

Even when they are dried and brittle, old cattail stems still provide shelter to many animals that cross the frozen marsh during the winter. Look for eastern cottontails, marsh rabbits, ring-necked pheasants, and wild turkeys huddling in the windshadow of cattail clumps. Under the ice, muskrats and fish remain alive, and under-the-mud turtles breathe a sort of muddy oxygen.

When the ice begins to thaw, frogs, toads, and salamanders return to the open water of marshes to breed. The thick clusters of plants cut down on wave action, giving these amphibians a quiet harbor in which to lay their eggs. Insects are also laying their eggs between, under, and on the plants, providing an abundant source of food to quick-tongued frogs. In turn, the amphibians give wading birds, snakes, and land mammals something to hunt for.

Breeding birds also come to the marshes in droves. The air is loud with the courtship calls of red-winged blackbirds and others fighting for a patch of marsh in which to nest. The still-standing stalks of last year's plants provide valuable nesting sites for rails, coots, purple gallinules, and other waterfowl. Young ducklings are initiated in the art of paddling in the new growth of cattails, bulrushes, and smartweeds. As a bonus, each plant harbors the larvae of various insects, providing the high-protein diet that ducklings need. Ducks such as mallards and teals dabble for waterweed

PIED-BILLED GREBE

and other submerged plants in the shallow end of the marsh. The tubers of arrowhead ("duck potato") are especially popular with migrating waterfowl when they are fueling up for their southern trek.

Farther out, white-beaked, ducklike birds called coots turn over the floating leaves of water lilies to find tasty snails for their nestlings. Small frogs that have just developed legs and absorbed their tail also linger near the pads for protection. In the center of the marsh, canvasback ducks and redheads dive to nibble their favorite foods, such as water celery and pondweed.

The marsh's productivity is legendary. With sun and water in ample supply, plants fill every available space. Thanks to an abundance of decay organisms, the nutrients in fallen plants and animals are quickly recycled back into the community, encouraging even more growth. Compared with the surrounding uplands, a marsh can seem like a lush oasis of life. Many species have evolved special adaptations that enable them to exploit these riches.

Birds in the marsh, for instance, are adapted to perch on vertical stems (watch for wrens and blackbirds balancing neatly between two stalks), perform vertical takeoffs from small spaces, or even impersonate the reeds, as bitterns do. Pied-billed grebes build nests that float, while other birds nest in dense congregations, without having to worry so much about land predators that they'd find if they were in the uplands.

Like any habitat, however, the marsh is not a utopia. In fact, the most successful species are those that are not solely dependent on the marsh. The truly flexible species concentrate on the edges of the marsh, where they can escape to the uplands if the wetland dries up or floods over.

Red-winged Blackbird

You can't help but notice them. In the spring, it seems that every other stalk in the marsh is topped with a blackbird, puffing up his crimson epaulets and singing his "con-quer-ee" song. In the fall, clouds of migrating

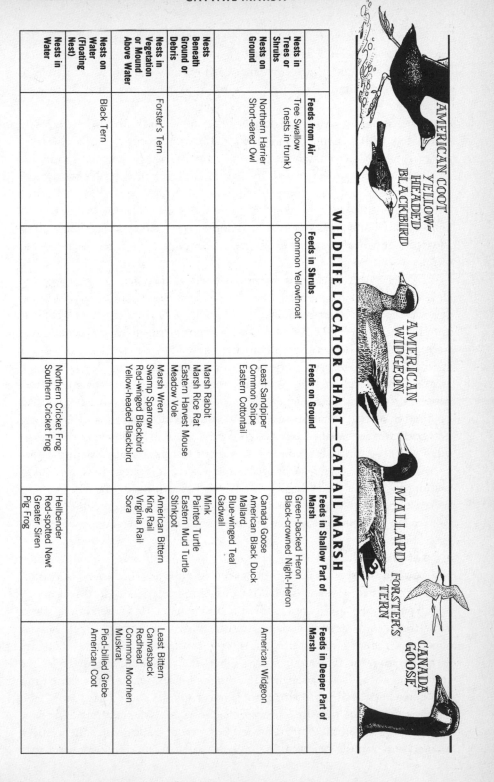

WILDLIFE LOCATOR CHART—CATTAIL MARSH

	Feeds from Air	Feeds in Shrubs	Feeds on Ground	Feeds in Shallow Part of Marsh	Feeds in Deeper Part of Marsh
Nests in Trees or Shrubs	Tree Swallow (nests in trunk)	Common Yellowthroat		Green-backed Heron Black-crowned Night-Heron	
Nests on Ground	Northern Harrier Short-eared Owl		Least Sandpiper Common Snipe Eastern Cottontail	Canada Goose American Black Duck Mallard Blue-winged Teal Gadwall	American Widgeon
Nests Beneath Ground or Debris			Marsh Rabbit Marsh Rice Rat Eastern Harvest Mouse Meadow Vole	Mink Painted Turtle Eastern Mud Turtle Stinkpot	
Nests in Vegetation or Mound Above Water	Forster's Tern		Marsh Wren Swamp Sparrow Red-winged Blackbird Yellow-headed Blackbird	American Bittern King Rail Virginia Rail Sora	Least Bittern Canvasback Redhead Common Moorhen Muskrat
Nests on Water (Floating Nest)	Black Tern				Pied-billed Grebe American Coot
Nests in Water			Northern Cricket Frog Southern Cricket Frog	Hellbender Red-spotted Newt Greater Siren Pig Frog	

AMERICAN COOT
YELLOW-HEADED BLACKBIRD
AMERICAN WIDGEON
MALLARD
FORSTER'S TERN
CANADA GOOSE

birds look like plumes of dark smoke in the sky. Redwings are immensely successful, and with a fall population of 400 million, they are the most numerous land bird in North America. But why have they been able to increase so phenomenally? Are there more marshes now than there used to be?

Surprisingly, marshes are only half the story. Blackbirds, now so closely associated with marshes in our imaginations, probably began as birds of upland fields. They may have moved to the marshes when the conditions in the fields grew too crowded. In the marsh, blackbirds find a cornucopia of insect foods and little competition. They return to upland fields later in the summer, however, to feast on grain and seeds. This ability to exploit the best of both worlds comes in handy when changes occur in either environment. If a marsh dries up in a drought, for instance, the birds can simply switch to fields.

It seems the blackbirds haven't nested in marshes long enough to develop true marsh-bird adaptations, however. For instance, rails and bitterns use grasses as camouflage when predators are near, but blackbirds simply fly away. A curious nesting accident also points to their recent arrival here. Blackbirds sometimes attach their nests to two stalks of cattails. If the cattails grow unevenly, the nest tips and the eggs roll out, a mistake that natural selection will no doubt iron out in time. In the meantime, however, the lopsided nests don't happen often enough to have a real effect on the population. Marshes are still crawling with nestlings in the spring.

Look for red-winged blackbirds—perched on a cattail along the marsh edge (yellow-headed blackbirds take over the center ring), singing a territorial song or feeding on insects. After breeding season, look for flocks feeding in upland fields during the day and returning to marshes at night to roost. Late in August, when molting, they stay in the marshes during the day to hide. In late September, they flock to the uplands again before migrating.

Length: 7–9½ inches.

Look for nests—deep, woven baskets of grass attached to reeds, rushes, or cattails above water or built in a bush, typically less than 6 feet above the ground. The male attracts 3 or more females to his territory, mates with them, and then defends all the nests from predators. Each female chooses her mate, not by the characteristics of the male himself, but by how lucrative his real estate looks. Once she settles in, she defends her subsection of the territory against the other females, while at the same time the polygamist male is battling for their right to stay. They both have legitimate agenda: for him, the more females he has, the more offspring he can sire; for her, the more crowded the territory, the greater the chances of predators raiding her nest.

Listen for—a loud, bravado "con-quer-ee" call, often made with the wings slightly spread to show off the male's epaulets—his badge of maturity and eligibility. Blackbirds also give a "chack" call and an alarm whistle. If you listen very carefully by a breeding site, you may hear the female tearing cattail leaves for her nest.

Muskrat

The haystack houses of these water-loving rodents are a familiar site on most marshes. To build them, muskrats pile aquatic plants such as cattails and bulrushes atop a foundation of mud, branches, and other debris. As they cut down plants and dredge up mud around the house, they create a "moat" of open water that protects them from land predators. To form the chamber inside the house, the muskrat gnaws a tunnel up from the foundation almost to the top, chewing out a cavity that sits above the waterline. As the roof settles, the muskrat munches away at the lowering ceiling (a nutritious job) until the chamber provides a liberal layer of headroom.

You may notice some smaller "outbuildings" around the marsh called feeding houses. These are basically platforms of vegetation that the muskrats have roofed over to give themselves weatherproof, incognito places to eat. These are especially important in cool weather, when the muskrat's naked tail and feet make it vulnerable to a deep chill in the water.

When ice caps the marsh, the muskrats build yet another structure called a "push-up." They begin by gnawing a 4- to 5-inch hole in the ice, through which they pull or push up vegetation to make a 12- to 18-inch lumpy pile over the hole. This vegetation is usually enough to keep ice from closing the hole. A small cavity within this pile gives them a way station on their under-ice excursions—a place to rest, feed, and breathe. Their winter fare includes roots, stems, and tubers that they find under-water. In a pinch, they can even eat the walls of their own homes!

Look for muskrats—swimming in still marshes with no current and plenty of cattails. In the North, the marshes should be at least 3–4 feet deep, so they won't freeze all the way to the bottom in winter. Here's how to tell a muskrat from a beaver: muskrats are 10 times smaller and some-times hold their skinny tails out of the water when swimming, while beavers have wide, flat tails that trail underwater. Occasionally you can catch musk-rats feeding on platforms or sunning themselves on their "decks" during the day, but they are most active at twilight. In spring and fall, muskrats may be on land, even far from the water, looking for new quarters. Drought, high water, or an "eat-out" (when large numbers of muskrats strip all the cattails from a marsh) may force them from their original marsh.

Length: Head and body, 10–14 inches; tail, 8–11 inches.

Look for houses—randomly arranged in the marsh. A house may be some distance from open water, but usually has water-filled channels that connect it to the pond. Muskrats may also den in burrows in the banks.

Look for feeding houses—smaller versions of lodges, used for protection when feeding.

Look for push-ups—small piles of vegetation on an ice-covered marsh, used for feeding, resting, and breathing. Push-ups help extend a muskrat's feeding range under the ice.

Look for feeding debris—piles of mussel shells on feeding platforms, or floating rafts of uprooted cattails.

Look for tracks—in pairs, separated by a stride of 3 inches. The hindprint, 2–3 inches long, is twice as long as the foreprint. Sometimes only four of the five toes print. Look for the drag mark of the skinny tail.

Listen for—the squeals of young muskrats. Adults are rather quiet, except during mating when the female can squeal like a bird. As you approach a marsh, you may hear a loud splash as a muskrat plops from the bank, warning its comrades of your presence.

Cricket Frog

Given the choice of contestants in a frog-jumping contest, you'd be wise to put your money on a cricket frog. There are three species in the East (northern, Blanchard's, and southern cricket frog), and every one of them is a good leaper. Although they are only about an inch long, they are able to spring nearly 3 feet per leap, which is equivalent to you jumping about 200 feet. Their "series of erratic hops" is so characteristic that it is the single feature that most field guides recommend for easy identification in the field. Catching them for closer study is not nearly so easy.

When a frog leaps, its forelimbs lift the body up and aim it. The hind legs swing open from the hip joint, and the thighs and calves extend to propel the frog upward and forward. The ankles and hind feet roll off the ground, giving a little extra "kick." Like any well-aimed projectile, the frog takes the most efficient flight path through the air (45 degrees). As it travels, it shuts its eyes and withdraws them into its mouth cavity for protection. Landing is the most stressful part of the leap. After the forelimbs break the fall, the chest hits the ground, followed by the rest of the underside. With the hind limbs flexed and pressed against the body, the frog is ready to take to the air once again.

For cricket frogs, the destination is usually the safety of water. They move through the water in much the same way as they leap, but without the vertical component. When they kick their legs back, the water spreads open their webbed feet and gives them something to push against, thus propelling them forward. As they pull their legs back up to their body, their webbed feet fold shut, slicing through the water like feathered oars. Besides humans doing the breaststroke, frogs are the only animals that move this way through the water.

Look for cricket frogs—in the shallow edges of lakes, ponds, and marshes, wherever there is abundant emergent vegetation. Northern cricket frogs can be found resting on algal mats or leaves of spatterdock. Blanchard's cricket frogs are said to like the more open, sandy, or muddy edges of wetlands. Southern cricket frogs are mainly in coastal plain lowlands and river bottoms. They may be seen both day and night and are easiest to find when they are calling.

Length: 5/8–1½ inches.

Look for egg masses—about 200 eggs per female, attached to aquatic vegetation in surface clusters of about 10–15 eggs.

Listen for—a metallic, cricketlike "gick gick gick gick" that sounds like two pebbles being clicked together. It starts slow, then accelerates to a rapid pace for 20–30 beats before decelerating. They begin to call in April and May but their choruses may be heard later in the summer too, even during the day. Rain often prompts frogs to call.

STINKPOT

Cocoplum

Southern Bayberry

Bald Cypress

SNAIL KITE

EVERGLADES RAT SNAKE

ANHINGA

Apple Snail

Buttonbush

WOOD STORK

MARSH RABBIT

Resurrection Fern

Marsh Rabbit

Everglades

WHERE TO SEE THIS HABITAT:

Florida: Big Cypress National Preserve; Everglades National Park; Loxahatchee National Wildlife Refuge

Everglades

BEGINNINGS

Long before humans wandered to the continent's tip, the Florida peninsula was covered by a warm, shallow sea. Beneath its placid surface, generations of marine organisms mated and multiplied, filtering down to the bottom as they died. Their shells and fragments pressed layer upon layer to create a 2-mile-thick base of porous limestone. As the level of the Atlantic dropped, the sea drained from the land, leaving a few large lakes still sparkling in the sun.

Lake Okeechobee has been called the "liquid heart of Florida." The river that flows from it is hard to spot from the air, because it flows under a waving prairie of sawgrass, a type of sedge that grows nearly 10 feet high. The land is so flat and so gently tipped that the river flows in a sheet (40 miles wide and 6 inches deep) rather than cutting a deep channel. This sawgrass river even has a huge bed and banks, but they're hard to see with the unaided eye. At one time, the river flowed a full 100 miles to the sea, but has since been interrupted in places by drainage, road-building, and housing developments. Thankfully, some of the land has been included in park systems, where it is carefully managed.

One of the best ways to view the entire river is from an airplane. The golden prairie grows on a limestone bed covered by a 5,000-year-old mantle of peat, marl, and soil—the largest single body of organic soils in the world. Occasionally, you'll see the shimmer of open water in the sawgrass. These are sloughs (pronounced "slews")—channels where the glades water deepens and has a noticeable current. Many animals depend on these sources of water during dry periods.

Also from the air you can see tree islands rising from the sea of sawgrass, ranging from a quarter acre to many thousand acres in size. Some of them are tear-shaped, rounded at the northern end where sediments pile up and tapered toward the south. Several distinct plant communities flourish on these islands, depending on whether the land was once elevated (hammocks), or sunken into a depression (heads).

HAMMOCKS AND HEADS

Hammocks are raised at least a foot above the level of the marsh, high enough for trees to keep their roots above the water so they can get oxygen. Tropical hardwoods are most common here, along with shrubs and woody vines. As leaves and twigs from the hardwoods decay, they release acids that dissolve the edges of the limestone base, creating a moat of water around the island. Throughout its interior, potholes may also be eaten through the limestone base, then filled with water, aquatic plants, and often, with alligators.

Cypress heads, bayheads, and willow heads get their start in low rather than high spots. These pools are populated at first by water lilies and other aquatic plants that die, decay, and begin to build up a layer of peat and marl (clay and calcium carbonate deposits). The aggressive Coastal Plain willows are often the first trees to colonize the borders, "marching" into the pools as they multiply. With their trunks completely submerged, their bushy canopies look as though they are floating. When enough muck or peat has built up the bottom of the basin, other swamp trees such as baldcypress or redbay can become established. Baldcypress sheds its needles each year, adding to the acidity of the waters it grows in. This acid dissolves more limestone, making the pond even larger. The moisture that remains in these depressions is extremely important to animals during dry periods, when water levels in the marsh can drop as much as 4 feet.

GARDENS IN THE AIR

Some of the most unusual inhabitants of tree islands are the orchids and other plants that grow *over* your head. These plants, called epiphytes or air plants, are uniquely adapted to compete in a crowded, shady environment where growing space is at a premium. Instead of jockeying for ground space, air plants take root on branches in the canopy of trees, using their roots for anchors. They don't panhandle nutrients from their host; instead they manufacture their own food and get water and traces of nutrients

CHARACTERISTIC PLANTS:

Sawgrass Prairie:
Trees and Shrubs:
buttonbush
Coastal Plain willow
dahoon
greenbriers
southern bayberry
Herbaceous Plants:
alligator weed
arrow arum
cattail
duckweed
floating hearts
fragrant water lily
lizard's tail
maidencane
pickerelweed
royal fern
sawgrass
smartweeds
spatterdock
upright primrose-
   willow
water pennywort

Tree Islands:
Trees and Shrubs:
baldcypress
cocoplum
Florida nectandra
Florida strangler fig
gumbo-limbo
leadwood
live oak
marlberry
paradise-tree
paurotis-palm
pigeon-plum
pondcypress
possumhaw
redbay
royalpalm
satinleaf
stoppers
sweetbay
tamarind
torchwood
West Indian
   mahogany
willow bustic

Air Plants:
cowhorn
giant wild pine
resurrection fern
sword fern

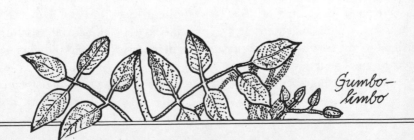

Gumbo-
limbo

DUSKY PIGMY
RATTLESNAKE

GREEN
TREEFROG

from the air. Their dustlike seeds travel easily on the wind, spreading these plants from island to island.

Because they are "rooted" in the air, epiphytes experience great extremes of drought and humidity. To survive the dry times, many have a reduced number of leaves or thick skins that resist wilting. Others store water in thick stems called pseudobulbs or collect rain in leaves shaped like vases. Others have structures that are specially formed to condense dew. Besides nourishing themselves in this way, these water collectors are a drinking fountain for tree-climbing animals and a breeding puddle for mosquitoes and small treefrogs.

FIRES AND ALLIGATORS: KEEPERS OF THE GLADES

The everglades have a wet season (summer) and a dry season (winter). When the water level drops in winter, the mud flats crack in the sun and the sawgrass becomes tinder-dry—perfect fodder for lightning fires. In southern Florida, where there are more lightning storms than almost any other place in North America, these fires can be frequent. In normal years, they are a rejuvenating force, causing many kinds of plants to sprout even more profusely. Even the devastating fires that occur during heavy droughts have their purpose. Wildfires burn the trees on some of the islands, and keep them from expanding to take over the glades (thus the name "EV-ERglades"). Now that natural fires are blocked by unnatural structures such as roads, land managers must set artificial fires to keep the glades in their original state.

American alligators do their own land or, rather, water management in deep-water pools called "alligator holes." Sometimes the alligators move into already existing holes in the downstream end of a slough or into an acid-created pothole on a tree island. Other times, the alligator digs its own hole where instinct tells it the water table is close to the surface. They enlarge and deepen their holes by breaking the ground with their powerful tails and using their snouts to shovel debris up onto the rim of the pool. In time, a dense thicket of Coastal Plain willows, buttonbush, southern bayberry, or other plants grows on this tossed-up "mulch." Alligators help stock their own aquarium by keeping the center open and free of choking vegetation. This open water attracts fish, frogs, and other edibles, which in turn attract birds and mammals that also become part of the alligators' menu.

WHAT'S IN IT FOR WILDLIFE?

Like many of the habitats in this book, the everglades are both irreplaceable and endangered. Besides being a key player in the Gulf of Mexico's water cycle, this 100-mile-long "river of grass" is an oasis for wildlife from surrounding communities. Animals from the hot, dry pinelands, for instance, use the everglades as a watering hole. Other outside visitors include hundreds of migrating species that use the glades for refueling or resting. Finally, the everglades support their own native population of species that couldn't live anywhere else.

Animals native to the everglades were drawn here not just because it was wet, but also because it was dry for part of the year. The drawdown and rejuvenation have shaped the whole ecology of the region. Take the wood stork, for example. These storks need an inordinate number of small fish to feed their young—440 pounds per family during the breeding season. Collecting these fish one by one would be an energy-intensive venture anywhere else but the everglades. Here, the annual drawdown creates shallow, half-evaporated pools where fish are crowded together. The storks merely need to find a pond full of gasping fish, then quickly collect what they need for the day. They are so dependent on these drawdowns that even a few days of heavy rain around breeding season will discourage the entire population from nesting.

Unfortunately, our draining and damming have interrupted much of the natural wetting and drying cycles of the everglades. Many species that depend on them are already extinct, and those in trouble include the snail kite and the American crocodile.

The sloughs and tree hammocks are meccas for wildlife, especially during the dry times. Alligator pools in the everglades can remind you of

DOUBLE-CRESTED CORMORANT

REDDISH EGRET

TRICOLORED HERON

LITTLE BLUE HERON

LIMPKIN

PURPLE GALLINULE

WILDLIFE LOCATOR CHART—EVERGLADES

	Feeds from Air	Feeds in Tree Canopy	Feeds on Ground	Feeds While Standing in Water (Wades)	Feeds Underwater (Dives or Swims)
Nests in Tree Canopy	Brown Pelican American Swallow-tailed Kite		Raccoon	Little Blue Heron Tricolored Heron Reddish Egret White Ibis Roseate Spoonbill Wood Stork	Double-crested Cormorant (also nests on ground) Anhinga
Nests on Ground	Northern Harrier		Dusky Pigmy Rattlesnake	Limpkin (also nests in shrubs)	
Nests Beneath Ground or Debris		Green Anole	Marsh Rabbit Marsh Rice Rat Meadow Vole Eastern Glass Lizard Everglades Rat Snake		Mink Alligator Snapping Turtle Spiny Softshell American Alligator American Crocodile Mud Snake
Nests in Vegetation or Mound Above Water	Snail Kite		Purple Gallinule Marsh Wren Red-winged Blackbird Yellow-headed Blackbird	American Bittern Least Bittern King Rail	Round-tailed Muskrat
Nests in Water		Green Treefrog			

the water holes in the African Serengeti. If you visit one, be sure to take a camera and expect several hours of great wildlife viewing. Thanks to the alligator's efforts, you may see unusual concentrations of raccoons, river otters, spiny softshell turtles, two dozen species of snakes, and ten species of waterbirds. Crowds of fish and aquatic invertebrates wait out the drought in these pools, emigrating in the spring to repopulate the flooded plain. Without these refuges to rekindle them, the everglades communities would eventually flicker out.

Snail Kite

Kites, the kind that children (of all ages) fly, were named for the soaring, darting, swallowlike flight of this beautiful group of birds. If you ever travel to the everglades, by all means go see these snail kites; it may be your last chance. There are now only about 560 snail kites in existence—a full 500 more than we had in the 1960s, but still perilously close to extinction. Their future hinges on two factors: the amount of moisture in the fragile everglades and the fate of the tiny apple snail.

Apple snails live submerged in shallow, marshy pools, and come to the surface only to lay eggs or to feed and breathe. A kite plies the air above these pools for hours until it spots one of the bobbing snails. Without missing a beat, it swoops down, dips one long leg into the water, and hoists the snail up to a feeding perch. Using its specially curved beak, the kite reaches deep into the recesses of the snail's shell, clips the back muscle, and pulls the juicy morsel out in one piece. Although kites are capable of eating other foods, snails are their staple, and without them, kite numbers would soon thin out.

Unfortunately, the droughts that plague the everglades tend to dry up the pools that snails live in. At one time, the water storage capacity of the vast everglades was large enough to buffer the effects of a dry year. But now, after our draining and canal-building, the everglades can't bounce back as quickly, and neither can the snail kite.

Droughts also lead to nesting failure. In normal years, the kites build their nests in shrubs a few inches above the water. In dry years, when the water recedes beneath these shrubs, the snail kites head for the cattails in deeper water. They need this water under their nest so that ground predators can't get to the eggs or nestlings. The loosely constructed stick nests prove too bulky for the cattails, however, and they often collapse before the kite can raise its brood.

This is a classic example of what happens when an animal is shut out of its preferred habitat. Though it may settle somewhere else, it may not succeed in the new habitat. (See What Happens When a Habitat Changes? on page 26.) Thankfully, wildlife managers are aware of the snail kite's plight and often transfer these nests to sturdy, artificial platforms. In many cases, the kites accept these as their own.

Look for snail kites—hunting 5–30 feet above water and marsh grasses, bill pointed downward, watching for snails. They flap their 45-inch-wide wings slowly, with occasional glides in between. They may also perch surprisingly close to you on a dead branch, scanning for snails. Watch the sky for males making swooping flights to impress potential mates. They tuck their wings and descend sharply for 6–15 feet before snapping the wings open and rising again. Groups often roost together in leafless, drowned bushes.

Length: 17–19 inches.

Look for nests—either in bushes growing in water or in dense clumps of cattails, often in colonies of a half-dozen or more pairs. Nests are sloppily built platforms of sticks, 1 foot across and 3–15 feet above the water. A single parent has to make 60 trips a day to feed a brood of 3.

Listen for—the harsh "kor-ee-ee-a, koree-a" the kites use to greet one another. They cackle when an intruder nears the nest. These vocal threats rarely lead to violence though, since the kite's relatively weak talons are no match for most predators.

Mink

In a mink, you can find all the qualities of the weasel family wrapped up in one mammal. It's long and thin like a weasel, it releases musk like a skunk, it has webbed feet like an otter, and it can even climb trees like a marten if it has to. But, as is often typical of "jacks of all trades," the mink has no real specialty. It isn't skinny enough for weasel burrows, nor can it aim its musk as well as a skunk, see underwater as well as an otter, nor climb as agilely as the marten. What the mink does have going for it, however, is its flexibility.

Minks have evolved catholic tastes, and can easily switch to whatever diet item is most prevalent in a particular season or habitat. In summer, they feast on fish, frogs, snakes, salamanders, muskrats, mice, chipmunks, and birds. In the North, when the birds fly south and the frogs burrow underground, minks switch to a diet of winter-active rodents such as rabbits and voles. They aren't particularly choosy about where they hunt; as long as water is involved, it can be a stream, pond, marsh, bog, swamp, slough, or puddle. And unlike some animals that have a restricted range, minks are willing to travel for their dinner. Males may take 5–7 days to inspect more than 25 square miles of prey habitat.

Muskrats are one of the mink's favorite finds. By culling out the weak, young, or very old members of the muskrat population, this supposed "enemy" of muskrats actually helps improve muskrat breeding stock. Minks can also be clever anglers, and have been seen driving fish into a shallow part of the marsh, then feasting on those that are beached.

Most predators, in turn, find the mink a difficult quarry. Minks have sharp teeth, claws, musk, and a ferocious disposition. They are more than willing to take on animals larger than themselves. When trapped, the wily mink will bite off its own foot or even bury itself, trap and all, to get away.

Look for minks—prowling along the edges of wetlands, looking for prey in every hole, hollow tree, log, root tangle, pile of brush, and dark crevice. They also travel over dry land to look for a meal. Minks are active mainly at night, although the abundance of cones (color-sensitive cells) in their eyes suggest that they may have been daytime hunters long before human interference caused them to adjust their habits. In more remote areas, you may still see them out during the day. Trapping of minks is no longer a threat to the population since only 10 percent of fur coats are made from wild mink these days. It takes 75 minks to make one full-length coat, and most are raised on mink ranches. The real threat is the draining of wetlands, stream channelization, and dam building.

Length: Males—head and body, 13–17 inches; tail, 7–9 inches. Females—head and body, 12–14 inches; tail, 5–8 inches.

Look for dens—in "borrowed" muskrat houses (they often eat their hosts), in hollow logs, beneath tree roots, or in 8- to 12-foot-long burrows in the bank. Look for the 2–5 entrances above water level or a vertical plunge hole on the surface of the ground, leading 2–3 feet straight down to the den. Minks may store food in their dens.

Look for droppings—in 2-inch-high piles outside dens. They are slate-colored, bluntly cone-shaped, and segmented, made up of dirt, hair, fur, feathers, and bones.

Smell for—a musky odor left by minks as a territorial marking, a courting signal, or a show of alarm.

Look for tracks—1–1⅜ inches long, on muddy shores. Minks bound in a hunchbacked gait, placing their hind feet in or near forefoot tracks.

Listen for—chuckling, defensive screams, hissings, and warning squeaks.

American Alligator

In 1791, when naturalist William Bartram toured the American South, he wrote: "The alligators were in such incredible numbers and so close together from shore to shore that it would have been easy to have walked across on their heads." Nearly a century and a half later, so many of these reptiles had been made into shoes and handbags that they were in danger of extinction. Thankfully, laws were enacted to stem the tide of gator slaughter.

Given half a chance, alligators are quite capable of rebuilding their populations. The females are model mothers, building a clever nest that rivals any in the natural world. The huge mound of decaying vegetation is a natural composter, using the heat of decomposition to keep the eggs warm.

The female begins by clearing a site for her nest—tearing vegetation out by the roots, mashing it down, or scissoring it off with her large jaws. She then piles the vegetation into a cone-shaped mound, using her snout and tail to push it tightly into place. She makes frequent trips to the waterway to pluck additional water plants to build up the cone, which she finally levels at the top. Then, to form a large, bowl-shaped hollow in the top of the mound, she begins to pinwheel on her belly, pushing off with one foot. Into the hollow, she packs mud and more aquatic plants until it is filled to the top again. She hollows out a smaller depression in this "liner," just large enough to lay her eggs, which number between 25 and 60. Using debris she has pulled from the nest, she covers the eggs, and then smooths the large cone with her body.

The eggs incubate for 9 weeks, with the female standing guard nearby. The temperature control is crucial. Researchers have found that if the eggs are kept below 86 degrees F, they will all turn out female; if kept above 93 degrees F, they will all be male. If the female senses that the nest is drying out, she will crawl around on it to wet it. Evidently, her thermostat control works; most broods appear to be an even mix of males and females. The 8- to 10-inch hatchlings will stay with their mother for 1½ years. By the time they are finally adult-size, there are few animals (besides poachers) that they will have to fear.

Look for American alligators—prowling the wilder waterways with just their eyes or snout showing above the water. They may occasionally climb on shore to bask (reptiles use the heat or cold of the environment to regulate their body temperature). Their feeding method is to slowly sneak up on a prey animal and surprise it—swimming beneath a duck and pulling it down, for instance. They can swallow a duck in one gulp, sealing their air passage with their tongue so as not to drown while dining. If the prey is too large to be swallowed in a gulp, they may shake it violently until it breaks apart. Watch for alligators under heron colonies, waiting patiently for a nestling to fall overboard.

Length: 6–19 feet.

Look for nests:—mounds of mud, leaves, and rotting vegetation, 5–7 feet in diameter and 1½–3 feet high. Use caution from spring to late summer, when there may be an anxious mother guarding the nest.

Listen for—a throaty, bellowing roar of the male during breeding season. As he roars, glands under his chin spray jets of a musky fluid that can be smelled miles away. The female bellows too, but not as loudly as the male. The young gators utter moaning grunts: "y-eonk, y-eonk, y-eonk" (try saying "umph-umph-umph" in a high pitch with your mouth closed).

ALLIGATOR
SNAPPING
TURTLE

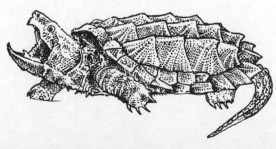

sedge rhizomes

NORTHERN HARRIER

NORTHERN PINTAIL

MEADOW VOLE

Common Sedge

SEDGE WREN

Blue-joint

Fowl-meadow Grass

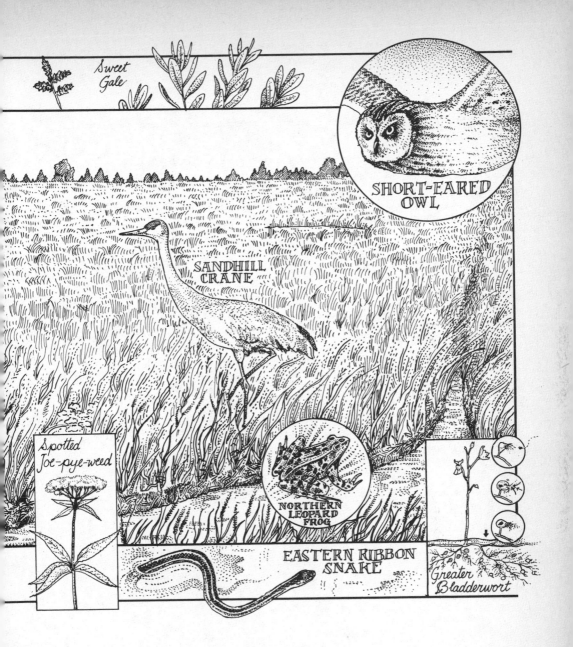

Sweet Gale

SHORT-EARED OWL

SANDHILL CRANE

Spotted Joe-pye-weed

NORTHERN LEOPARD FROG

EASTERN RIBBON SNAKE

Greater Bladderwort

Sedge Meadow

WHERE TO SEE THIS HABITAT:

Maine: Moosehorn National Wildlife Refuge

Michigan: Hiawatha, Huron-Manistee, and Ottawa national forests; Seney National Wildlife Refuge

Minnesota: Agassiz, Rice Lake, Sherburne, and Tamarac national wildlife refuges; Chippewa and Superior national forests; Minnesota Wetlands Complex

New York: Adirondack Forest Preserve; Iroquois and Montezuma national wildlife refuges

Wisconsin: Chequamegon and Nicolet national forests; Horicon, Necedah, and Trempealeau national wildlife refuges

Sedge Meadow

BEGINNINGS

Sedge meadows often crop up in old lake beds after the water has drained and the ground is no longer wet enough for a cattail marsh. The sedges persist because they can tolerate an occasional flood, yet stand on their own without a constant covering of water. To find the first inklings of a sedge meadow, look along the edges of old lakes and shallow streams. In the Far North, you'll also find sedge meadows bordering bogs in a complex landscape known as patterned peatlands.

Unfortunately, some people view sedge meadows as worthless flatlands, producing nothing more than mosquitoes. Chances are they have never seen the salmon-colored glow of the sedge at sunset or watched the northern harrier cruise the tops of the rippling blades. The uncommon wildlife that thrive here do so because the meadow offers a unique mix of terrestrial and aquatic habitats.

Like many of our vital habitats, sedge meadows are fragile and sensitive to disturbances that upset their moisture supply and chemical balance. Draining, road construction, peat mining, or even nearby beaver dams can transform sedge meadows into shrub thickets, tamarack swamps, or dry grassy meadows. With their passing, the wildlife community that depends on sedge meadows loses a home.

THE MEADOW MAKER

A good way to tell sedges from look-alike grasses is to remember that "sedges have edges." Try rolling a stem in your fingers; sedge stems have three flat sides, while grass stems are smooth cylinders.

The moundlike stepping-stones you use to work your way across a meadow are called tussocks. These clumps of sedge stems come up year after year and live to an old age. To start another tussock, the clump sends out a horizontal, satellite stem known as a "rhizome," or it extends a rootstock under the ground. A new plant will arise as much as a foot away from the parent plant.

Sedge shoots sprout, not in the spring like most plants, but in late summer. The tiny shoots remain green all through a winter locked in snow and ice. They bolt from the gate as soon as the ice thaws, gaining a critical head start in growth over other wetland plants. As the sedges die, more and more leaves, matted roots, and rhizomes are added to the soil, creating a dense, fibrous peat—the perfect growing medium for the meadow maker.

Another reason sedges dominate wet meadows is that they can withstand the characteristic up-and-down water levels. Their aerial stems are tall enough to remain above the water, even when the marsh is flooded. When water levels drop, the leaves can fold up neatly to conserve moisture.

WHAT'S IN IT FOR WILDLIFE?

To a mouse-sized rodent, the 2-foot-high blades of sedges, grasses, and rushes can seem like a towering jungle. Because the tussocks are so densely packed with leaves, they make good cover for arctic shrews, meadow voles, and other small animals foraging for insects and seeds. The tangle of last year's dead leaves and rhizomes also makes a tightly knit fabric under which to burrow. When traveling between tussocks, these animals must be

---

CHARACTERISTIC PLANTS:

Herbaceous Plants:

		Scattered Shrubs:
angelica	panicled aster	narrowleaf meadow-
bedstraw bellflower	purple meadow rue	sweet
blue-joint	purple-stemmed aster	sandbar willow
Canada anemone	rattlesnake grass	speckled alder
common cattail	rushes	sweet gale
field horsetail	sedges	
fowl-meadow grass	sensitive fern	
golden ragwort	southern blue flag	
goldenrods	spotted joe-pye-weed	
greater bladderwort	swamp milkweed	
marsh bellflower	water horehound	
marsh marigold		

---

on constant alert for northern harriers and short-eared owls, two birds of prey that are attracted to the high rodent population here.

Many ground- or shrub-foraging birds also find safe feeding in the sedge meadow. The triangular seeds of sedges are relished by birds such as rails, grouse, sparrows (swamp and Lincoln's), snow buntings, and common redpolls. Insects attracted to the rank growth keep wrens, swallows, and common snipes busy. Watch the tops of small bushes or tall stalks for singing yellowthroats and swamp sparrows.

Thumbprint ponds rich with algae and tiny floating animals offer late-developing tadpoles the sheltered water and food they need to mature into adult northern leopard frogs. Trigger-quick egrets and herons often snap up the unsuspecting frogs that float on the surface at breeding time. In fall, winter, and early spring, shallow water frequently covers the meadow, giving dabbling ducks such as mallards, northern shovelers, pintails, and blue-winged teals a place to rest and feed. Nearby, elevated tussocks keep the nests of sedge wrens and Le Conte's sparrows from getting wet.

Northern Harrier

The hawk flies low and liltingly across the tops of the sedges. Its head is pointed down, patiently combing the dense sea of blades. Suddenly a blade parts, and the retreating form of a meadow vole flashes in the gap. The harrier overshoots, then somersaults back, hovering for a moment like a gigantic hummingbird. In a blur of speed, it dives down, extends its talons, and gracefully plucks a limp form from the meadow.

Watch carefully now. A female harrier flies to meet the hunter, and they twist and turn together in midair. Finally, the hunter drops the vole and the female tucks her wings for a headfirst descent. At the last moment, she swoops beneath the falling vole, snatching it before it lands. You've just seen an aerial food pass, performed some 15–20 times a day when females are bringing food to the young in the nest. When the nestlings get a little older, they will fly out themselves to receive food via the pass.

These aerobats are also tireless travelers. They spend 40 percent of their day plying the meadow, covering some 100 miles a day in their search for rodents, shrews, rabbits, frogs, snakes, and even insects. Whenever they can, they catch a ride on air currents, tilting their wings into a slight "V" and rocking their bodies from side to side. They are listening as hard as they are watching. These hawks have a ruff of feathers around their face that directs sound to their ears, allowing them to detect the sound of shuffling paws up to 18 feet away. As they get closer, they can pinpoint the source of the sound to within a millimeter. Their eyes are also built for picking up detail from a long distance. Hawk eyes are packed with a million visual receptor cells—five times more than we humans have.

BOBOLINK BLUE-WINGED TEAL KING RAIL VIRGINIA RAIL SORA COMMON SNIPE SWAMP SPARROW Le CONTE'S SPARROW

WILDLIFE LOCATOR CHART—SEDGE MEADOW

	Feeds from Air	Feeds in Tree Canopy	Feeds on Ground	Feeds While Standing in Water (Wades)	Feeds in Water (Dabbles or Swims)
Nests on Ground	Northern Harrier Short-eared Owl	Common Yellowthroat (also nests in shrubs)	Sandhill Crane Common Snipe Sedge Wren Le Conte's Sparrow Sharp-tailed Sparrow Lincoln's Sparrow Bobolink		Mallard Northern Pintail Blue-winged Teal Northern Shoveler Northern Water Snake Eastern Ribbon Snake
Nests Beneath Ground or Debris			Northern Short-tailed Shrew Meadow Vole Southern Bog Lemming		Water Shrew Painted Turtle Spotted Turtle
Nests in Vegetation Above Water			Swamp Sparrow	King Rail Virginia Rail Sora	Common Moorhen
Nests in Water			Pickerel Frog Northern Leopard Frog		

It is interesting to note that the nighttime counterpart of the northern harrier, the short-eared owl, is equipped with similar hunting apparatus: a round, disklike face to amplify sound, ultrasensitive eyes and ears, and a low, quartering flight. Indeed, the habitat dictates the adaptations, even across species lines.

Look for northern harriers—skimming along the tops of sedges, 10–30 feet above the meadow. They roost on the ground in groups of usually less than 10, but occasionally as many as 50.

Length: 17½–24 inches.

Watch for courtship flights—or "skydances" in the spring. The male ascends steeply to 60 feet, rolls or somersaults at the top, then dives down to within 10 feet of the ground before swooping upward again. He performs as many as 70 of these U-shaped flights in a row, thus advertising his willingness to mate and to defend his territory. Later in the season, the female will join him in aerobatic feats, and they will spend much time flying together.

Don't disturb nests—on the ground in a protected hollow, or built as high as 18 inches above the water, on a clump of sedge or willow, or on a stick foundation. The nest typically measures 13–20 inches across and 3–10 inches deep. Other harriers may be nesting as close as 200 yards away.

Listen for—a nasal "pee-pee-pee" or a sharp whistle when on the nest.

Meadow Vole

At ground level, where the grass blades rise like tree trunks, a small mouselike rodent finds a new plant blocking one of its regular routes, called a "runway." It immediately bites at the base until the plant falls, and then cuts it up into smaller pieces that are easier to eat. Other voles are elsewhere in the meadow, also cutting grasses to keep their runways open. There may be as many as 4.6 miles of runways crisscrossing the meadow that you walk through on your way to work. But have you ever seen a vole?

Consider the fact that a female vole, under ideal conditions, is capable of producing 1 million descendants in her lifetime. A single acre of grassland may hold up to 200 of these living lawn mowers, all eating up to 60 percent of their body weight daily and reproducing prolifically. In a full-scale explosion, it's a wonder our meadows aren't shaved bare.

The fact is that nature's system of checks and balances is always at work regulating the vole population. Almost everything that eats meat eats voles, from snakes to bobcats. In fact, voles compose up to 85 percent of the diet of some hawks and owls, making them a premier link in the food chain and an invaluable source of meadow energy. Thus, the average vole lives only 2–3 months, long enough to have about three litters.

Despite these controls, vole numbers tend to swell every 3–4 years. The crowded conditions usually lead some voles to abandon the habitat. It seems that those that stay at home are genetically different than those that leave to colonize new territory. The colonizers have more reproductive potential, it seems, while the stay-at-homes, the defenders of territory, are by nature more aggressive. This riddle is not completely solved, however.

Look for meadow voles—running in the open between runways or on top of the snow for short distances. Since exposure makes them vulnerable to predators, these forays are usually conducted at top speed. They are active around the clock, but peak times are dawn and dusk. In winter, they are most apt to be stirring during the day.

Length: Head and body, 3½–5 inches; tail, 1²/₅–2³/₅ inches.

Look for runways—shallow, 1-inch-wide ruts in the soil, worn by the paws of innumerable voles and other rodents that also use the runway system. Arched grasses usually form a roof over the runway. Look for 1½-inch-wide holes in this roof, especially visible in the spring when snow has matted down the vegetation. Starting at a hole, part the grasses carefully to "unzip" the roof and expose the runway. In the winter, voles tunnel under the insulating blanket of snow.

Look for droppings—in piles at intersections in the runway system.

Look for grass clippings—lining the runway and in piles around burrow entrances.

Look for gnawing—at the base of shrubs and small trees. Voles sometimes eat a band of bark around trunk, thus girdling and killing the tree.

Look for nests—small, round balls of grasses, 6 inches in diameter, tucked into burrows or under boards, rocks, or logs.

Look for skulls—of meadow voles in the pellets of indigestible fur and bones that hawks and owls cough up. Red-tailed hawks and great horned owls may eat 2 or 3 of these voles a day.

As the snow melts—look for meandering ruts in the snow, 1½ to 2 inches wide. These were vole tunnels during the winter, but their roofs are now melted off by the sun.

Look for tracks—⅝–½ inch long. The foreprint has four toes printing, and the hindprint shows five. The pattern varies, but when jumping, the tracks are 2–4 inches apart.

Listen for—the squeaks of fighting voles. They often battle when they meet in runways, rolling in a great ball together and boxing with their forepaws. At breeding season, as many as 90 percent of the males bear scars from these fights.

Northern Leopard Frog

If you took biology lab in high school, chances are you may have dissected a northern leopard frog. They are widely collected for this purpose, and further reduced in some areas by toxic amounts of agricultural chemicals. Losing leopard frogs disrupts the food chain for a great many predators, including snakes, turtles, birds, weasels, fish, minks, and raccoons. Besides being a vital food source, frogs are also predators of many kinds of spiders, snails, sow bugs, and insects, including those that harm farm crops.

To lure females, the males call out with a rumbling snore. They float atop the water as they call, and groups of these spread-eagle suitors can look like skydivers in formation. After breeding and laying eggs in the shallow pools, the frogs return to the waving sedges to hunt insects.

Tadpoles may transform by midsummer, or it may take as long as 2 years for them to lose their tail, trade their gills for lungs, grow new front legs, and lengthen their hind legs. As their diet switches to insects, they must also shorten their digestive tract and revamp their sense of smell to monitor scents in the air instead of water.

For the first year, newly metamorphosed frogs tend to stay close to the safety of the pools. When you walk along the shore, they may hop before you in a thousand directions, like kernels of corn popping. Adults wander farther away, returning to watery places when the weather gets cold. The homing instinct of frogs is very keen. Even on cloudy nights, without using smell or hearing, these frogs can find their way home if displaced.

Leopard frogs pile up in groups on the bottom of ponds to hibernate, occasionally taking a swim beneath the ice. If the pond is shallow enough, it may freeze through to the bottom, depriving the frogs of oxygen or encasing them in ice. The population eventually recovers, however, freshened by the large number of eggs laid by newly arriving frogs. According to Wisconsin herpetologist Richard Vogt, a single female leopard frog can lay 6,000 eggs!

Look for leopard frogs—breeding in pools between March and April. Adults are in grasses and sedges throughout summer, but juveniles stick close to pond borders. When approached, they hunker down in preparation for a fast leap. When picked up, they may squirt a foul-smelling liquid.

Length: 2–5 inches.

Look for egg masses—500–1,000 in a clump. The eggs are dark (perhaps to enhance solar heating), covered with jelly, and attached to submerged sticks, sedges, or grasses.

In October and November—look for groups of leopard frogs on the shores of ponds, streams, or lakes, preparing to submerge for the winter.

Listen for—a many-pulsed snoring call in March or April, beginning at dusk. Leopards have at least three types of calls: the mating snore, a croak that sounds like rubbing your finger across a rubber balloon, and a loud chuckle that may establish territory.

COMMON
REDPOLL

Speckled Alder

STAR-NOSED
MOLE

MOOSE

Marsh
Fern

ALDER FLYCATCHER

Pussy willow

YELLOW WARBLER

Skunk Cabbage

Red-osier Dogwood

PICKEREL FROG

AMERICAN WOODCOCK

Earthworm

Alder root nodule

Shrub Swamp

WHERE TO SEE THIS HABITAT:

Maine: Moosehorn National Wildlife Refuge

Michigan: Hiawatha, Huron-Manistee, and Ottawa national forests; Seney National Wildlife Refuge

Minnesota: Agassiz, Rice Lake, Sherburne, and Tamarac national wildlife refuges; Chippewa and Superior national forests; Minnesota Wetlands Complex

New Jersey: Great Swamp National Wildlife Refuge

New York: Adirondack Forest Preserve; Iroquois and Montezuma national wildlife refuges

Wisconsin: Chequamegon and Nicolet national forests; Horicon, Necedah, and Trempealeau national wildlife refuges

West Virginia: Monongahela National Forest

Shrub Swamp

BEGINNINGS

You'll find shrub swamps in lowlands that are too dry for sedge meadow plants but too wet for upland trees such as quaking aspen and paper birch. Dried-up sedge meadows, drained beaver ponds, old marshes, or the edges of lakes and streams are likely candidates for a shrub swamp. Conditions are fertile compared with other types of saturated lands. The soil is rich and black, and less acidic than that of bogs. Flowing rivulets bring a pulse of oxygen and fresh nutrients to the roots of plants. Speckled alder, the most abundant tree in the swamp, further improves the real estate.

Alder invades with abandon, forming a twisted maze of purple-black to reddish-brown branches that can be taxing to walk or, rather, to climb through. Alder is a member of the legume family, and like the plants used to rejuvenate fallow fields, it enriches the soil wherever it grows. Lumpy "nodules" in its roots harbor bacteria that extract nitrogen from the air and convert it to a form plants can use. Alder distributes this valuable nutrient with a bumper crop of leaves that carpets the swamp floor each fall. This mulch helps support a diverse gallery of herbs such as rough bedstraw, virgin's-bower, and crested wood fern. Wedged among the alders are tall, wispy pussy willows and squat clumps of red-osier dogwood. Patches of skunk cabbage sprout from the rich muck, hiding the posthole-deep hoofprints of moose.

As long as water is moving through them, alder swamps are likely to remain shrubby. Once they start to dry up, they may convert to black ash or red maple. Or, in swamps where the predecessor was a burned black spruce bog, the future may belong to needleleaf trees (usually northern white-cedar). For the most part, however, as long as the swamp remains swampy, speckled alder and pussy willow will rule the roost.

IT PAYS TO BE FLEXIBLE

Occasionally, flood waters will rake through the swamp, drowning grasses and pulling at the bases of the shrubs. Alder, willow, and dogwood, unlike many trees, are able to put up with "wet feet" for a while without drowning. Their multiple, clumped stems are also supple enough to bend without breaking.

The weight of the winter's first wet snowfalls often bows over pliable young alder stems, creating a hidden maze of pockets under the snow. Beneath these snow-laden branches, a snowshoe hare can pass the coldest winter days shielded from biting winds, hidden from its predators, and surrounded by tasty young plant shoots. When the spring sun frees the alders of their burden, the resilient branches arch back up to the light, producing the sprawling shape they are known for.

Alder and willow are also flexible in the ways they reproduce. Their seeds float on the wind or are carried in the stomachs of birds and mammals, to be later "planted" in droppings. These shrubs can also sprout from the base of old plants, from underground stems, or even from their own branches in a process called layering. To see this, gently lift a lower branch and look for white roots dangling from the underside. A new plant will spring up where the branch touched the soil, thus helping the alder or willow extend its empire.

CHARACTERISTIC PLANTS:

Trees and Shrubs:	Herbaceous Plants:	
blueberries	arrowleaf tearthumb	sensitive fern
buttonbush	blue-joint	skunk cabbage
narrowleaf meadow-	bulrushes	spotted joe-pye-weed
sweet	crested wood fern	turtlehead
pussy willow	goldenrods	virgin's-bower
red-osier dogwood	marsh fern	Virginia bluebells
smooth gooseberry	panicled aster	
speckled alder	purple-stemmed aster	
sweet gale	rough bedstraw	
viburnums	sedges	

SONG SPARROW

YELLOW-BELLIED FLYCATCHER

WHAT'S IN IT FOR WILDLIFE?

During the warm season, the moist shade of an alder thicket provides a cool refuge for many kinds of wildlife. Moles and shrews build their "highways" under the weave of trailing plants. Elusive star-nosed moles dive for worms in the rivulets trickling around alder stems. Nearby, American woodcocks probe the mud with their sensitive, pencil-thin bills. They are looking for earthworms that seem to gravitate toward the nitrogen-rich soil around alder roots. Above, gray catbirds feather their nests in the fragrant, leafy branches, and yellow warblers pluck a beakful of fluffy seeds from the pussy willows. Deep inside the thickets, female moose seek seclusion before giving birth to their spindle-legged calves.

In the summer, moose and snowshoe hare pass by the ubiquitous alder in favor of the more palatable willow leaves and shoots. (Willows, by the way, contain the chemical used to make aspirin.) Skunk cabbage is even more unpopular than alder because its leaves contain oxalic acid, a noxious chemical defense. Black bears don't seem to mind, however, and you can find them feeding liberally on skunk cabbage in the spring.

In the fall, alder catkins are picked clean of their seeds by colorful redpolls and chickadees, while deer and grouse eat the twigs and buds. In winter, willows are often tall enough to stick up through the snow and provide buds for grouse, as well as twigs and bark for beaver, white-tailed deer, moose, and snowshoe hare.

American Woodcock

Secreted by its cinnamon-colored, leaflike plumage, a woodcock may be right under your nose before you see it. Yet it has certainly seen you. These birds have 360-degree vision, thanks to eyes set far back on their golf-ball-sized head. Their range of vision overlaps in the front, giving

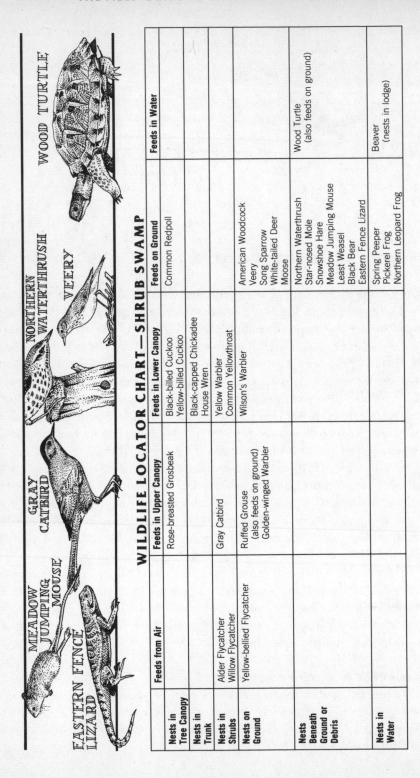

EASTERN FENCE LIZARD

MEADOW JUMPING MOUSE

GRAY CATBIRD

NORTHERN WATERTHRUSH

VEERY

WOOD TURTLE

WILDLIFE LOCATOR CHART—SHRUB SWAMP

	Feeds from Air	Feeds in Upper Canopy	Feeds in Lower Canopy	Feeds on Ground	Feeds in Water
Nests in Tree Canopy		Rose-breasted Grosbeak	Black-billed Cuckoo Yellow-billed Cuckoo	Common Redpoll	
Nests in Trunk			Black-capped Chickadee House Wren		
Nests in Shrubs	Alder Flycatcher Willow Flycatcher	Gray Catbird	Yellow Warbler Common Yellowthroat		
Nests on Ground	Yellow-bellied Flycatcher	Ruffed Grouse (also feeds on ground) Golden-winged Warbler	Wilson's Warbler	American Woodcock Veery Song Sparrow White-tailed Deer Moose	
Nests Beneath Ground or Debris				Northern Waterthrush Star-nosed Mole Snowshoe Hare Meadow Jumping Mouse Least Weasel Black Bear Eastern Fence Lizard	Wood Turtle (also feeds on ground)
Nests in Water				Spring Peeper Pickerel Frog Northern Leopard Frog	Beaver (nests in lodge)

154

them highly accurate binocular vision such as hawks have. Their view continues all around the sides of their head, then overlaps again in the back to give them another window of binocular vision! To make room for these backset eyes, their ears have shifted forward onto their cheeks, and their brain has crowded back toward the base of their skull.

The woodcock's wraparound eyes developed as a way to watch for predators when their bill was buried to the hilt in mud. They spend much of their lives head-down like this, while sensitive nerve endings in their bill "listen" for the vibrations of earthworms in their beds. A woodcock may plant its "antennae" in one spot, then suddenly pull up and scurry to a spot farther away, where it has sensed an earthworm stirring. If you watch carefully, you may see a woodcock stamp its feet to get earthworms to wriggle and give themselves away. Their bill is long, nearly a quarter of their total body length, and flexible at the tip so that it can open up underground to pinch their prey. The serrations help them hold onto the slippery worm and overcome the tug caused by its anchoring bristles.

Unfortunately, the woodcock's passion for earthworms puts it in danger wherever pesticides are used. Because earthworms pass large volumes of soil through their digestive tracts, they tend to accumulate toxic amounts of these chemicals. And woodcocks, in turn, eat large numbers of these tainted worms.

Look for American woodcocks—resting, raising young, and feeding in shrub swamps during the day, then moving to upland fields half an hour after sunset to roost for the night. In the spring, look for courtship flights in clearings that have scattered shrubs and small trees to protect the birds from aerial predators. The trees immediately ringing the clearing must be low enough to allow clearance for low-angle takeoffs. The flight begins with a gurgle and an insectlike "pent pent" sound. The male then planes up from the field, circles overhead, and drifts back down like a leaf on the breeze. He may fly a dozen times to impress his mate.

Length: 11 inches.

Look for jab marks—in the mud, where woodcocks have inserted their pencil-thin bills in pursuit of earthworms.

Look for nests—in cuplike depressions on the forest floor, within 50 feet of an edge. If you disturb a female on her nest she will reluctantly fly away, usually dragging her tail and dangling her legs low to the ground in an attempt to distract you from the nest.

Listen for—a "tuko" and "pent pent" before the courtship flight, and the twitter of wings as the male circles overhead. The twitter is caused by wind strumming the front of the feathers. Other calls include "wick-wick-wick," a scolding "cac-cac-cac-cac," a hawklike "keeee," and a catlike call when flushed.

Star-nosed Mole

In the natural world, being a specialist sometimes means sacrificing other skills. Take the blind and clumsy mole, for instance. When it comes to digging, moles are the epitome of form and function. Their hair is hinged and reversible; it lays just as flat whether they are moving forward or backward in their burrow. Their forelimbs don't drop below their body like most animals' but, rather, work like flippers, extending straight out from their sides. Their hands are huge, and the skin at the edges of the fingers is flattened to achieve a paddle effect. Long claws tip each finger. Their shoulder blades are enlarged and their breastbone deeply ridged to hold a powerful set of chest muscles—the "hydraulics" of the shoveling forepaws. Because of these specialized features, however, moles can't run as swiftly as their cousins the shrews. And, in the dim light of their subterranean homes, they've lost their vision.

To compensate, they've evolved a trigger sensitivity to touch. Their hands, face, feet, and tail are covered with bristles that warn them, much like cat's whiskers do, about what's in their path. Around their sensitive nostrils they have a rosette of 22 pink, fleshy, fingerlike projections. These "Eimer's organs" are chock-full of nerves and blood vessels that are sensitive to touch, vibrations, pressure changes, chemical sensations, and possibly heat. These feelers can curl together to protect the nostrils when the mole is digging, and bloom outward when it enters the water.

Instead of relying on their eyes to find them food, moles use their strange flippers to dig for dinner. Their "convenience foods" are the insects and other items that simply fall into shallow, underground tunnels. A single mole may eat nearly 80 pounds of food a year, which equals, for instance, 8,000 earthworms. To eat an earthworm, the mole begins at one end and sucks (like a kid with a piece of spaghetti). Strangely enough, this tiny worm hunter has 44 teeth—more than wolves, bobcats, bears, and most other mammals in North America. This mouthful of cutlery comes in handy when the star-nosed mole takes on mollusks and crayfish.

Perhaps because of the high water table in swamps, star-nosed moles are often found foraging aboveground, in the water, or in shallow ruts called runways. Once outside the safety of their burrows, they are easy (though not very tasty) prey for hawks, meat-eating mammals, and even fish.

Look for star-nosed moles—year-round, most active at night, foraging aboveground for earthworms, slugs, snails, and small bits of plant food. They may also venture out during the day if it's cloudy or raining. Don't forget to look for them zigzagging in the water, more often in winter than in summer.

Length: Head and body, 4½–5 inches; tail 3–3½ inches.

Nests are underground—3 to 12 inches below the surface but above the high-water line, usually in a knoll of higher ground. Moles enlarge a section of tunnel and fill it with grass and leaves. You may also find a grass nest on the ground under logs.

Look for ridges—of soil pushed up by the mole's burrowing. When the mole burrows deeper, the ridge will stop, then reappear when the mole surfaces again. You've heard about moles "repairing" tunnels that have collapsed. It may not be fussiness that causes them to do this. They may simply be redrilling already-broken soil because it is easiest to work.

Look for molehills—mounds of ejected soil (up to 6 inches high) at the 1½-inch-wide mouths of deep tunnels where moles rear their young and forage in winter. Molehills are most visible in the spring and fall when building is at its peak. To eject a buildup of soil, moles turn a slow somersault in their tunnel, and then push out this soil with their forefeet. Several muddy layers make the mounds look like the "mud chimneys" of crayfish.

Look for droppings—in or outside of runways, tiny and irregularly curved.

Listen for—the wheezing of sleeping moles, and the shrill cries of nestlings in ground nests.

Moose

A close encounter with a 7-foot-tall, half-ton moose is sure to get your adrenaline flowing. Imagine how your ancestors must have felt, stalking giant mammals even larger than this with handmade tools. When you're standing close to a moose, even the cartoonish dewlap, beady eyes, and bucket nose take on an aura of the magnificent.

The moose's great size is an adaptive trait that has helped it to survive in its northern habitat. A moose loses less body heat than a deer, for instance, and is comfortable down to a very chilly − 40 degrees F. With a stomach that can hold 112 pounds of food, the moose has plenty of storage space for fuel. They actually eat 50–60 pounds of browse a day, reaching up to 11 feet for twigs and leaves—far above the heads of other browsers. To get to the top of saplings they can't reach, moose simply walk over them, bending them down to a convenient height. Their long legs enable them to wade deep into lakes for aquatic plants, or to negotiate snowbanks that would slow wolves, bobcats, or deer. In very deep snow, they will sometimes crawl on the surface, using their bent legs like snowshoes.

Despite their bulk, moose can gallop at a brisk 35 miles per hour, but can also be surprisingly quiet when they detect danger. They can slip through even the densest woods without snagging their 7-foot-wide antlers or betraying their presence with sound.

Young moose are not nearly so adept; their struggles through the thickets make them a prime target for bear and wolves. Besides being a bit awkward, they are also rather trusting. Calves have been known to follow any kind of animal, including a human, during their impressionable first months. Consequently, female moose are vigilant mothers; they spend 1½ years teaching and defending their calves. Threats to the calf's life are not taken lightly. The mother usually keeps her calf in front of her when they travel so she can mount a rear-attack against predators. She begins by flattening her ears, raising her hair, and stiffening her lip—equivalent to shaking her fist. If you're even considering staying to see what happens next, remember that one slap from a moose's sharp forehooves can kill or cripple a strong wolf!

Look for moose—in thickets any time of day or night. They alternate a few hours of activity with a few hours of rest. Spot them by looking for the darkest horizontal line in a field of vertical bushes. The flat, tan palms of antlers catch the sun, and can be spotted up to a mile away. Also look for moose wading in the inlets and outlets of lakes where the water is shallow and filled with sodium-rich aquatic plants. You may see a "decorated" moose rise from the water with slimy green stalks dripping from his antlers.

Size: Head and body length, 6¾–8½ feet; tail length, 6¾ inches; shoulder height, 5–6½ feet.

Look for wallows—in rutting season (September and October), males urinate in and paw up 10-foot-square patches of earth. Both sexes roll in these muddy hollows as part of the mating ritual. A female will spread out on a wallow to claim it, and rival females will work tirelessly to get her to leave.

Look for rubbing trees—or saplings that males thrash their antlers against to help scrape off the bloody strips of drying "velvet." Velvet is the blood-rich skin that covers the antlers when they are developing. Males will use their 75-pound, 7-foot-wide rack to attract females and fight with other males. A honeycombed core enables the rack to give somewhat under stress. Antlers are shed between December and March, but are rarely found because they are eaten so quickly by mice and other gnawers of the forest floor.

In the winter—moose often travel to dense stands of mixed needleleaf and broadleaf trees. They form loose colonies, using each other's trails to save energy in deep snow.

Look for tracks—in deep, posthole depressions in wet mud or snow.

The prints are cloven, 6½ inches long, with signs of a dewclaw (a digit above the true hoof).

Look for browse lines—chewed-off twigs and gnaw marks on the branches up to 11 feet. The flexible upper lip of the moose acts almost like an elephant's trunk, extending its reach just a little farther.

Look for piles of droppings—that resemble extra-large deer or porcupine droppings. In the summer, their droppings are softer, and form cow pies or clumps.

Listen for—the locomotivelike bellow of a male, the plaintive moan of a female, and an assortment of croaks, barks, whines, and hoglike grunts. To get a moose's attention, try imitating their sounds. Pouring a bucket of water over the side of your canoe may sound like a moose urinating and may rouse a curious investigator.

YELLOW-BILLED CUCKOO

Black Spruce

OLIVE-SIDED FLYCATCHER

LYNX

PALM WARBLER

Round-leaved Sundew

Northern White-cedar

Tamarack
GREAT GRAY
OWL

Northern
Parula nest

Leatherleaf

SOUTHERN
BOG LEMMING

FOUR-TOED
SALAMANDER

Sphagnum
Moss

Northern
Pitcher
Plant

Bog and
Bog Forest

WHERE TO SEE THIS HABITAT:

Maine: Acadia National Park; Moosehorn National Wildlife Refuge
Michigan: Hiawatha, Huron-Manistee, and Ottawa national forests; Isle Royale National Park; Seney National Wildlife Refuge
Minnesota: Agassiz and Rice Lake national wildlife refuges; Chippewa and Superior national forests; Voyaguers National Park
New Hampshire: Wapack National Wildlife Refuge
New Jersey: Great Swamp National Wildlife Refuge
West Virginia: Cranberry Glades (Monongahela National Forest)
Wisconsin: Chequamegon and Nicolet national forests

Bog and Bog Forest

BEGINNINGS

Bogs are pockets of the cold north, filled with leftovers from the glacier's passing. Today you can visit a bit of the north country as far south as West Virginia by traveling to a bog. To get the full effect, go on a sultry summer day. Though the air around you may be in the 90s, you need only dip your feet in a boggy pool to feel the 45-degree chill of a northern snow-fed lake.

To learn the bog's beginnings, we have to go back 10,000 to 12,000 years, when the ice cap that extended down to the Ohio River was retreating for the last time. Cold winds blowing off the glacier kept the land refrigerated in a wide fringe around its base. The only plants that could grow here were hardy boreal species such as black spruce and tamarack. As the edge of the melting glacier moved back to the North, the Arctic plants were replaced by oaks, pines, and maples—all better suited to the warmer climes.

Certain low spots in the landscape held onto their Arctic characteristics, however. These were areas where the glacier had left a block of ice stranded in a pile of debris. When the ice finally melted, the debris slumped, creating a kettlehole. No streams flowed into or out of this basin, so the water sat unstirred. These cold, stagnant pools were a perfect prelude to a bog.

Modern-day bogs also form in isolated ponds or in hollow pockets where water seepage and cold air collect. The bog begins when sedges growing along the banks spread out over the water, forming a floating shelf. Sphagnum moss grows in lumpy mounds atop this mat, and where it is thick enough, small shrubs such as leatherleaf take root. The water is so cold and acidic that decay organisms can't do their job of breaking down plant remains. Instead, the mat thickens, and plant remains filter down under the shelf. Eventually, the lowering mat meets the rising bottom. Along the edges, where the mat is grounded, a ring of dense, brooding spruce and tamarack trees begins to invade. If left undisturbed for years, the bog forest may slowly become less acidic and may change into a northern white-cedar forest.

THE GIANT SPHAGNUM SPONGE

Next time you're in a bog, pick up some sphagnum moss. Squeeze the air-filled cells to empty them, then dip them in the water. As you watch them fill with water, you'll discover why sphagnum is the keeper of the bog, responsible in many ways for making the habitat what it is. Sphagnum grows in a deep, spreading mat that absorbs 25 times its own weight in water (no wonder American Indians used sphagnum for diapers!). This giant sponge imprisons the water and keeps it from circulating. Like a greenhouse shade, the mat also prevents sun from warming the layers below.

The cold, locked-up water is a hostile place for many kinds of life, including agents that break down plant remains. You may have noticed that the open water of a boggy pool is the color of strong tea. Now you know why: it's been "steeping" in the preserved remains of its own plants for decades. Nutrients that would normally be released through decay are imprisoned in these plant bodies for years. Because no inflowing streams bring new nutrients, plants must rely on the meager offerings of dust, rain, and minute ground seepage. To be competitive here, a plant must be able to make the most of this spartan diet.

CARNIVORES WITH ROOTS

To supplement what they manufacture, some plants nab nitrogen as it crawls or flies by. These insect-eating plants are some of the most fascinating in all the plant world.

One of the better known carnivores, the pitcher plant, emanates fragrance from its innocent-looking vase of red and green leaves. Insects drawn by the smell land on the graceful lip of the vase, then quickly lose their footing on the slippery inner surface. Even if they regain a grip halfway down, their escape is blocked by downward pointing hairs. With each step, their legs pick up globs of loose platelets, further bungling their progress. Before long, they are on a one-way trip to the bottom of the vase, where a deadly cocktail of rainwater laced with enzymes and bacteria awaits them. The potion slowly liquefies the insects so they can be absorbed by the plant's cells.

As proof that no habitat goes unexploited, look inside the mouth of a pitcher plant. You may see a tiny mosquito larva that is not in its death throes but, rather, is thriving on the feasts that "drop by." Opportunistic spiders weave their webs across the mouth of the vase, and treefrogs wait on the lip, hoping to snare an easy meal without falling in themselves.

CHARACTERISTIC PLANTS:

Trees and Shrubs:
balsam fir
birches: bog, paper,
    and yellow
black ash
black spruce
blueberries
bog rosemary
common winterberry
dwarf raspberry
eastern hemlock
Labrador tea
large cranberry
laurels: pale and
    sheep
leatherleaf
northern holly
poison-sumac
red maple
red-osier dogwood
rhododendrons
swamp fly honey-
    suckle
swamp white azalea
sweet gale
tamarack
water willow
white-cedars: Atlantic
    and northern

Orchids:
fringed orchids
grass pink
lady's slippers: pink
    and showy
large twayblade
rose pogonia

Carnivorous Plants:
bladderwort
butterworts (south)
pitcher plants: hooded
    (south) and north-
    ern
round-leaved sundew
trumpets (south)

**Other Herbaceous
    Plants:**
cottongrass
creeping snowberry
false Solomon's seal
feather mosses
goldthread
marsh blue violet
marsh marigold
naked miterwort
sensitive fern
sphagnum mosses

Sphagnum Moss

165

A DESERT THAT FLOATS

Believe it or not, the plants of the water-logged bog have a lot in common with those of parched deserts. Both have adaptations that help them hold onto water in the face of drying winds and hot sun. Many of the leaves are leathery, with a tough, waterproof coating. Others have dense wool on the undersides and edges that curl down to keep water vapor from escaping.

But why do plants that are literally perched on a pond need all this special gear to conserve water? Why don't their roots simply imbibe more water to compensate for the loss? The reason is the same one that may have caused you to yank your foot out of the chilly bath: the water is cold! In fact, the roots of bog plants can be slightly frozen as late as July while their leaves up above are baking in 100-plus-degree temperatures. Roots can't absorb cold water very well, and when it's acidic, the trouble magnifies. Just like plants in a desert, the thirsty bog plants can't afford to lose a single drop.

WHAT'S IN IT FOR WILDLIFE?

Despite the adversities, a colorful community of tenacious plants and animals does make its home on the bog. Burrowing rodents such as Arctic shrews, bog lemmings, and meadow voles carefully avoid the damp lower layers of peat. Their runways and nests are in the dry upper layers, within or atop sphagnum moss hummocks. Short-eared owls and great gray owls patrol these hummocks, hoping to catch one of the residents unawares.

Bog pools are breeding grounds for the few amphibians, such as four-toed salamanders and mink frogs, that can tolerate the highly acidic conditions. Ubiquitous reptiles such as painted turtles and garter snakes also make an appearance here. You won't see aquatic creatures such as fish and most tadpoles, however, because the humic acid that turns the bog water brown can damage their gills.

Bog forests are dark, damp places, crisscrossed with fallen logs and leaning trees. The branches are draped with the wispy strands of old man's beard (a lichen), and the lumpy ground is covered with a moss that muffles sound. Because the trees grow so close together and are so prone to tipping in the soft moss, these forests are sometimes hard for a person to travel through. Those same qualities make them an ideal hiding place for many shy northern species.

Black-backed woodpeckers feed on the darkened trunks of dead trees, while northern saw-whet owls raise young in the cavities. Lynx hunt snowshoe hare from inclined logs, and spruce grouse feed on needles and leathery heath leaves. Tiny birds such as warblers, kinglets, and chickadees scour spruce and tamarack boughs for insect larvae, while northern parula warblers fashion their nest in a hanging purse of old man's beard. Songbirds and red squirrels pry seeds out of the tiny spruce cones. In northern white-cedar swamps, the needle-chomping larch sawfly is often present in large numbers, feeding many a swamp bird and its young.

Some seasons are busier than others at the bog. In spring, sparrows and warblers usually build their ground nests on the open bog. Migrant groups of sandhill cranes may stop here on their northward flight, breaking the stillness of the bog with their gruff, rattling cries. Fall brings black bears to the cranberries and blueberry bushes, and may entice migrant birds to stop if the crop is large enough. Winter in white-cedar bogs can be standing room only as white-tailed deer huddle for warmth, food, and easy travel in the snow. After a winter of stripping the white-cedar branches as high as their teeth can reach, you can see a visible browse line in these "yards."

Palm Warbler

Depending on where you live, and what time of year you look, you're likely to find the palm warbler in an assortment of habitats. During the spring and summer, these birds are most strongly associated with northern bogs, where they build their nests on clumps of sphagnum moss. They are one of the first warblers to return to these northern breeding grounds, often arriving while nights are still crisp and the muskeg is still icy underfoot.

In the fall, they migrate toward their wintering grounds in Florida, Cuba, and the West Indies, where the "palm" in their common name seems to make more sense. On the way, they feed in mixed flocks of as many as 50 birds at a time. Their associates include sparrows, chickadees, vireos, creepers, and other warblers. These flocks feed mainly in open, grassy, or shrubby country and along the edges of roads.

Once on their wintering grounds, the warblers inhabit weedy fields and open pine forests with saw-palmetto in the understory. They are common or even abundant in Florida, where they feed on insects, seeds, and berries on the ground or in small bushes within 10 feet of the ground. They are successful insect hunters, devouring as many as 60 insects a minute. Their favorites are beetles, ants, caterpillars, gnats, mosquitoes, flies, and mayflies.

Look for palm warblers—on the ground, searching for insects in open bogs during the warm months. During the fall and winter, look in drier open fields and shrubby woods farther south. They walk with a gliding

SNOWY OWL · BLACK-BACKED WOODPECKER · GRAY JAY · NORTHERN SAW-WHET OWL · GOLDEN-CROWNED KINGLET · WINTER WREN · SNOWSHOE HARE

WILDLIFE LOCATOR CHART—BOG AND BOG FOREST

	Feeds from Air	Feeds in Upper Canopy	Feeds in Lower Canopy	Feeds on Trunk	Feeds on Ground	Feeds in Water
Nests in Tree Canopy	Great Gray Owl Olive-sided Flycatcher	Gray Jay Golden-crowned Kinglet Ruby-crowned Kinglet Solitary Vireo Northern Parula Pine Grosbeak Red Crossbill Pine Siskin	Swainson's Thrush		Rusty Blackbird Purple Finch	
Nests in Trunk	Northern Saw-whet Owl		Boreal Chickadee	Three-toed Woodpecker Black-backed Woodpecker	Winter Wren (also nests in stump)	
Nests on Ground	Snowy Owl Short-eared Owl	Spruce Grouse (also feeds on ground) Tennessee Warbler	Nashville Warbler		Sandhill Crane Common Snipe Palm Warbler Connecticut Warbler Lincoln's Sparrow White-throated Sparrow Snowshoe Hare White-tailed Deer Moose Four-toed Salamander Eastern Garter Snake	Ring-necked Duck Eastern Ribbon Snake
Nests Beneath Ground or Debris					Northern Waterthrush Arctic Shrew Smokey Shrew Pygmy Shrew Southern Red-backed Vole Meadow Vole Southern Bog Lemming Lynx Smooth Green Snake	Painted Turtle Spotted Turtle Bog Turtle
Nests in Water				Gray Treefrog	Carpenter Frog	Mink Frog

motion, body tilted and tail pumping up and down with each step. Near migration, look for them feeding in mixed flocks of 6–10 birds.

Length: 4½–5½ inches.

Look for nests—set deeply into hummocks of sphagnum moss, protected overhead by black spruces. They occasionally set their nests in the lower branches of these trees.

Listen for—a trill: a series of short notes repeated rapidly with only a slight change in pitch. Their "thi-thi-thi-thi . . ." has been compared to the chipping sparrow's song. At the beginning of the nesting season, males may sing from higher perches, moving to the lower branches as the season wears on.

Lynx

Like windblown silk, the wildcat slinks along the edge of the bog, 500 fluid muscles rippling beneath its coat. It keeps its head lower than its shoulders, sniffing a snowshoe hare trail that is rich with fresh scent. An old tamarack leans into the swamp, and the lynx climbs it, ears twitching and stubby tail jerking. With eyes pinned to the trail below, it settles into a frozen crouch to watch and wait. Before long, the trail-maker dashes by, and the lynx explodes from the perch, closing the distance between them with a few graceful bounds.

For a medium-sized cat like the lynx, the snowshoe hare is perfect prey: small enough to overcome, but large enough to fill its 3-pounds-of-meat-a-day requirement. The energy it spends hunting a large hare is well rewarded; to find enough mice or voles to make up the same amount of meat, the cat would have to spend a lot more energy on the hunt. This way, it can spend much of its winter resting and conserving its precious heat.

A single lynx needs at least 200 snowshoe hares a year to stay alive and feed its young. Like any economy based on one crop, the lynx is vulnerable to the boom-and-bust cycles that characterize hare populations. One year, an area may be literally hopping with hares, and the next year, the population will drop to one-twentieth of its former size. Lynx numbers respond accordingly, riding a roller coaster of crash and resurgence every 10 years or so.

Lynxes' eyes are adapted to react quickly to sudden darkness. This allows them to see well, for instance, when a chase takes them from a sunlit snowfield to a deep tamarack swamp. Their eyes are set in the front of their head to deliver a wide field of overlapping (binocular) vision, which gives them the depth perception needed to pick out a ghostly white hare against a ghostly white background.

Look for lynx—hunting along snowshoe hare trails in heavily wooded swamps. They are night hunters by nature, but may be found traveling during the day in remote areas. Look for them on inclined logs, perched and alert, or all spread out, basking like a house cat on a sunny windowsill. They are twice as large as house cats, and have distinctive muttonchop ruffs, plus long ear tufts that enhance their acute hearing. Their 4-inch-by-4-inch feet look like furry mops, and help them walk atop the snow without sinking in.

Length: Head and body, 32–36 inches; tail, 4 inches.

Look along the road—for the green shine of their eyes in car headlights.

Look for dens—in extensive, unbroken forests, far from human dwellings. They prefer hollows created by upturned tree roots or bent-over needleleaf branches. Also look in thickets, among rocks, or in hollow logs.

Look for tracks—4 inches by 4½ inches wide. In the winter, they grow stiff hairs on their footpads that make their tracks indistinguishable.

Listen for—the soulful wailing of male cats during breeding season.

Four-toed Salamander

Four-toed salamanders live in a habitat that is off-limits to most moist-skinned amphibians. The humic acid in the bog water damages the gills of most species, and the soil is impoverished by a mantle of evergreen needles. Despite the adversities, four-toed salamanders wriggle happily within the layers of sphagnum moss and leaves, seemingly unaffected by the caustic acid all around them.

Because they have no lungs, four-toeds breathe through their skin and the mucous membranes in their mouth. The sodden, fog-choked northern swamps provide just the right amount of moisture needed to transfer oxygen from the air to capillaries that lie just beneath their skin. Four-toeds also "drink" water through their skin to keep their metabolism and other processes on track.

Salamanders spend the first 6 weeks of their lives swimming and breathing through gills in the open water at the center of the bog. Curiously, their eggs are not laid in the water itself, but in the roots of grasses or mosses just above the water's surface. Many females lay their eggs together, leaving the guarding chores to just one female, in a kind of communal daycare. When the larvae hatch, they wriggle furiously, along with their 50 or so compatriots, trying to free themselves from the jellylike mass. Gravity finally helps them, and they plop, one by one, into the water.

In their transformation to adults, they will lose their gills, resorb their tail fins, and undergo great skeletal and muscular changes. When they crawl onto land, they continue to live a rather secretive life, crawling from log to log under the protective tangle of springy moss.

Finding a four-toed salamander is a real treat for professional and amateur alike. You can identify them by counting their toes—the hind feet have four digits instead of the usual five. Also characteristic are their tails, flattened at the point where they attach to the body. It is here that the tails break off easily when grabbed by a predator. By the time the predator realizes its mistake, the torso is usually safely hidden.

Look for four-toed salamanders—on the ground, under logs, or in the litter of shady woods, especially those carpeted with sphagnum moss. They are most active at night and around open ponds. In the spring, look for them crawling along the bottom of ponds looking for a mate, or occasionally surfacing for air. Adults are also found in broadleaf forests when they are not breeding. If you frighten a four-toed, it may curl its tail up over its body, tempting you to grab this disposable piece so that the rest of the body can get away.

Length: 2–4 inches.

In the winter—they crawl underground and hide within the decaying root systems of trees.

Look for eggs—hanging in clusters from mosses or roots at the water's edge. The female lies on her back to deposit 30 or more eggs 2½–7 inches above the water's surface. In communal nest sites, as many as 1,100 eggs have been found.

MINK FROG

American Elm

Green Ash

SILVER-HAIRED BAT

RACCOON

WOOD FROG

Trumpet-creeper

Boxelder

Northern Floodplain Forest

WHERE TO SEE THIS HABITAT:

Illinois: Crab Orchard, Chautauqua, and Mark Twain national wildlife refuges
Indiana: Hoosier National Forest; Muscatatuck National Wildlife Refuge
Iowa: De Soto National Wildlife Refuge
Massachusetts: Great Meadows National Wildlife Refuge
Michigan: Shiawassee National Wildlife Refuge
Minnesota: Minnesota Valley National Wildlife Refuge; Upper Mississippi River National Wildlife and Fish Refuge
New Jersey: Great Swamp National Wildlife Refuge
Ohio: Wayne National Forest

Northern Floodplain Forest

BEGINNINGS

The seasonal spill of water over a river's banks is actually a healthy part of the river's year. As the shallow lake spreads under the boughs of the surrounding trees, it deposits a blanket of rich, fertilizing soil called alluvium. By slowing down the water on the upstream end, the floodplain lessens the burden for downstream communities. It is only when we build vacation homes or agricultural fields on this floodplain that the high water becomes an insurance liability. (For more about floodplain dynamics, see Southern Floodplain Forest, page 185.)

THE TREES THAT HOLD DOWN THE BANK

Willows and green ashes are well suited to life at the ragged edge of a stream. When their roots have been in high water for a while, they are stimulated to form new, air-filled roots to take the place of those killed by the flood. At the same time, tiny openings in the bark called lenticels expand, allowing air to move more easily into the tree. But unlike most plants, these trees are also able to switch to an oxygenless form of respiration when necessary.

Farther back from the water's edge, behind the willows, eastern cottonwoods grow on a long "levee," a low ridge running parallel to the river on each side. Levees are made up of layers of heavy, coarse sediments that the river dumps when it overflows its banks. Because of the large size of the grains, groundwater doesn't ooze to the surface of the levee easily, and surface water usually leaches straight through. The cottonwoods that colonize these bits of higher ground put down deep taproots early—a much needed precaution against drought.

Under the cottonwoods, you'll find seedlings of silver maple, boxelder, American elm, ash, and hackberry. If they are not wiped out by a flood, they may survive to take over when the cottonwoods die. Tangled vine communities of bur cucumber also grow, well adapted to come back quickly after the tearing, destructive forces of the floods. Occasionally, where the sun breaks through the canopy, you'll find a pure glade of ferns.

Farther back from the river, you can see the next stage of succession— the maple, elm, and ash forest that takes over after the cottonwoods. The trunks of silver maples rise 80 feet above the floodplain, still bearing the marks of mud from the high waters of spring. When the river reaches this far back, it finally lays down the finer clays and silts that it has carried suspended in its water. In this rich muck, annual plants take their chances between floods.

In the low spots on the floodplain, ponds of water called sloughs (pronounced "slews") are holdovers from the last flood. They usually fill with marsh plants such as arrowhead, water arum, and pickerelweed. Given enough time to build up sediments, the floor of these basins will eventually rise and dry out enough to become a sedge meadow.

Still farther back, American beech and tulip-poplar make their stand, close enough to the river to benefit from the moist soils, but far enough not to be seriously flooded.

WHAT'S IN IT FOR WILDLIFE?

You might think that floodplains are a dangerous place for wildlife to be. On the contrary, they offer all the attractions of a wetland: drinking water, edible aquatic plants and animals, rich soil wriggling with earthworms, and shallow ponds alive with salamanders, frogs, and snakes. The huge trees of the floodplain are an extra attraction, offering leafy canopies for nesting, large crops of seeds and nuts, and trunks riddled with nesting cavities and bark insects. This combination of broadleaf forest and moist lowland makes the floodplain vital not only to its residents but also to animals that visit from the uplands.

Of course, in any habitat that can suddenly be submerged under a foot or more of moving water, there is always an element of risk. Floodplain animals have learned to swim well or to move to higher land (or up a tree) when the water level rises. For other animals, the temporary ponds are a blessing. A layer of water, for instance, can make food all the more accessible to waterfowl. Migrating ducks can float among the submerged trunks, safely dabbling ("tipping up") for acorns and seeds on the forest floor beneath them. Colony nesting birds such as herons, cormorants, and egrets

CHARACTERISTIC PLANTS:

Trees and Shrubs:
American bladdernut
American elm
American holly
American hornbeam
ashes: green, pump-
   kin, and others
black walnut
boxelder
buttonbush
coralberry
cottonwoods: eastern
   and plains
deerberry
eastern burningbush
elderberry
hackberry
hickories: shagbark
   and shellbark
maple: red and silver
oaks: northern pin,
   swamp white,
   water, and others
possumhaw
red mulberry
river birch
slippery elm
speckled alder
sweetgum
sycamore
willows: black, peach-
   leaf, and sandbar
winged elm
witch-hazel
yellow-poplar

Vines:
American black cur-
   rant
bur cucumber
climbing bittersweet
common moonseed
greenbriers
poison-ivy
trumpet-creeper
virgin's-bower
Virginia creeper
wild grape
wild yam

Herbaceous Plants:
ferns: Christmas, cin-
   namon, ostrich, and
   royal
great ragweed
green dragon
groundnut
hog peanut
jack-in-the-pulpit
jewelweed
mayapple
nettle: stinging and
   wood
sedges
sweetflag
trout-lily
turtlehead

Trumpet-Creeper

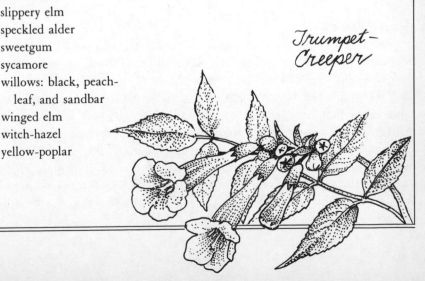

build their nests in the branches above the ponds, enjoying the temporary immunity from land predators.

When the waters subside, the fertile silts often sprout a salad of grasses, herbs, and mushrooms (including morels!), relished by rabbits, white-tailed deer, eastern harvest mice, and other mammals. Water-tolerant shrubs such as willow provide nesting cover for yellow warblers and other songbirds. Some of the trees eventually succumb to the stresses of root-dunking, creating another important habitat for hollow tree nesters such as raccoons, wood ducks, Virginia opossums, flying squirrels, owls, and woodpeckers. Perching kingfishers, flycatchers, and hawks find ample dead limbs from which to spot prey and launch their attacks.

As anyone in the flat heartland knows, a river floodplain provides a corridor of dense, wild vegetation in an otherwise monotonous landscape of agricultural fields. This forest becomes a place of refuge for upland animals, especially toward the end of hunting season and during severe winters.

GRAY TREEFROG

EASTERN HARVEST MOUSE

Wood Duck

What perches on trunks like a woodpecker, tightropes on branches like a squirrel, and paddles in the water like a duck? Thanks to their adaptive design, multitalented wood ducks are at home on water, land, or air. Their feet, able to propel them through water, also have sharp claws and strong hind toes to help them perch on tree limbs. Their legs are farther forward on their body than puddle ducks', giving them the balance they need to walk and run on land. With their broad, maneuverable wings, they can lift straight up out of a water hole or deftly thread their way through an obstacle course of trunks and branches. Finally, their bill, which is narrower than that of most ducks, helps them pick seeds, acorns, and nuts up off the ground.

The best place to look for a woodie is everywhere in its habitat. They use the flooded trees and snagged debris in the river for protection from predators, and on land they waddle from bush to bush, combing the ground for acorns. Sometimes they perch on the limbs of trees, or mount an exposed sandbar to preen. For variety, they upend in shallow water for succulent, aquatic plants or abundant insects. In the spring, try following the female deep into the woods as she shops for nesting cavities. Come back in a few weeks, and you may see the spectacle of wood duckling training.

After only a day of feeding the new hatchlings in the nest, it's time to introduce them to the watery part of their habitat. To coax them to leave the nest, the mother begins calling to them from a nearby tree. In response, they jump up inside the cavity, as far as they can, heading for the entrance hole that may be 3–4 feet above the bottom of the nest. With each try, they sink their sharp, downcurving claws into the cavity wall to anchor themselves. When they finally reach the light of day, they jump into thin air without hesitation, falling as much as 60 feet to the forest floor. Because they weigh only an ounce, they touch down lightly and without damage.

When the entourage is finally assembled, the mother herds them into a long line and leads them on a slow, cautious journey to the water's edge. This journey, which may take an entire day, must make a great impression on the young ducks. When it comes time for the daughters to raise *their* young, they will somehow find their way back to their own birthplace.

Look for wood ducks—resting, preening, or roosting in water with plenty of flooded trees and other debris for cover. They look for water that is less than 18 inches deep. If water levels change (as they often do in floodplain forests), woodies simply move to new sites. Their home ranges are very flexible—a telltale sign of living in a fluctuating habitat. They fly to the woods to feed on insects, seeds, acorns, berries, and nuts. In late summer, look for males that are molting their old feathers and growing new ones for the migration flight. The plumage at this time, called eclipse plumage, is drab. It allows the duck to be inconspicuous at a time when it is without flight feathers. At night, look for wood ducks roosting in pairs or in flocks of 10–15. In fall and winter, these roosting flocks may number in the several thousands.

Length: 17–20½ inches.

Look for cavity nests—more than 30 feet above the ground, in trees that are at least 16 inches in diameter. The nest was probably created by pileated woodpeckers. The entrance is ideally 4 inches high and 3 inches wide, and there's enough floor space inside for 10–15 young. Contrary to the old wives' (or husbands') tale, wood ducks do not fly straight into their nest holes at top speeds (47 miles per hour). Instead, they check their flight before entering, often perching on the trunk, using their stout tail as a

WILDLIFE LOCATOR CHART—NORTHERN FLOODPLAIN FOREST

	Feeds from Air	Feeds in Upper Canopy	Feeds in Lower Canopy	Feeds on Trunk	Feeds on Ground	Feeds in Water
Nests in Tree Canopy	Cooper's Hawk Red-shouldered Hawk Silver-haired Bat	Warbling Vireo Northern Parula Northern Oriole	Yellow-billed Cuckoo American Redstart		Wood Thrush	Great Egret Green-backed Heron
Nests in Trunk	Barred Owl		Prothonotary Warbler (also feeds on trunk)	Red-headed Wood-pecker Red-bellied Wood-pecker Pileated Woodpecker	Northern Flying Squirrel Raccoon	Wood Duck Common Goldeneye Hooded Merganser
Nests on Ground	Whip-poor-will				American Woodcock Veery Four-toed Salamander Massasauga	Eastern Ribbon Snake
Nests Beneath Ground or Debris	Belted Kingfisher Indiana Myotis (nests in caves)				Virginia Opossum Eastern Harvest Mouse Woodland Jumping Mouse	Mink River Otter Wood Turtle (also feeds on ground)
Nests in Water				Gray Treefrog	Spring Peeper Wood Frog	Central Newt

GREAT EGRET

RED-BELLIED WOODPECKERS

RED-HEADED WOODPECKER

BARRED OWL

COMMON GOLDENEYE

HOODED MERGANSER

WARBLING VIREO

brace. It may take the female 10 days of "shopping" to find the right site.

Listen for—a very distinctive, squealing "weeeeek weeeeek," made by the hen as she flees through the trees. The male's cry is uttered more softly. When the female leaves the nest for feeding, she lands on the water with a loud cry, informing her mate that it's time for him to take over nest duty.

Silver-haired Bat

Silver-haired bats emerge in the evening to dine on insects rising from the river. Their wide wings and small body give them a tremendous amount of airlift, which allows them to decelerate and turn at slow speeds without stalling. This fluttery and erratic flight is a trademark of their unusual hunting style.

Bats use a process called echolocation to locate and catch prey. As they zig and zag, they send out a stream of high beeps, and then "read" the echoes that come back. When the sound waves hit something, such as a flying insect, the bat increases its beeps from the cruising rate of 20/second to 250/second. The insect is moving, the bat is moving, and the sound waves boomerang in just millisecconds. Somehow the bat "computes" the time it takes for the sound to return, then compares the frequency of the echo with the frequency of the beep it sent out. This reveals a detailed picture of how big the prey is, how far away it is, how fast it's flying, and in what direction it's moving. It's a built-in system that makes our mechanized sonar seem clumsy.

The silverhairs' keen maneuverability helps them keep their prey before them, even when the prey is doing its level best to get away. Some insects have mastered ways to elude clever bats. When moths and lacewings hear the bats' high-pitched "search" calls, they fold their wings and drop into a downward spiral. Tiger moths have gone one step farther. By scraping together grooves on their chest, they emit ultrasonic clicks that actually jam the bat's navigational system. Our latest look at the scoreboard shows that bats are still evolving ways to counteract these insects. Some species have simply raised their calls to a higher frequency that the moths can't seem to hear (not yet, at least—stay tuned).

Look for silver-haired bats—flying less than 20 feet above water or in and out of the trees along a stream bank. Look for the silver tips on the ends of their fur. They come out earlier in the evening than most bats. Trout anglers have had silverhairs authenticate their trout flies for them— the bats, thinking the lure was an actual hatch of an aquatic insect, swooped down for a closer look!

Size: Length, 3–4 inches; wingspan, 10–12½ inches.

Look for roosting bats—in dense foliage of trees, in abandoned woodpecker cavities, in tree hollows, behind loose bark, or in old crow nests.

Look for migrating bats—flying as high as 10,000 feet to their hibernating zones farther south. They will stay up north a little longer than most bats, however, lowering their body temperature to 23 degrees F without suffering frost damage. When they finally leave, high winds may knock them off course. Some exhausted bats have been found on ships miles from shore. When resting during their flights, they'll check into buildings, abandoned quarries, old fenceposts, piles of lumber, or railroad ties.

Listen for—a high-pitched squeak and chatter as a bat flies by. This bat's "transmissions" are lower in range than most bats', and some humans can hear them.

Wood Frog

It's not easy being the only frog hopping in the Arctic Circle (that's how far north they breed). For one thing, a wood frog lacks the heavy fur and fat of other cold-weather animals. And because it's an amphibian (animals that breathe in part through their skin), our northernmost frog needs to stay moist at all times. To keep both warm and moist during the winter, it hibernates in shallow depressions under the forest floor, blanketed by leaves and litter. Despite this insulation, a string of subzero days may freeze the soil and put the hibernating frogs on ice. Instead of digging deeper or shivering, the frogs do what we would do—they freeze solid. Their eyes become opaque, their organs become cut off from oxygen and nutrients, and eventually, their bodies harden.

Come spring, however, wood frogs do something we could never do—they thaw out alive! Their secret is the same biochemical process that many creatures employ to get through stressful times—they manufacture glucose from carbohydrates stored in the liver. The unusual twist is that wood frogs manufacture an astounding amount of glucose at an astoundingly fast rate. As soon as the mercury dips into the lower digits, they load their system with 60 times the normal amount of glucose, about 37 times the amount that we humans could tolerate! Interestingly, the frogs can handle this much sugar without the normal diabetic coma most animals experience.

Glucose is one of the wonder chemicals known as cryoprotectants. Like a biological antifreeze, glucose ensures that only those fluids outside and between cells will freeze, while fluids within cells will remain liquid. This way, delicate cell walls are not broken by expanding ice crystals.

When spring comes, wood frogs are the first to wiggle their toes. They begin breeding explosively even before the ice is off the ponds. The idea is to get a head start so their tadpoles will be large enough to defend themselves by the time predators, such as salamanders, are ready to hatch.

Also, by breeding earlier, wood frogs can exploit breeding pools in the floodplain before they dry up.

Look for wood frogs—breeding in the backwaters of large rivers or in floodplain pools. After laying their eggs, they move into the moist leaf litter beside the water, relishing the shade and humidity that lush floodplains offer. When predators such as garter snakes, minks, and birds threaten, they hop into brush piles, into grass hummocks, or under leaves.

Length: 1³/₈–3¹/₄ inches.

Look for egg masses—a globular lump of up to 3,000 eggs laid in shallow water, usually at the base of a sedge clump or small drowned bushes. Up to 300 frogs may lay their eggs in one spot, so that the eggs in the center are kept as much as 12 degrees warmer than the icy surrounding water. Egg laying seems to have its dangers, however, and females are occasionally found entrapped and drowned in the large jelly masses.

Listen for—a chorus of sharp, coarse "waaaduck"s that sound like ducks quacking. Listen near water.

PILEATED WOODPECKER

Water Hickory

YELLOW RAT SNAKE

Overcup Oak

SWAMP RABBIT

VIRGINIA OPOSSUM

Waterlocust

Opossum

Southern Floodplain Forest

WHERE TO SEE THIS HABITAT:

Alabama: Choctaw National Wildlife Refuge

Arkansas: Big Lake, Felsenthal, Wapanocca, and White River national wildlife refuges

Florida: Apalachicola National Forest; Big Cypress Swamp; Corkscrew Swamp Sanctuary; Osceola National Forest

Georgia: Okefenokee and Savannah national wildlife refuges

Illinois: Chautauqua National Wildlife Refuge; Shawnee National Forest

Louisiana: Kisatchie National Forest; Catahoula, D'Arbonne, Delta, and Sabine national wildlife refuges

Mississippi: Delta and De Soto national forests; Hillside, Morgan Brake, Panther Swamp, and Yazoo national wildlife refuge

Missouri: Mingo and Squaw Creek national wildlife refuges

North Carolina: Pungo National Wildlife Refuge

South Carolina: Francis Marion National Forest; Congaree Swamp National Monument

Tennessee: Cross Creeks, Hatchee, and Reelfoot national wildlife refuges

Texas: Big Thicket National Preserve

Virginia: Great Dismal Swamp National Wildlife Refuge

West Virginia: Monongahela National Forest

Southern Floodplain Forest

BEGINNINGS

"Flood" is a relative term—a uniquely human concept. If you live in the Mississippi delta or along many of the rivers that meander their way across the coastal plain to the Atlantic Ocean, you know that rivers regularly rise past their banks, creating a shallow lake on the adjoining flatlands. In some floodplain forests, this is a twice-a-year affair, occurring in late winter, and once again in spring. You can read how high the last water was by the rings of flotsam left on the tree trunks.

In their natural context, these periodic inundations are not floods. They are, in fact, a rejuvenating tonic for the forests, as well as a safety valve for natural communities downstream.

A swollen, fast-running river is usually cocoa brown, choked with sand, silt, and clay it has picked up each mile along the way (1,300 miles in the Mississippi's case). By jumping the banks and widening its channel, the river is forced to slow down. As it slows, it loses the power to transport its cargo of silt, and a blanket of nutrient-rich soil filters down to the floor of the floodplain. By slowing down and "cleaning" the floodwater, the floodplain protects the bays and estuaries downstream. These areas are extremely fragile and are a nursery bed for most of the commercial fish and shellfish that we harvest. Without the floodplains upstream, a massive pulse of fresh water and silt would tear into the estuary twice a year, overwhelming the saltwater-adapted life there.

This cycle of "flood" and deposition has been going on for ages. In fact, beneath parts of the Mississippi delta, there are no less than 30,000 feet of sediments that have been dragged down from the heartland. These deposits have built a landscape along the river, filled with basins, ridges, and sandbars. Characteristic plant communities inhabit these different spots, and by recognizing them, you can predict the lay of the land, even from the air.

WHAT REMAINS WHEN THE RIVER DRAINS

When a muddy river floods its banks, it begins losing momentum, causing it to drop the load of sediment it's carrying. The heaviest, coarsest particles are laid down first in a long "levee"—a ridge running parallel to the river. Even though it's closest to the water, the levee may have some of the driest sands around because water trickles quickly between the large grains. Cottonwoods growing on the levee don't seem to mind, however; they have deep taproots to find water during dry times.

As the river rises, the floodwater continues to spread back from the banks, slowing as it goes. The very finest particles are deposited last, on a wide plain called a "flat." Sometimes these fine particles lay down an impervious clay bed that water tends to collect in. These areas may be the last to dry out after the flood subsides.

Even farther from the water, the land may step up to an older floodplain created at a time when the river was wider. Neither the first nor the second floodplain is completely flat, however. Ridges may poke above the surface, showing where the levees of old streams were laid down. The beds of those old streams may have left shallow depressions called sloughs (pronounced "slews") between the ridges. Larger depressions, or areas where water is backed up and therefore always present, are called swamps.

An elevation difference of as little as 6 inches will determine whether a spot will be flooded, how deeply, and for how long. In each of these bumps, stairsteps, and bowls, different kinds of plants grow.

Baldcypress and water tupelo are found soaking in permanent swamps. Their trunks look like upside-down trumpets, with the base flared five times as wide as the upper trunk. They are also famous for their arching roots and curious "cypress knees." Soil catches around these buttresses and knees, gradually building a land base for trees that are more adapted to drier soil.

Trees such as overcup oak, red maple, waterlocust, and water hickory grow at slightly higher elevations where water doesn't stand as long or as deep. Areas that are flooded only during dormant seasons attract Nuttall oak, water oak, sweetgum, and willow oak. Sites near the high-water mark on old floodplains or ridges are flooded only occasionally, and are good sites for shagbark hickory, swamp chestnut oak, and post oak.

CHARACTERISTIC PLANTS:

Trees, Shrubs, and Vines:

ashes: Carolina, green, and pumpkin
baldcypress
black willow
blackgum
boxelder
buttonbush
common persimmon
eastern cottonwood
hackberry
hickories: shagbark and water
maples: red and silver
oaks: cherrybark, northern pin, Nuttall, overcup, post, Shumard, swamp chestnut, water, and willow
pecan
peppervine
possumhaw
redbay
river birch
swamp-privet
sweetgum
sycamore
trumpet-creeper
water elm
waterlocust
water tupelo
wild grape

Herbaceous Plants:

On the Shore:

American wisteria
Dutchman's-breeches
giant cane
jack-in-the-pulpit
Spanish moss
spring beauty
trout-lily

In the Water:

fragrant water lily
greater bladderwort
pickerelweed
yellow flag
yellow pond lily

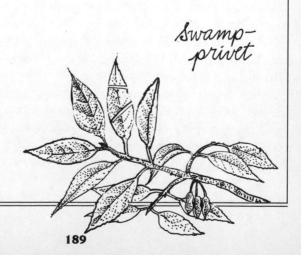

swamp-privet

189

SOUNDING THE ALARM

Bottomland forests are the South's most productive living communities. In their humid, tangled depths, more than 70 commercial species of trees grow, and more kinds of flowering plants, birds, mammals, reptiles, and amphibians grow here than anywhere else in the South. There are five times the number of game animals and ten times more birds in the hardwood swamps than there are in the surrounding pinelands. Only coral reefs and tropical rain forests compare with these forests in terms of productivity.

This is hardly surprising when you consider all that the bottomlands have going for them. As if growing in a giant greenhouse, they are bathed in abundant sun and water, and regularly receive "energy subsidies" in the form of nutrients and minerals from upstream. Further nutrients are lavished on the land when the flood subsides, and the riffraff of leaves, logs, and branches begins to decay. This decaying humus holds water like a sponge for later use by trees and plants. Then, instead of spending energy to acquire water and nutrients, plants on the floodplain can spend their energy being productive—putting on more leaves, more girth, and more fruits. A single water oak can produce a staggering 28,000 acorns a year. These and many other trees grow to their largest size and achieve their fastest rates of growth in these rich river bottoms.

Unfortunately, these engines of productivity are being snuffed out at an alarming rate. In the Mississippi delta alone, 20 million of the original 25 million acres of bottomland hardwoods have been eliminated—turned into soybeans, suburbs, or reservoirs. Some species that depended on these forests have all but disappeared from the area, including the cougar, red wolf, and ivory-billed woodpecker. The Carolina parakeet, now extinct, used to distribute cypress seeds in its droppings; without this service, the balance of the bottomland hardwoods has been forever changed.

Removing the bottomland hardwoods is like cutting a vital organ out of the river's "body." Inevitably, the rest of the system, headwater to outlet, will pay for the needless act. Thankfully, concerned citizens long ago began the fight to save these lands before the last was drained, dammed, or channeled for other uses. For rare species such as Mississippi kite, American swallow-tailed kite, Bachman's warbler, and Swainson's warbler, the rescue may come not a moment too soon.

WHAT'S IN IT FOR WILDLIFE?

Wherever the floodplain undulates, even slightly, a new habitat is available for a certain plant. These subtle differences allow various tree species to grow next to each other, intermingled with dense shrubs, vines, and ground plants. Because these plants produce acorns, berries, and seeds on differing schedules, some type of food is always "in season."

Just as in tropical rain forests, the canopy is a world unto itself. Tremendous vertical variety exists, providing different compartments for wildlife—whether they be singing perches, foraging niches, foliage screens, or nesting sites. The shelter doesn't disappear in the winter months, either; many of the trees are broadleaf evergreens that hold their leaves throughout the year.

Most of these broadleaf evergreens have showy flowers and nectar, which, along with their richly patterned bark, support large numbers of insects. In turn, a whole host of insect-feeding birds, reptiles, and amphibians are attracted to these trees. The same flowers that attract insects in the growing season eventually bear fruit, seeds, and nuts to support other wildlife in the fall and winter.

Shelter and nesting opportunities are also unique and plentiful in the floodplain forest. Butt rot, a common affliction in trees here, creates roomy cavities at the base of trees that are perfect denning places for bobcats and bears. Higher up on the trunk, disease may enter a tree where a branch breaks, creating a cavity that later becomes home to a screech owl, a flying squirrel, or a wood duck. Downed logs are also a characteristic of this habitat (try walking through these forests without climbing over one). Hollowed out, these provide shelter for mink, otter, and raccoon, as well as a walkway for land animals when the water is high.

REDBELLY
WATER SNAKE

PROTHONOTARY WARBLER

COMMON GRACKLE

YELLOW-CROWNED NIGHT-HERON

SWAINSON'S WARBLER

BLUE-GRAY GNATCATCHER

AMERICAN SWALLOW-TAILED KITE

MISSISSIPPI KITE

WILDLIFE LOCATOR CHART—SOUTHERN FLOODPLAIN FOREST

	Feeds from Air	Feeds in Upper Canopy	Feeds in Lower Canopy	Feeds on Trunk	Feeds on Ground	Feeds in Water
Nests in Tree Canopy	American Swallow-tailed Kite Mississippi Kite Red-shouldered Hawk Short-tailed Hawk Seminole Bat	Blue-gray Gnatcatcher Red-eyed Vireo Northern Parula	Yellow-billed Cuckoo American Redstart	Yellow-throated Warbler	Rusty Blackbird Common Grackle	Double-crested Cormorant Anhinga Little Blue Heron Yellow-crowned Night-Heron Wood Stork
Nests in Trunk	Barred Owl Great Crested Flycatcher		Tufted Titmouse Prothonotary Warbler	Red-headed Woodpecker Red-bellied Woodpecker Pileated Woodpecker	Raccoon	Wood Duck
Nests in Shrubs		Bachman's Warbler (very rare)	Swainson's Warbler (also feeds on ground)		Golden Mouse	Limpkin
Nests on Ground				Black-and-white Warbler	Common Snipe American Woodcock Southern Copperhead Canebrake Rattlesnake	Western Cottonmouth Redbelly Water Snake Yellowbelly Water Snake Black Swamp Snake Western Ribbon Snake
Nests Beneath Ground or Debris	Belted Kingfisher		Yellow Rat Snake		Virginia Opossum Southeastern Shrew Southern Short-tailed Shrew Marsh Rabbit Swamp Rabbit Marsh Rice Rat Eastern Harvest Mouse Cotton Mouse Hispid Cotton Rat Five-lined Skink	Mink River Otter Striped Mud Turtle Alligator Snapping Turtle Mud Snake Rainbow Snake
Nests in Water		Bird-voiced Treefrog Green Treefrog Pine Woods Treefrog			Spotted Salamander Southern Cricket Frog Oak Toad Little Grass Frog Upland Chorus Frog Southern Leopard Frog	Central Newt Pig Frog

Springtime floodwaters provide a warm, shallow spawning area for aquatic life. Small invertebrates, snails, and crayfish become food for larger animals like frogs, fish, young wood ducks, and wading birds. Some of these provide food for still larger otters, minks, herons, and egrets. Winter floods cover nuts, seeds, and acorns with a few inches of water, making them available to dabbling ducks that feed by "tipping up" in shallow water.

If the floodwaters remain for unusually long periods of time, they may kill certain trees, again enriching the entire community by creating openings important to swamp rabbits, eastern harvest mice, cotton mice, and raccoons. Sparrows, common grackles, and migrating waterfowl carefully scour these openings for the seeds of grasses and other plants. Dead standing trees provide feeding sites for woodpeckers and bark gleaners, and nesting cavities that will house generations of animals.

Permanently flooded sites are excellent foraging areas for wading birds such as herons, anhingas, or double-crested cormorants. Moist mud flats without vegetation attract shorebirds such as American woodcocks and common snipes.

Barred Owl

The wise, unblinking eyes of a barred owl are part of its sophisticated, night-hunting arsenal. Their eyeballs are huge (almost as large as ours) and have oversized pupils able to take in lots of light. An extra supply of "rods," minute visual cells that register light, allow them to see in 1/100 of the light that we would need.

Their eyes are placed close together on the front of their face, so that the right and left fields of vision overlap somewhat, giving them three-dimensional, binocular vision. This three-dimensional sight covers a 70-degree arc, which is ten times wider than that of most birds. In this range, their vision has depth; prey objects stand out from a matching background so their position is easier to compute for an accurate strike. So accurate in fact is the barred owl's aim that it is usually correct to within 1 or 2 degrees (the width of your little finger held at arm's length).

Unlike most birds, which have flat, disklike eyes, owls' eyes are tubular, and can't be rotated in their sockets the way ours can. To compensate, owls' necks are remarkably flexible, enabling them to turn their head 270 degrees so they can look directly behind them.

Even without their sight, barred owls would usually be able to locate their prey by sound alone. Their ear openings are larger than those of other birds, and are placed far apart on either side of a wide face. The right ear opening is shaped differently than the left, and one is positioned slightly higher on the head than the other. These asymmetries cause sounds to register sooner or be a little louder in one ear than the other. By taking these two "readings" and triangulating, the owl is able to pinpoint the source of sound, even as it scurries beneath the leaf litter.

To carry them swiftly to their target, barred owls have a full 4 feet of wings. When you consider that their body weight is only 22–28 ounces, you can see why they can glide so far. Their feathers are softer than those of most other birds and are frayed on the leading edges to deflect air smoothly and silently. Unsuspecting prey literally never hear what's coming until the squeeze of powerful talons is upon them.

Barred owls practice a kind of family planning that is directly related to the quality of their habitat. If the small mammal population is low for some reason, barred owls may not nest that year, waiting for food sources to rebound. When they do have a brood, they space out the hatching of the nestlings so that the youngest may be a full 3 weeks behind the rest. If hard times fall on the family, this youngest owlet often becomes food for the larger siblings.

Look for barred owls—perched on dead branches or stubs of decaying trees at dusk, beginning their nightly search for prey. They prefer woods that have an open understory so they can fly and attack prey easily. Red-shouldered hawks hunt this same area during the day. The two species therefore do not compete directly for prey, and may even be found nesting close together. To communicate with owls at night, try imitating their calls or kissing the back of your hand (sounds like an injured mouse). Look for them roosting in trees during the day (the lower branches are often white-washed with excrement). American crows will often raise a ruckus around the roosting owl to get it to leave.

Length: 17–24 inches.

Look for nests—in cavities, up to 80 feet high, in the trunks of dead, beetle-riddled trees that are at least 20 inches in diameter. A telltale sign is a strand of gray fluff dangling from the opening. Owls will also hunt from these nest trees. If holes are unavailable, they may use deserted crow, squirrel, or red-shouldered hawk nests.

Look for pellets—large, compact balls of "indigestibles"—fur, feathers, and bones—on the ground beneath roosts. Owls cough these up after they digest their meal. The pellets keep sharp bones from cutting their digestive tract, and they also scrape away bacteria in their throat as they come up. Pick apart dried pellets (wear gloves!) to find whole skulls and other remnants of the owl's prey.

Listen for—"Who-cooks-for-you? Who-cooks-for-you-all?" repeated twice, with the accent on the "you." Barred owls are famous for their maniacal laughter, doglike barks, hissing, and wildcat caterwauling, especially in February or March (the "months of madness") when they are courting.

Swamp Rabbit

Swamp rabbits are never far from water. They don't hesitate to dive right in, whether it's to travel from place to place or to hide from enemies. Rather like the American alligator that floats with just its eyes above water, swamp rabbits can float incognito past predators, keeping only their nose above the surface.

They are also well adapted to the occasional superflood, when water overwhelms their living space for a long period of time. Rabbits and other floodplain organisms must either swim, evacuate, or crowd together on limited patches of higher ground. Swamp rabbits have evolved ways to cope with this crowding, one of which is to "delay" the birth of their young by reabsorbing the embryos back into their bodies.

A group of swamp rabbits may provide you with hours of interesting behavior-watching. The males are organized in a hierarchy, so that subordinate males attempt to avoid contact with the male directly above them in rank. When they "hear" the vibrations of an approaching rabbit, they freeze or quickly zigzag away. This cuts down on fighting among reproductively active males. The less they fight, the more energy they will have for foraging and mating.

When swamp rabbits do fight, their encounters can be ferocious. Two males will stand on their hind feet, striking each other with forepaws and teeth. Their hind feet are also clawed, and as they jump up in the air to slash one another, they sometime leave a nasty gash. These fights are occasionally to the death.

Look for swamp rabbits—feeding on grasses, sedges, berries, and tree seedlings in floodplain openings. To confuse predators that are following their scent, swamp rabbits will walk the length of a log, turn around and retrace their steps, and then hop off to the side, traveling at right angles to the log. When the predator gets to the end of the log, the scent trail mysteriously ends. They are most active at night, but emerge from their daytime hiding places well before sunset in late spring and summer.

Length: Head and body, 14–17 inches.

Look for forms—matted-down hiding places in tangled marsh vegetation, briar bushes, low crotches or cavities of trees, the green tops of stumps, cane patches, open grassy areas, or holes in the ground.

Look for runways—trampled in the vegetation by the hopping of many rabbits.

Look for nests—slight depressions filled with grasses and rabbit hair.

The female bites off pieces of her breast hair to line the nest and cover her young. This gives them access to her nipples and keeps the young warm while she is away from the nest. In baldcypress swamps, nests made of Spanish moss and rabbit fur are often placed between two "cypress knees."

Look for droppings—on elevated objects such as stumps.

Look for tracks—in groups of four. The foreprints are almost round, and about 1 inch wide. The hindprints are elongated and 3–4 inches long. When running, the forepaws are used as fulcrums, so the hindpaws print ahead of the forepaws. Hindprints may be cut short when the rabbit is moving quickly.

Listen for—foot thumping of alarmed rabbits.

Bird-voiced Treefrog

Sounds are evocative; they can send our imagination back to the very first time we heard them. For many people, the beautiful whistle of a bird-voiced treefrog evokes images of a brooding cypress forest in the thick of a summer's night.

Frogs call to attract mates and to settle territorial disputes with other males. The calls are generated by vibrations in their vocal cords set up when the frogs exhale a large volume of air and contract muscles in their bodies. As the frogs call, they inflate a balloonlike sac under their chin. The sac works like the sounding board of a piano, and allows the frog to emphasize certain frequencies or filter out others.

Treefrogs have inner ear organs that are specially tuned to pick up the frequency that is unique to the species. Even in a chorus of a dozen different frogs, bird-voiced treefrogs have no trouble picking out the call that is meant for them. With practice, you can also learn to identify which "instrument" in the chorus is speaking.

Bird-voiced treefrogs climb onto the lower branches to deliver their song. Unlike leaping frogs that have meaty thighs, treefrogs have long, skinny legs—perfect for walking and balancing on limbs. Their bodies are flattened to even out their weight distribution, and their belly skin "gives" so they can spread it flush against any surface. The famous "suction cups" at the tips of their toes have an underlayer of fibrous, pilelike skin that meshes with irregularities to help the frogs cling to rough, dry surfaces. A mucous layer beneath each disk helps them cling to smooth, damp surfaces such as leaves. Cartilage between the last two bones of their toes allows the toe tip to swivel backward and sideways to hook around twigs.

Look for bird-voiced treefrogs—at night in baldcypress, water tupelo, and other trees growing in standing water. The males call from 3–5 feet above the water, perched in shrubs or vines that grow among the trees.

Handling this frog may give you a runny nose or watery eyes due to skin secretions that are designed to protect them.

Length: 1⅛-2⅛ inches.

Look for eggs—laid in masses in the water between March and September.

Listen for—a birdlike whistle, "wit-wit-wit . . . ," repeated 20 times or more. It sounds like someone calling a dog.

GOLDEN MOUSE

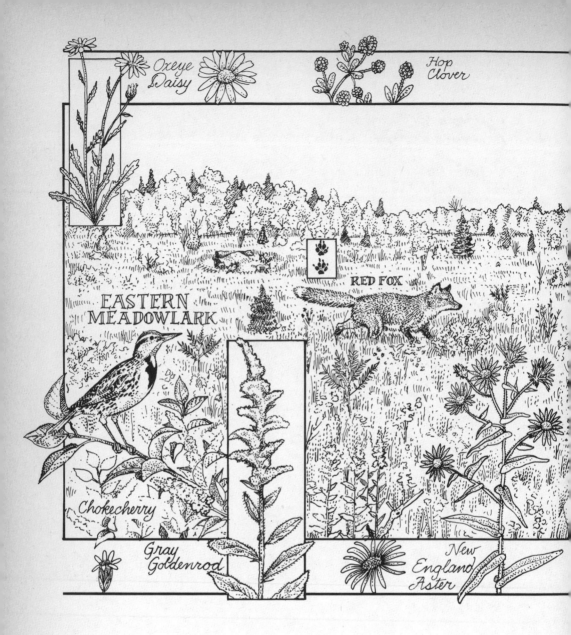

Oxeye Daisy

Hop Clover

RED FOX

EASTERN MEADOWLARK

Chokecherry

Gray Goldenrod

New England Aster

RED-TAILED HAWK

Common Yarrow

EASTERN BLUEBIRD

EASTERN HOGNOSE SNAKE

SOUTHEASTERN SHREW

Common Strawberry

Orange Hawkweed

Grassy Field

WHERE TO SEE THIS HABITAT:

Large fields are common throughout the East. This is just a sampling; there are many more.

Alabama: Wheeler and Eufaula national wildlife refuges
Indiana: Muscatatuck National Wildlife Refuge
Iowa: De Soto National Wildlife Refuge
Michigan: Shiawassee National Wildlife Refuge
Minnesota: Agassiz, Rice Lake, and Tamarac national wildlife refuges
Mississippi: Holly Springs National Forest; Hillside and Mississippi Sandhill Crane national wildlife refuges
South Carolina: Carolina Sandhills National Wildlife Refuge.
Tennessee: Tennessee National Wildlife Refuge
Texas: Aransas National Wildlife Refuge
Vermont: Missisquoi National Wildlife Refuge
Wisconsin: Chequamegon National Forest; Trempealeau National Wildlife Refuge

Grassy Field

BEGINNINGS

Most openings are temporary "haircuts" in the forested cover of the eastern United States. If untouched by plow, cattle, herbicide, flood, or fire, a field usually yields to a thicket, which finally withers under the shade of a woodland. Each community of plants prepares the ground for the next community by aerating the soil, fertilizing the ground with leaves, and creating an awning of shade. The species that can best tolerate shade usually prevail, but this "succession" of various plant communities can take centuries.

Sometimes, the field-to-forest scenario is interrupted, and a particular stage persists for years and years. Fields that remain grassy are a fine example of this. The secret of their staying power is a tightly woven, impenetrable sod layer—the result of years of grass growth.

Grasses have dense, fibrous root systems and a unique way of spreading. Think of the grass in your lawn. Each tuft sends out underground runners called rhizomes that pop up as grass tufts some distance away. The new plants develop their own fibrous roots, put out more runners, etc. Eventually, the soil beneath the surface is choked with miles of roots. You get a glimpse of this when you pull up a clump of grass and get a cubic foot of root-bound soil along with it.

On top of the soil, decomposing grass blades lie like jackstraws in an equally complex fabric. This helps to keep moisture in, but also to limit the fortunes of other plants that may want to put roots down through this thick mat. Plants that do force their way down must then compete for water with the sophisticated monopoly of grass roots.

Only a few plants, among them asters, goldenrods, and hawkweeds, manage to work their way into the sod mat. They have a secret weapon, however. Poisonous compounds called phenols are washed into the soil when rain hits their decaying leaves. Pioneering trees, already struggling to share water and nutrients with grass and bracken fern, wither and die when these poisons flow into their roots, thus giving the weeds free rein.

THE STAYING POWER OF SOD

How does sod like this develop to begin with? First, the grass must be favored for several years in order to build up such an impressive mat of fiber and roots. Other plants, such as broadleaf tree seedlings, must be discouraged. Years of being grazed by cattle can do this to the land, by weeding out all but the low-lying plants such as grasses that can withstand their constant "pruning." The hooves of the animals also compact the soil, adding another obstacle to invaders.

Sod is also likely to form in topographical hollows called frost pockets—dips in the landscape where cold, heavy air rolls down from the uplands and becomes trapped. Frost often forms here, even on relatively mild summer nights. If these pockets don't get the morning sun, they can stay frosty for hours, killing all but the cold-tolerant grasses. Once grass dominates for a few years, its formidable sod mat will ensure its continued rule.

Grasses are also successful on sandy sites that have been abused by fire, poor farming practices, or erosion. The worst sites lose their stabilizing plants and become subject to sand-stealing winds. In the same way that grasses come to the rescue on coastal beaches, grass clumps may also take root and eventually stabilize these inland "sandblows."

Grassy clearings that are sprinkled with mature but stunted trees are called savannas, oak barrens, or pine barrens. They often develop in areas that have frequent fires. The fires keep the trees from spreading, and the ashes fertilize a new flush of grasses.

WHAT'S IN IT FOR WILDLIFE?

Fields, like aquatic habitats, are often visited by animals that don't necessarily live there year-round. They may come only at certain times of day, or in certain seasons when food in other habitats is scarce. Part of the magic of a field is that it is so different from the habitats that surround it.

Because they are in the sun for much of the day, fields are among the first places to lose their snow cover. Grasses may begin to green-up here

CHARACTERISTIC PLANTS:

Saplings, Shrubs, and Vines:

aspens: quaking and bigtooth
bayberry: northern and southern
beaked hazel
black cherry
brambles
chokecherry
common juniper
common persimmon
downy serviceberry
eastern redcedar
gray birch
hawthorns
multiflora rose
pines: eastern white, Virginia, loblolly, and others
shortleaf pine
smooth sumac
sweet-fern
sweetgum
Virginia creeper

Herbaceous Plants:

asters
black-eyed Susan
bracken fern
broomsedge
camphorweed
common lamb's-quarters
common milkweed
common mullein
common ragweed
common strawberry
crab grass
goldenrods
haircap moss
hop clover
horseweed
Kentucky bluegrass
little bluestem
orange hawkweed
oxeye daisy
pearly everlasting
pokeweed
poverty grass
Queen Anne's lace
reindeer moss
thistles
yarrow

Gray Goldenrod

Hop Clover

long before other fresh foods are available. Browsers such as white-tailed deer are regular customers, eager to have succulent food after a winter of feeding on less-preferred woody browse. Look for hibernators such as woodchucks and snakes basking in the warm sun, seemingly shaking off the drowsiness of a long internment.

Flowering plants also abound in fields, and with them come insects drawn by the fragrance and nectar. Birds know this, and many sit perched on small shrubs or nearby trees, sallying out at intervals for a midair snack. On the ground, grasshoppers provide meaty morsels for northern harriers. Flickers probe into mounds of sand, hoping to disturb a hidden colony of juicy ants. On fresh aprons of sand outside fox dens, look for tiny frolicking kits well camouflaged against their sandy backdrop.

The loose, workable soil of a field is attractive to burrowers such as ground squirrels, eastern hognose snakes, toads, and meadow voles. Voles also build aboveground runways, eating the grass as they clear it away. Grass seeds are a favorite of all kinds of rodents. The bristling blades hide the nests of several ground-dwelling birds, including horned larks, sparrows, northern bobwhites, and killdeer. In addition to cover, the parents find a convenient supply of insects to fill their nestlings' gaping beaks. Aerial predators such as red-tailed hawks and short-eared owls have a privileged view of the bustling meadow, and they watch the runways and burrow entrances carefully. For them, the field's openness makes it an ideal choice of hunting habitat.

GRASSHOPPER SPARROW

AMERICAN KESTREL

UPLAND SANDPIPER

Eastern Bluebird

Nothing says "spring" as artfully as a returning flock of bluebirds. They arrive on their northern breeding grounds early, and are sometimes caught by late winter storms that force them to crowd into cavities by the dozen. In this case, it's not the worm that the early bird is after, but a suitable nesting cavity. Bluebirds don't have the luxury of building their own nest holes because their bills are too weak. Unless they can find an old woodpecker hole or a natural cavity rotted out of a tree, they won't be able to nest.

Bluebirds aren't the only ones looking for this kind of real estate, however. Tree swallows, house wrens, northern flickers, deer mice, flying squirrels, and even wasps set up housekeeping in cavities. The most threatening competitors are two which have been introduced to this country—the house sparrow and the European starling. A few decades ago, the housing crunch began to wear down the bluebird populations, and they started disappearing from their old haunts. Besides having to compete for a home, bluebirds, like songbirds everywhere, were also suffering from the sting of farm pesticides such as DDT.

Thankfully, the public noticed, and communities decided to do something to reverse the trend. DDT was banned, and thousands of bluebird houses were strung up along fences and roads. Today, builders of "bluebird trails" apply basic ecological principles to give the birds a further leg up. Houses are placed in pairs to take advantage of the guarding instincts of the bluebird's competitors. If a tree swallow nests in one of the boxes, it will defend the immediate area from other birds *of its kind*. Bluebirds, being an entirely different species, are free to set up house next door, within the force field of the other bird's territory.

Although this "reservation" system helps boost the bluebird's chances, the competition for remaining sites is still keen. Female bluebirds that can't find cavities of their own will often lay their eggs in another female's nest, thus tricking the owner into raising their young. No wonder nesting bluebirds are so quick to chase any female that flies too near!

Look for eastern bluebirds—singing on small shrubs or fence posts, or dropping to the ground to feed on caterpillars, grasshoppers, crickets, and beetles. Areas with poor soil and sparse ground cover are best, especially if dead trees with cavities are nearby for nesting. They also hawk insects from the air or pick them off leaf and twig surfaces. Fruit makes up nearly a third of their diet. Bluebirds are able to perch even when sleeping because of their specially formed feet. A backward-pointing hind toe automatically grasps their perch if they sway backward. In fall and spring, watch for waves of bluebirds in migrating flocks.

Length: 7 inches.

WILDLIFE LOCATOR CHART—GRASSY FIELD

	Feeds from Air	Feeds on Ground	Feeds Beneath Ground
Nests in Tree Canopy	Red-tailed Hawk Eastern Kingbird Loggerhead Shrike		
Nests in Trunk	American Kestrel Eastern Screech-Owl	Eastern Bluebird	
Nests on Ground	Short-eared Owl Common Nighthawk	Sharp-tailed Grouse Northern Bobwhite Killdeer Upland Sandpiper Horned Lark Vesper Sparrow Savannah Sparrow Grasshopper Sparrow Sharp-tailed Sparrow Bobolink Eastern Meadowlark Eastern Cottontail Eastern Garter Snake	
Nests Beneath Ground or Debris	Turkey Vulture Burrowing Owl	Southeastern Shrew Least Shrew Woodchuck Thirteen-lined Ground Squirrel Oldfield Mouse Hispid Cotton Rat Meadow Vole Meadow Jumping Mouse Red Fox Six-lined Racerunner Eastern Fence Lizard Prairie Kingsnake Milk Snake Smooth Green Snake	Eastern Mole Badger Eastern Hognose Snake

Look for nests—typically 5–12 feet up in natural cavities, woodpecker holes, rotting fence posts, or artificial bird boxes. Here are specs so you can build your own: a box 8 inches in height, with a floor 5 inches by 5 inches, and an entrance hole 6 inches above the floor and 1½ inches in diameter. Fasten the box 5–10 feet above the ground, and place another box 20–25 feet away.

Listen for—"chir-wi" of flying or perching bird. Males sing a more musical, liquid "tru-a-lly, tru-a-lly!"

Southeastern Shrew

Shrews are a demanding lot. Although they are smaller than mice, they need a constant supply of food and water to fuel their tiny, hyperactive bodies. Their heart beats an extraordinary 1,200 times a minute, and their gut, even when full, empties in a short 3 hours. To counteract this demanding nature, they live in environments where they can find plenty of food. They scurry haphazardly in their search for prey, and can detect something as small as the microscopic nematode or as large (to a shrew) as the giant earthworm. Other foods include spiders, butterfly larvae, slugs, snails, centipedes, and vegetation. Even the parasites that inhabit the shrew's own body are not exempt when it comes to mealtime.

Another evolutionary "trick" they've learned is to reingest their own feces to get nutrients such as vitamin B and potassium that they may not have absorbed the first time around. If you ever see a shrew curled up, grasping its hind legs with its forelegs, and nibbling its anus, you'll know that it's having its dinner—again.

Because they are so tiny, shrews are always giving away a lot of their heat. Compared with their volume, they have a vast amount of skin area through which heat can escape. Their small size, however, affords them the luxury of crawling under "blankets"—layers of decaying leaves, grasses, sedges, and vines—to keep warm.

Look for southeastern shrews—especially in moist parts of open fields. Try sitting still and focusing on the small. Remember that although their hearing is acute, they are not likely to be able to "figure" out anything as large as a still human being. If you're lucky, you may see a caravan of 4–7 young shrews coming from the nest. The young bite onto the rump of the sibling ahead of them, forming a sinuous lineup behind and attached to the mother.

Length: Head and body, 2–2½ inches; tail, 1–1½ inches.

Look for runways—very tiny matted-down trails around the bases of grass and sedge plants. They are usually covered over with leaves and grass blades, forming a tunnel. Shrews forage in these runways, as well as those of mice and voles. They may also dig pencil-sized burrows, leading with their flexible, sensitive snouts. Watch them emerge with insect prey seized in their jaws.

Look for nests—Small balls of clipped vegetation in runways.

Listen for—birdlike chirps and high-pitched screams when shrews are disagreeing. The pitch and intensity of these cries may give a clue as to the status of the caller. If a defending resident has a formidable vocalization, the intruder may back down without a fight. This helps settle disputes without injury. Though you can't hear it, some shrews bounce ultrasonic calls off the walls of their runways, using a sort of sonar ("echolocation"— see Silver-haired Bat, page 181) to extend their senses.

Eastern Hognose Snake

When you walk through an open field, you're a Goliath in a tiny forest of grasses and weeds. Even so, the hognose snake may not see you coming. Snakes can't see as clearly as birds and mammals, nor can they hear you in the traditional sense, because they have no ear openings. Instead, the hognose snake picks up the vibrations of your footsteps transmitted from the ground to its inner ear via its jawbones! Scientists believe even its lungs may play a part in picking up your vibrations.

If for some reason it can't get away from you in time, the snake will treat you to a performance that hundreds of thousands of years of evolution have perfected. First it lifts its head and "hoods" its neck in a good imitation of a cobra. Large black patches on either side of its neck make it look like a much larger animal. It hisses loudly, then strikes out like a viper (but without the dangerous venom). A slow-motion film of the attack would show something surprising; for all its ferociousness, the snake is actually harmless, and its fake strikes are delivered with a closed mouth.

As Act II begins, you can start to relax. Instead of following through with its attack, the snake suddenly writhes on the ground as if suffering, with mouth agape, tongue protruding, and blood seeping around its teeth. It gulps air to appear bloated. For its climax, it rolls onto its back and, after a few violent jerks, goes completely limp. Fluid discharges from its cloaca for a touch of authenticity.

The performance is flawless, as long as the actor is allowed to remain on its back. It you flip a "dead" hognose, it will flop itself right back over. Presumably, not many of its wild predators are as curious as naturalists tend to be. Many predators such as birds of prey are easily fooled by a limp, lifeless-looking snake. Once movement stops, the raptor's attack reflex turns off, and it goes looking for a more lively meal. If you wait a while after a "death scene," you'll see the limp snake lift its head, check to see that the coast is clear, then slowly slither away.

Look for eastern hognose snakes—sunning in sandy, weedy areas, or burrowing underground to escape high temperatures. Look sharp; the snake's light coloring blends seamlessly with the sandy soil and dry grasses. It uses its upturned snout (its "hog nose") for digging out toads that live in burrows. The teeth at the back of its mouth are designed to puncture inflated toads and make them easier to swallow. Unlike most animals that are poisoned by the toads' alkaline skin secretions, the hognose can easily digest them. It will also enter the burrows of other small animals to take shelter or find a meal.

Length: 20–45½ inches.

Look for nests—in shallow cavities in loose soil in spring and fall. As many as 45 eggs, but the mean is 20.

Listen for—the hiss of a "performing" snake.

SMOOTH
GREEN SNAKE

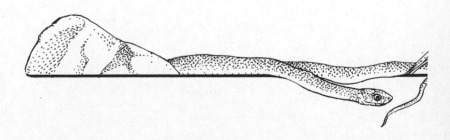

Northern Bush honeysuckle

Smooth Sumac

Sassafras

Gray Birch

GRAY CATBIRD

STRIPED SKUNK

Bracken Fern

Wild Grape

NORTHERN BLACK RACER

Chokecherry

Red Raspberry

Pin Cherry

WHITE-TAILED DEER

RUBY-THROATED HUMMINGBIRD

AMERICAN GOLDFINCH

FIVE-LINED SKINK

Beaked Hazel

Downy Serviceberry

Shrub-Sapling Opening/Edge

WHERE TO SEE THIS HABITAT:

Shrub-sapling openings are common throughout the East. Look in any area that has been recently disturbed by fire, logging, storms, insects and diseases, or flooding.

Shrub-Sapling Opening/Edge

BEGINNINGS

A shrub-sapling opening is a forest in the making—a way station on the road from field to forest, yet an important habitat in its own right. Which shrubs and saplings you'll find will depend on how the land was used in the past and what kinds of trees, shrubs, and herbs were around when the field was first being colonized.

There may be some clues in the field that will help you decipher how the land was used before it was abandoned. Flat-topped stumps, for instance, are a graphic reminder of the crosscut saw or chainsaw. Scarred ground covered with the pink blossoms of fireweed or the scrubby umbrellas of jack pine points to fire in the recent past. In New England, a low stone wall shows the boundary of a farm field. Sometimes, you can still find the furrows of cultivation or old cow paths beneath the dense covering of shrubs and saplings. When you see these, hunt in the woods somewhere near the field to find a crumbling foundation or an ancient root cellar.

Very dense thickets or trees with multiple stems may indicate that woody rootstocks were present beneath the field even as it was being used. Perhaps the aboveground portions of these trees were grazed by cattle, burnt back by fire, or mowed twice a year in a hayfield. The roots remained alive, and when released from their "pruning," the trees went wild, fueled by an already mature root network.

Remember when you're reconstructing the scene, however, that natural forces also play a part in creating openings. A forest may fall prey to diseases, high winds, insect outbreaks, beaver flooding, or lightning fires. The original forest may or may not grow back the way it was. Once the shady canopy is removed, sun bombards and dries the soil; there are no leaves to block the force of rains and no roots to stop erosion. The climate at ground level becomes one of extremes: high temperatures during the day, quick cooling and even frost at night. The shrubs and saplings that invade these areas must be specially suited to survive temperature swings while competing feverishly with an army of other colonizers. Their adaptations put them in a special class of plants called "pioneers."

GETTING THERE FIRST: STRATEGIES OF THE PIONEERS

Very often, the first plants to blossom above a once-cultivated field are exotic (not native) annuals—fascinating plants that are perhaps unfairly called "weeds." They persist because they are endowed with adaptations such as finely segmented leaves that expose a minimum of surface area to

CHARACTERISTIC PLANTS:

Taller Saplings:	Shrubs and Vines:	Herbaceous Plants:
aspen: bigtooth and quaking	beaked hazel	black-eyed Susan
birches: gray and paper	blackberries	bracken fern
black cherry	brambles	broomsedge
black locust	climbing bittersweet	common lamb's-quarters
chokecherry	common juniper	goldenrods
eastern redcedar	downy serviceberry	largeleaf aster
eastern white pine	glossy buckthorn	milkweeds
hawthorns	greenbriers	oxeye daisy
pin cherry	hedge bindweed	pokeweed
red-osier dogwood	northern bush-honey-suckle	Queen Anne's lace
sassafras	poison-ivy	thistles
white ash	purple-flowering raspberry	wild sarsaparilla
	red raspberry	yarrow
	smooth sumac	
	staghorn sumac	
	Virginia creeper	
	wild grape	

the moisture-robbing sun, and deep taproots that find water far beneath the dry, baked surface.

Over the next couple of years, the hardy perennials begin to take over. Plants such as goldenrod, wild aster, milkweed, pokeweed, raspberry, and blackberry sprout from rootstocks that spread under the ground. At the same time, shrubs such as beaked hazel, witch-hazel, bush honeysuckle, and red-osier dogwood begin to find their way into the field. Twined around these shrubs and making their bid for light are wild grape, bittersweet, Virginia creeper, greenbrier, and poison-ivy.

These plants recondition the soil by shedding nutrient-filled leaves and eventually adding their own decayed remains to it. Tree seedlings begin to appear among the shrubs, profiting not only from their slight shade but also from their soil-building service.

TREES OF THE FUTURE FOREST

In New England, eastern white pine and eastern redcedar are often the first trees to invade old fields. Both have lightweight seeds that are sail-equipped so they can travel on the wind, and both are tough enough to germinate in the turf of old grazed pastures or hayfields.

On their way through the field, squirrels may visit these pioneer trees, often stopping to bury the seeds of oaks or hickories—seeds that would otherwise be too heavy to get there on their own. Birds also stop at these perches, and as they defecate, they often deposit seeds from one of their favorite fruits—the pin cherry. After a few years, you may notice a circle of cherries growing around the pine or redcedar perch. Other typical old-field invaders include sumacs, common persimmon, sassafras, plums, and black cherry.

In the lake states, where logging and fires destroyed nearly all of the original white pines, the great invaders were aspens, birches, and jack pine. Aspens can travel up to a mile by means of a lightweight seed (3 million to the pound!); in the fall, a wind full of these fluffy seeds looks like a snowstorm. Even more effective is the aspen's habit of spreading into an opening by "suckering." Suckers sprout from underground roots, and as anyone who has ever cut down an aspen can tell you, suckers are stimulated by cutting. For every felled tree, 15 or more may sprout in its place, each a genetic duplicate of the parent.

Farther south, in the southern needleleaf region, the transition from old field to forest begins with crab grass and annuals, proceeds to horseweed followed by broomsedge, and culminates in a seeding-in of pitch, longleaf, slash, loblolly, or shortleaf pine.

THE IMPORTANCE OF EDGE

The busiest zone (and the most productive for wildlife watchers) is the edge, where the opening blends into the taller forest around it. This band of edge supports a distinct community of birds and mammals that depend on both forest and opening. Here on the edge, they can conveniently commute from one habitat to the other to satisfy their needs. Red bats, for instance, roost under the loose bark of forest trees by day but feed on the wing in nearby clearings each evening. Indigo buntings glean tiny seeds from the ground in grassy fields, nest in protective cover of dense shrubs, and sing incessantly from exposed perches near the top of young saplings.

The edge is also used as a stopover place when moving from the dense cover of the forest to the scanty cover of the field. Cautious wildlife pause here to get the lay of the land before they expose themselves. In turn, field dwellers often resort to the thickets temporarily when predators threaten. If you add these visitors from forest and field to the residents that specialize in this zone of "in-between," you can see why edges have three times the variety of most other communities.

For all its advantages, the edge is in some ways an "ecological trap." Sharp-eyed hawks and egg-eating mammals frequent field-forest borders and clearings because of the unusual concentration of nesting songbirds there. Edge environments also attract the brown-headed cowbird, which, instead of building its own nest, secretly deposits its eggs in the nests of many other birds. The invaded birds usually wear themselves to a frazzle trying to raise the young cowbird, which might be several times larger than their own young.

WHAT'S IN IT FOR WILDLIFE?

When a forest is cleared, species that depend on dense forest interiors (ovenbirds and wood thrushes, for instance) lose a place to live, but many other species gain a new home. The jumble of fallen tops and branches creates hundreds of nest sites and protected resting spots for birds and small mammals that need shelter from the eyes of winged hunters. Woodpeckers also flock to decaying limbs, in search of the beetles and borers that are hard at work dismantling the debris. Wherever dead trees are still standing, the habitat becomes even more attractive, luring cavity nesters such as Carolina wrens and red-headed woodpeckers.

The succulent grasses and flowering plants are a green feast to grazers such as white-tailed deer that may visit the opening like clockwork every day. On the ground level, seeds from these plants are eaten by voles, mice, and other rodents. The insects that pollinate the blossoms are hungrily devoured by many songbirds that perch on nearby saplings to sing their territorial songs. The shrubs and brambles in a field may produce up to 30 times more fruit than their counterparts in the woods. No wonder wildlife such as birds, skunks, rabbits, and even bears congregate here.

Besides the direct benefits of food, cover, and nesting sites, many of the plants in shrub-sapling openings provide indirect services that you may not think of. The large leaves of grapevines protect young bird fledglings from the full heat of the sun, for instance. Other plants may not be a nest site, but may be used as building material. For example, the down of cinnamon fern is used as a nest lining by ruby-throated hummingbirds, eastern wood-pewees, and various warblers. Other shrubs are soil conditioners, preparing the way for the forest trees that will one day support a different community of animals.

The openness of this habitat attracts aerial predators, such as hawks and owls, and displaying birds such as American woodcocks, which need a generous "takeoff" radius. Wildlife also visit openings because they are sunny, warm places to recuperate from a cold night or a heavy rain. Next time you're camping in a downpour, hike to an opening when the sun comes out and see for yourself. If you're hiking in late winter, visit south-facing slopes—the first to lose their snow cover and expose coveted green plants.

Ruby-throated Hummingbird

The tiny hummingbird, no longer than your thumb, is packed with amazing adaptations. They are the only birds that can not only hover in one place and fly straight up and down but also fly backward. Their wings beat an incredible 2,000–3,000 times a minute, getting lift and power not only on the downstroke but also on the upstroke. If you could slow down the blur of their wings, you'd see why. Each hovering stroke is a smooth, horizontal figure eight in which the hummingbird turns its wing completely over, rotating it from the shoulder joint. This way, the front edge of the wing cuts the air both coming and going, thus keeping the hummer suspended. By tilting the plane of the wing back, it can fly up and backward like a living helicopter. By tilting it down, it zooms forward at speeds up to 30 miles per hour.

RED BAT · MOURNING DOVE · INDIGO BUNTING · YELLOW-BREASTED CHAT · NORTHERN FLICKER · BROWN THRASHER

WILDLIFE LOCATOR CHART—SHRUB-SAPLING OPENING/EDGE

	Feeds from Air	Feeds in Upper Canopy	Feeds in Lower Canopy	Feeds on Trunks	Feeds on Ground	Feeds Beneath Ground
Nests in Tree Canopy	Red-tailed Hawk Ruby-throated Hummingbird Least Flycatcher Red Bat Hoary Bat		American Goldfinch		Mourning Dove Brown-headed Cowbird	
Nests in Trunk	Eastern Screech-Owl		Carolina Wren	Red-headed Woodpecker	Northern Flicker	
Nests in Shrubs			White-eyed Vireo Chestnut-sided Warbler Prairie Warbler Yellow-breasted Chat Indigo Bunting		Gray Catbird Blue Grosbeak Brown Thrasher Golden Mouse	
Nests on Ground		Blue-winged Warbler Golden-winged Warbler			American Woodcock Rufous-sided Towhee Field Sparrow Song Sparrow Dark-eyed Junco Eastern Cottontail White-tailed Deer Eastern Garter Snake	
Nests Beneath Ground or Debris			Rough Green Snake		Hairy-tailed Mole Eastern Chipmunk Woodchuck Eastern Harvest Mouse White-footed Mouse Coyote Ermine Least Weasel Striped Skunk Eastern Box Turtle Five-lined Skink Mole Kingsnake Milk Snake Eastern Coachwhip	Southeastern Pocket Gopher Badger Eastern Hognose Snake

The muscles that power this flight are massive, taking up 25–30 percent of their body weight. Their sternum is deeply keeled and reinforced with two extra ribs to help them endure the stresses of flight. Meanwhile, their oversized heart is beating 1,260 times a minute (when active) and their lungs (at rest) are expanding 250 times a minute. It's an energy output that's 10 times that of a person running 9 miles per hour.

Imagine for a moment how it would feel for you to live the life of a hummingbird. Say you weigh 170 pounds. You would burn 155,000 calories a day and evaporate 100 pounds of perspiration an hour. If you ran out of water, your skin temperature would soon reach the melting point of lead, and you'd eventually ignite! Now imagine yourself flying 600 miles across the Gulf of Mexico without stopping. Hummingbirds do it with only 2.1 grams of food inside them.

The fuel that keeps their engines humming comes from the nectar of 1,000 blossoms a day. The hummer's long, needle thin bill reaches down into the neck of tubular flowers and its grooved tongue sucks up the nectar with capillary action. The flower, in turn, has good reason for serving free nectar to the birds. Each time the bird imbibes, its bill becomes dusted with pollen, which in turn fertilizes the next flower the bird visits.

When it comes time to fertilize their own eggs, the male performs a beautiful pendulum flight in front of the female. So precise are his movements that it looks like he is swinging back and forth on a wire. As he flies, he shows off his shimmering throat patch, or "gorget." Although the feathers seem vibrantly colored, they actually have no pigment. The colors are caused by a phenomenon called iridescence, in which light is scattered by the laminated platelets on the feathers. The same phenomenon causes the swirling colors we see in soap bubbles.

Look for ruby-throated hummingbirds—breeding in mixed woodlands and visiting flowers at the sunlit edges. They are especially partial to red flowers such as salvia, trumpet-creeper, jewelweed, and thistle bloom. Also look for hummingbirds plucking insects out of spider webs, or feeding on insects trapped in the sapwells drilled by yellow-bellied sapsuckers. Hummingbirds bathe in puddles on large leaves, and may even be seen streaking through your sprinkler. Groups of hummingbirds sometimes swarm around large flowered trees such as buckeyes or lilac bushes.

Length: 3–3¾ inches.

Look for nests—walnut-sized knots, 1 inch in diameter, 10–20 feet above the ground on the saddle of a drooping branch. Nests are usually protected by vegetation above, but open below to a trail, clearing, or water. They are built of bud scales, decorated with lichens, and wrapped with spider webbing. The rim is curved inward to keep the two pea-sized eggs from tumbling out.

Listen for—the whir of wings in flight. At the bottom of the pendulum display, the males' wings buzz. Occasionally you can hear high-pitched squeaks as the males and females "bicker."

White-tailed Deer

White-tailed deer don't have to be coaxed to eat what's good for them; if given a choice of two menus, deer will instinctively choose the one with the higher nutritional value. Even if offered an unlimited amount of one of their favorite foods (e.g., Canada yew), deer will show uncanny restraint, eating some of their favorite, along with a variety of complementary foods. Evidently, some of their favorite plants produce small amounts of compounds that inhibit digestion; eating a bushel of these might concentrate these compounds and cause problems. By eating a mixture of plants, deer are able to fully digest all their food.

Deer also shift foods with the seasons, as their nutritional needs change. After their low-sodium winter diet, hungry springtime deer are drawn to aquatic plants such as horsetails and reeds that are rich in salts. They also travel to fields where the snow melts first so they can cash in on the new flush of spring growth. Deer even have a taste for lichens, and can be seen "barking up a tree" to nibble some green off its trunk. In summer, a plethora of foods becomes available, and deer may stay within a 2-to-3-square-mile area, using a few key trails to take them to productive feeding areas at dawn and dusk.

In winter, when broadleaf plants become scarce, deer are forced to switch to woody browse such as needleleaf boughs, which are less nutritious. Luckily, their bodies have put on layers of fat during the autumn, and their coats have been insulated with hollow winter hairs. At the same time, they go into a sort of walking hibernation: their metabolism slows, they don't move around as much, and they are actually able to survive on less food. In this geared-down state, deer become hardy and better able to cope with stress. When the snow depth reaches 16 inches, they group together in "yards," preferring northern white-cedar stands where they find food and a natural windscreen. With the eyes of the whole group on the lookout, each animal can spend more time feeding and less on surveillance. They also have access to a common system of tamped-down trails, saving them even more energy.

A deer herd is only as healthy as its habitat. The size of a buck's antlers, for instance, are not a function of its age, but of its nutritional health. Weak, small antlers may leave a buck in the dust when it comes to battles for reproductive dominance. Likewise, pregnant does that are hungry and poorly fed are likely to have only one fawn instead of two. If the food supply doesn't improve, the newborn is likely to die.

Look for white-tailed deer—feeding in shrubby areas at dawn and dusk. Stand still; deer have a harder time pinpointing a stationary object. Move a muscle, and you'll see them dissolve into the woods. Before they bound, they usually raise their tail to horizontal, then leave with a flip of the tail. This may warn other deer of approaching danger, or it may say to a predator: "Don't bother chasing me, I've seen you and am fleeing."

Length: Head and body, 4–6 feet; tail, 7–11 inches.

Look for deer trails—worn-down routes to and from feeding, bedding, and watering places. When following a trail, be sure to look behind you occasionally. Deer that have spotted you will often circle back to where you have just walked to get a whiff of your scent.

Look for day beds—on high ridges, on south-facing slopes in the sun, ideally with a good view of approaching predators. Deer will leave shallow, oval, body-sized dents in the grasses or leaves where they have slept. Look for chewed twigs, tracks, and a pile of 20–30 black droppings (pointed at one end) to confirm the presence of deer. If droppings are still warm, your deer might still be in the area. If it is summer, the droppings may be extra soft, like cow pies.

If you find an "orphan" fawn—leave it where it is. Mothers hide their fawns in two separate places to decrease the chances of both being found by a predator. The mother is probably just out feeding; she visits the fawns for milking 2–3 times a day.

Look for "scrapes"—patches of muddy, pawed-up ground that male deer urinate in to advertise their presence. They check these scrapes periodically, smelling for rival males or the scent of does that also visit the scrapes at breeding time. Once you find a scrape, try rattling two antlers together to imitate the sound of fighting bucks. You may draw a curious spectator. Don't overdo it, however; luring the same deer more than once is harassment.

Look for "bark rubs"—In the fall, bucks often "shadowbox" with small trees and shrubs to rub the blood-rich skin (called velvet) off their newly hardened antlers. Look for strips of the frayed, bloody velvet fluttering in the breeze near the worn-away bark. A scent gland on their forehead also spreads their chemical signature on the rubbed trees.

Look for antlers—shed from December to March. They are difficult to find because they are calcium-rich and thus quickly devoured by mice and other rodents.

In the winter—tracks and packed-down trails in lowland needleleaf stands are signs of a winter yarding site. Look for a "browse line"—nipped-off twigs as far up as the deer can reach. The ideal winter yards have nearby aspen stands where the deer can supplement their browsing.

Look for tracks—two-toed cloven hooves, like triangles pointing in the direction of travel. Common on deer trails or around water sources. Deer practice "perfect stepping"—placing their hind foot in or near the same track as their forefoot.

Listen for—the loud snort of a startled deer, whistles, whines and "whiews." Does murmur a low whine to their fawns, and the fawns bleat to their mother.

Five-lined Skink

The five-lined skink is one sharp lizard. It's born with a shiny black body, five yellow stripes, and a neon blue tail. As he ages, the male loses his bright stripes and the blue in his tail, acquiring a bright orange head that complements his aggressive nature during breeding season. The female's stripes don't fade quite as much, and she retains the blue in her tail. This color may save her life in more ways than one.

When the male is asserting himself during the breeding season, he chases all dull-colored skinks (adult males) out of his territory. The fights can be vicious at times. Females and young males, identified by their blue tails, are granted immunity from his attacks.

The blue tails are also a way to throw predators such as shrews, striped skunks, Virginia opossums, and snakes off the track. The predator usually homes in on the bright tail and strikes at it, causing it to break off. This severed tail continues to thrash wildly, keeping the predator occupied while the skink shimmies out of reach.

"Fragile" tails are built to break off. A wall of cartilage passes through each vertebra, creating a weak point where muscles and blood sinuses are also modified to allow an easy break. If in danger, a skink may even break off its own tail by pressing against something, thus leaving its pursuer with a wriggling calling card.

Losing a tail is a trick that works only once, and there are definite ecological costs associated with it. The new tail grows in slowly, for instance, and is never as long or as colorful as the last tail. Nor does it have fracture planes to allow it to break off easily. Besides, losing a tail means losing some fat that was stored there. This pantry might have gotten the skink through a food shortage, especially in winter or during drought. It also, of course, takes energy to grow a new tail, energy that must be borrowed from breeding or feeding activities. When a pregnant female loses her tail, her eggs may have lower mass, and thus less chance of surviving. In addition, a skink that loses the use of its tail, even for a short time, is not as well equipped to run, swim, balance, or climb.

The trade-offs have been weighed carefully in the long march of evolution, however, and for "blue scorpions," the benefits of losing a tail still seem to outweigh the costs.

Look for five-lined skinks—in cutover woods, where there are stumps, sawdust piles, and piles of rocks. They also live in open woods, near wooded bluffs, and on rocky, south-facing hillsides. They climb the lower trunks of trees occasionally, especially to bask on snags or stumps. They are wary when basking and usually slip out of sight before you have a chance to study them. Try poking around sawdust piles or peeling the dead bark of stumps to find skinks feeding on grubs and beetles that infest rotting wood. As they move, their tongues dart in and out, picking up chemical sensations that tell them about their environment.

Length: 5–8$\frac{1}{16}$ inches.

In the winter—skinks hibernate deep inside rotten logs, in sawdust piles, or under the ground, below frost level.

Look for eggs—under rocks, under logs, in rotted stumps, or in loose soil from April to June. The female will urinate on the eggs to keep them from drying out, or will turn them frequently to prevent microorganisms from growing. If an egg becomes addled, she usually eats it, shell and all, perhaps to keep predators from being drawn to the odor.

LEAST WEASEL

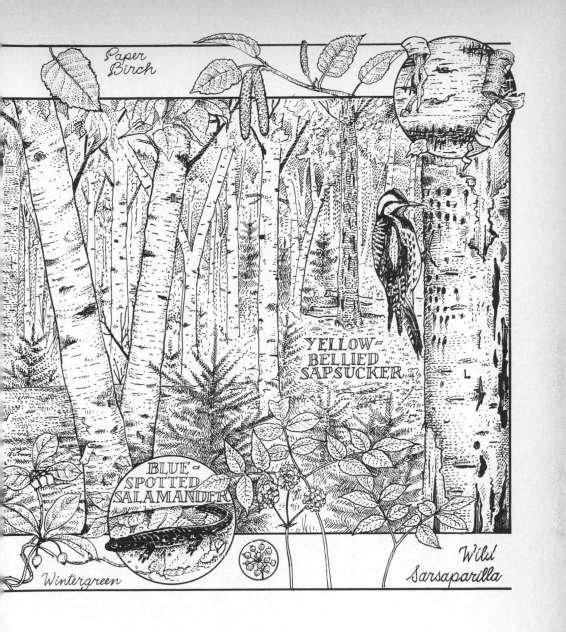

Paper Birch

YELLOW-BELLIED SAPSUCKER

BLUE-SPOTTED SALAMANDER

Wintergreen

Wild Sarsaparilla

Aspen-Birch Forest

WHERE TO SEE THIS HABITAT:

Maine: Moosehorn National Wildlife Refuge

Michigan: Hiawatha, Huron-Manistee, and Ottawa national forests; Isle Royale National Park; Seney National Wildlife Refuge

Minnesota: Chippewa and Superior national forests; Agassiz, Rice Lake, Sherburne, and Tamarac national wildlife refuges

New Hampshire: White Mountain National Forest

New York: Adirondack Forest Preserve; Iroquois and Montezuma national wildlife refuges

Vermont: Green Mountain National Forest

Wisconsin: Chequamegon and Nicolet national forests; Horicon and Necedah national wildlife refuges

Aspen-Birch Forest

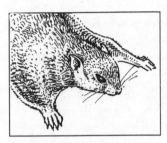

BEGINNINGS

Believe it or not, the northern aspen-birch forests are much like the loblolly or longleaf pine forests of the Southeast. Although they sport different leaves and grow in different climates, they perform the same role in the forest history of their region. Both are pioneer forests, coming in after a disturbance and preparing the ground for yet another kind of forest.

The disturbance that triggered the spread of the aspens and birches was caused by people. The first explorers who mapped the northwoods found mammoth pines nearly "scraping the rooftop of sky" and stretching from "horizon to horizon." Beginning in 1850, teams of men with oxen and crosscut saws made short work of the pines, leveling most of them in less than a century. In their wake, they left acres of dead branches and tops that stood hip-high in places. As the debris dried to kindling, hellacious fires broke out, killing the young growth and burning the seeds still left on the ground. Without the taller pines to lend new seeds, a forest that once characterized a region faded into history.

Quaking and bigtooth aspen trees that had been mixed among the pines were also burned to the ground, but underneath, their roots still lived. Like modern-day phoenixes, they sprouted from the ashes, growing as much as 4 feet a year for the first few years. Millions of their fluffy seeds fell onto the scarred expanses, and between the seedlings and the sprouts, the fire scar soon pulsed with green.

A RIPE HARVEST OF WOOD

Today, much of this forest is mature and starting to break down. In fertile soils, aspen-birch stands mature quickly (50–60 years), and just as quickly, the aged trees begin to disintegrate. Their trunks become riddled with heartrot, and as their inner wood softens, tree-hugging conks erupt on their bark. In a few short years, the rasps of wood borers and the ambitious threads of fungi will weaken the trees even further, until a gust of wind will one day lay them flat. As these fallen logs decay, they release nutrients that help feed the future forest waiting beneath the boughs.

If you look carefully at the tiny saplings on the forest floor, you'll see that the future may not belong to the aspens and birches. The qualities that allow these trees to excel on disturbed sites are handicaps when it comes to stable, understory growth. Adapted to the full-strength sun of an open field, these pioneers are usually stunted by the shade of their parent's branches. On the other hand, balsam fir, white spruce, sugar maple, American basswood, American beech, and eastern hemlock are all trees that can grow despite the shade. They simply wait out the aspens, growing slowly on the forest floor for decades. When the aspens begin to topple one by one, the shade-tolerant trees grow aggressively into the gaps the aspens leave. Eventually, if these are no major disturbances, they will overtop the dying aspens, changing the entire character of the forest.

CHARACTERISTIC PLANTS:

Trees, Shrubs, and Vines:

alders: American green and speckled

aspens: bigtooth and quaking

balsam fir (understory)

beaked hazel

brambles

chokecherry

mountain maple

northern bush-honeysuckle

paper birch

red-osier dogwood

sugar maple (understory)

white spruce

Herbaceous Plants:

bracken fern

bunchberry

Canada mayflower

goldenrods

lady fern

largeleaf aster

sedges

sensitive fern

sweet-fern

sweet-scented bedstraw

wild sarsaparilla

wintergreen (teaberry)

Sugar Maple

ROSE-BREASTED
GROSBEAK

BLACK-BILLED
CUCKOO

WHAT'S IN IT FOR WILDLIFE?

When you look at an aspen-birch forest in terms of wildlife, you have to consider at least two of its phases. The young forest is a thicket of dense pole-sized trees, offering an effective visual screen against predators, but not much understory vegetation for food. In these early years, the aspen leaves and buds themselves are within reach of browsers such as deer or moose. Beavers, snowshoe hares, and other mammals also eat the bark, twigs, and leaves of smaller aspens. Ruffed grouse lead their young on forays for insects, finding the dense stand a safe haven from sudden attack by northern goshawks or other predators. A host of songbirds, many of which are associated with shrub-sapling openings, can also be found in the young aspens.

As it ages, the aspen-birch forest fulfills different wildlife needs. The competition for sunlight leads to a natural thinning of the forest, with only the hardiest, most efficient trees reaching the canopy. In the winter, you may see the silhouettes of ruffed grouse up in the branches, feeding on male catkins (reproductive parts) and buds. The openings in the canopy allow sunlight to reach the forest floor, spurring the growth of berry-producing shrubs, succulent forbs, and even some grasses. Evergreens such as spruce and fir may be scattered among the mature aspen or sneaking up in the understory. These cone-bearers introduce a whole new food source, and are a drawing card for a wider variety of wildlife.

As the pioneering aspen and birch reach their peak, disease, insects, and storms begin to weaken them, and they begin to rot. Cavities form in

LEAST FLYCATCHER

ROSE-BREASTED GROSBEAK

BLACK-BILLED CUCKOO

VEERY

EASTERN CHIPMUNK

NORTHERN FLYING SQUIRREL

WILDLIFE LOCATOR CHART—ASPEN-BIRCH FOREST

	Feeds from Air	Feeds in Upper Canopy	Feeds in Lower Canopy	Feeds on Trunk	Feeds on Ground	Feeds in Water
Nests in Tree Canopy	Northern Goshawk Least Flycatcher	Red-eyed Vireo Rose-breasted Gros-beak	Black-billed Cuckoo American Redstart			
Nests in Trunk			Black-capped Chicka-dee	Yellow-bellied Sap-sucker	Northern Flying Squirrel	
Nests on Ground		Ruffed Grouse (also feeds on ground)			Veery Snowshoe Hare White-tailed Deer Moose	
Nests Beneath Ground or Debris		Porcupine			Eastern Chipmunk Long-tailed Weasel Marbled Salamander Ringneck Snake Milk Snake Smooth Green Snake	
Nests in Water					Blue-spotted Salaman-der Spotted Salamander Wood Frog	Beaver (nests in lodge) Red-spotted Newt

the trunks, creating hotly contested housing for squirrels, woodpeckers, nuthatches, chickadees, owls, and many other species. As the dead trees fall, they begin new lives as logs, providing a safe, moist refuge for salamanders, frogs, snakes, skunks, and weasels.

MARBLED SALAMANDER

Ruffed Grouse

If you thought the only sonic boom you could hear was that of a Concorde taking off for London, guess again. The male ruffed grouse creates sonic booms with his own wings during an acoustical display called "drumming." To begin, he mounts a well-chosen log, anchors himself with sharp claws, and brings his rounded, cupped wings all the way back, nearly to touching. He starts slow, bringing the wings completely forward and back a few times. At first, it's a heartbeat, then, like an engine turning over, it builds to a "brrrrrrrrrr." In the short 10-second burst, he may stroke his wings 50 times, creating a series of tiny air vacuums. The air rushing in to fill these vacuums creates the boom. Once it's up and running, the drumming sounds like a kettledrum, an ax chopping wood, or a farm tractor putt-putting over the fields. Grouse must think so too, for they are often seen following loggers or farmers on their rounds.

The male uses drumming as a way to tell other males in the vicinity that this is his territory. At the same time, he's appealing to a harem of potential mates. If an intruder steps into his territory, the grouse dismounts and begins to strut like a miniature tom turkey. He fans his tail, drags his wings, stiffens his neck ruffs to form a collar, bristles his red eyebrows, and wags his lowered head faster and faster. As he paces, he hisses to the same beat as his drumming. A lesser male soon gets the message and bows out. If the intruder is female, the display quickly grows gentler in preparation for mating.

Interactions between humans and grouse are equally as exciting. No matter how many times it happens, the powerful roar of a grouse flushing in front of you is guaranteed to get your blood racing. Banking on their camouflage to hide them, grouse wait until you are almost on top of them before rocketing out of the brush. Each parabolic flight sends them a little deeper in the brush just beyond you. Hunters often become hikers as they try to follow a grouse flush by flush into its escape grounds.

Look for ruffed grouse—in aspen-birch forests of all ages, feeding or roosting on the ground or in trees. Hens and chicks use shrub-sapling aspens for feeding. As the aspens grow taller (10–25 feet), the ground cover clears out, allowing adults to find each other for breeding. These young stands also make good winter cover, especially if they contain scattered conifers. Older stands of aspen (30–35 years) provide nesting sites and an important winter food source in the form of buds and catkins (male reproductive parts). In the fall, look in shrubby areas that are rich in fruiting shrubs such as gray dogwood, hawthorns, sumacs, or berry bushes. After you flush a grouse, try remaining perfectly silent. This may frustrate the grouse that is listening for you, and cause it to flush into view again.

Length: 16–19 inches.

Look for nests—shallow, leafy depressions on the ground, usually at the base of a large stump or under an overhanging branch, fallen log, or clump of bushes. They look for spots with plenty of leafy cover to protect them from predators such as great horned owls and northern goshawks. The female on the nest apparently loses her odor, which helps secrete her from hungry red foxes, bobcats, and striped skunks.

Look for drumming logs—on upper slopes in forests that are open at ground level, but have a ceiling of branches to shield the grouse from hawks and owls. The moss-covered log may have branches or roots at one end for extra protection. They return to the same logs time after time, until the top becomes worn away and the soil behind the log is "fanned" clear of leaves and scattered with inch-long, white droppings. The ground in front of the log may show the dragged wing marks left by the strutting grouse. Grouse also use boulders, tree roots, and dirt mounds for drumming sites.

Look for dusting depressions—shallow bowls in ant mounds or in the ruts of a forest trail where grouse wallow, covering themselves with dust. The dust may flush out parasites or improve the insulating quality of the bird's feathers by absorbing excess oil and moisture. Grouse also eat grit from roads to help break up food in their gizzards. Look for droppings at these sites.

In the winter—grouse dive into snowbanks to roost. Their breath melts a small hole at the surface. As they burst out, their wings leave marks on either side of the hole. Grouse grow "snowshoes"—furry combs on the sides of their toes—to help them walk atop the snow without sinking in. Try following these tracks.

Listen for—a throbbing drum roll lasting 10 seconds, then repeated every 5 minutes or so. The best time to listen is at dawn, at dusk, or on moonlit nights in the spring and fall. The low frequency (40 cycles/second) makes it hard for human ears to distinguish where the sound is coming from. Evidently owls can't pick up the noise either, and will sometimes fly right by a drumming bird. To sneak up on a drumming grouse, move forward when the bird is drumming so it can't hear you. Stop when it stops.

Long-tailed Weasel

When a weasel stalks a cottontail rabbit, it's like a house cat going after an animal the size of a white-tailed deer. The weasel is a skinny rodent, only 1½ inches in diameter, with short legs, a long tail, and a phenomenally ferocious demeanor. The weasel jumps on the rabbit's back before it has time to so much as tense a muscle. It wraps its tubular body around its victim, riding for dear life as the rabbit thrashes through the undergrowth, rolling over and over on the ground. Eventually, the weasel makes its way to the back of the rabbit's neck, where it delivers a precise surgical bite through the neck vertebrae, killing the rabbit instantly.

For the weasel, this aggressive, predatory nature is a survival tool, especially in cold weather. Their serpentine body shape, though it allows them to follow prey down tiny burrows, can be a hindrance when it comes to retaining heat. Compared to their body mass, weasels have a lot of skin area through which heat can escape. Unlike animals that can roll themselves into a sphere for warmth, the weasel can only manage to curl up on its side in a flattened disk. It also has short fur, again good for tunneling, but bad for insulating. A weasel, therefore, needs up to twice as much energy as other mammals of its size. For a female with young, this translates into a food requirement of two-thirds her own weight each day—comparable to a 125-pound woman eating 83 pounds of food a day! Also because of their svelte shape, their stomach can hold only an ounce of meat at a time. They are compelled, therefore, to hunt frequently and store what they cannot finish.

The need for constant fuel has led to an actual size difference between the males and females. Males are much larger, and thus exploit larger prey then females do. Going after different prey allows the weasels to live in the same habitat without putting stress on one another. Both males and females are equipped with the physical tools to track down prey and the spunk to take on animals 30 times their size. They have enormous stamina, and their senses of smell, hearing, and eyesight are remarkably keen, making them among the continent's most efficient predators.

Look for long-tailed weasels—bounding along the ground with arched back, like an inchworm in high gear. They move their head from side to side, sniffing every nook and cranny for possible prey. They usually walk 3½ zigzagging miles a night, though they don't venture more than a few hundred yards total from the den. During the day they nap, often in the burrows of mice, muskrats, or ground squirrels that they devoured the night before.

Length: Males—head and body, 9–10½ inches; tail, 4–6 inches. Females—head and body, 8–9 inches; tail, 3–5 inches.

In the winter—in northern regions, weasels replace their brown coat with a white one. The tip of their tail remains black, helping to confuse predators. The predator keys in on the black against the white snow and swoops down on it, usually missing the main body, and giving the weasel a chance to escape.

Look for dens—in shallow burrows (commandeered from prey species), in rock piles, under roots of trees or stumps, or in hollow logs. The nest is often lined with fur, feathers, bones, and other "trophies" of the hunt. Caches of as many as 100 mice and rats have been found in or near dens. Whenever weasels foul their nest, they cover it with grasses, resulting in a layered nest floor.

Look for pellets—of regurgitated fur.

Look for tracks—with four toes printing, in strides that vary from 12 inches to 20 inches when running. The hindprints, ¾ inch wide and 1 inch long, are twice as long as foreprints.

Smell for—a skunky odor discharged at the slightest provocation, or to mark territory. Females scent to let males know they want to mate.

Listen for—a characteristic, rapid "took-took-took." They also let out a raucous screech to startle their prey and their predators. When in pain, they squeal; when annoyed, they stamp their feet. Hunting weasels hiss, and females whistle a high-pitched reedy note when pursued by males.

Red-spotted Newt (Eft Stage)

After a good soaking rain, the forest floor may be alive with red efts, crawling up and over leaves by the thousands. These salamanders don't seem to be worried about predators, perhaps because their bright orange color serves as a warning, and their toxic skin secretions back it up.

The red eft is the middle-aged stage of the red-spotted newt. Newts begin their lives in the water, transforming into landlubbing efts after a few months. They trade in their smooth skin for rougher stuff, their flattened sculling tails for rounder ones, and their gills for lungs. After 3–7 years on land, the efts will reverse these transformations and wind up back in the water as newts. Perhaps witches were onto something when they called for eye of newt in their potions!

Besides their quick-change artistry, efts also seem to have an uncanny knack for finding their way back to the pond they were born in, even after years of being gone. Scientists suspect that their nervous system can somehow store internal "maps" of their environment. Studies have shown that they can detect the axis of the earth's magnetic field. Other navigational compasses may be odors, humidity gradients, landmarks, and the position of celestial bodies such as the sun.

Look for red-spotted newts—on the forest floor as efts, or in ponds during their newt phases (larval and adult). In ponds, look for newts swimming near the surface, drifting halfway down, or walking along the bottom. When temporary ponds dry up, newts burrow into the mud until water returns. In the forest, look for bold efts walking about in broad daylight. They feed on tiny insects and snails under logs.

Length: $2^5/8$–$5^1/2$ inches.

Look for eggs—300 or more, attached individually to leaves and stems of aquatic vegetation.

MILK SNAKE

Sugar Maple

American Beech

American Basswood

BROAD-WINGED HAWK

EASTERN CHIPMUNK

REDBACK SALAMANDER

RINGNECK SNAKE

Eastern White Pine

NORTHERN FLYING SQUIRREL

RED-EYED VIREO

Eastern Hemlock

Yellow Birch (prop roots)

False Solomon's Seal

Partridgeberry

Transition Forest

WHERE TO SEE THIS HABITAT:

Maine: Moosehorn National Wildlife Refuge
Michigan: Hiawatha, Huron-Manistee, and Ottawa national forests
New Hampshire: White Mountain National Forest
New York: Adirondack Forest Preserve
Pennsylvania: Allegheny National Forest
Vermont: Green Mountain National Forest
Wisconsin: Chequamegon and Nicolet national forests
In the mountains, below spruce-fir zone:
North Carolina: Blue Ridge Parkway; Pisgah and Nantahala national forests
Tennessee: Cherokee National Forest; Great Smoky Mountains National Park
Virginia: George Washington and Jefferson national forests; Shenandoah National Park
West Virginia: Monongahela National Forest

Transition Forest

BEGINNINGS

The transition forest is the overlap zone for two very different forest types. Coming down from Canada, the snowy needleleaf forests reach their southern limits here. At the same time, the broadleaf forests of the eastern United States extend as far north as they can. Where their ranges intersect, the two types mingle, dropping their needles and leaves on the same forest floor, and creating a habitat unlike any in North America.

This mingling of northern, southern, and resident species sets up unique relationships among the birds, animals, plants, insects, and other forms of life that live here. Only in a transition forest, for instance, could snowshoe hares (from the North) run next to eastern cottontails (from the South), while great gray owls dine on southern flying squirrels.

Just as this transition forest lies between northern and southern extremes, it also lies between low and high zones in the Appalachian Mountains. As you work your way down a mountain pass, you'll find the transition forest nestled just below the spruce-fir forests of the peaks, and above the oak-hickory forests of the base.

The roster of plant species changes as you move around the map, but sugar maple remains the common denominator, occupying more than half the area on most sites. It grows especially well on the rich, deep soils of "moraines"—undulating hills of sediments deposited more than 10,000 years ago, wherever the retreating glacier "paused." Yellow birch and eastern hemlock prefer moist or even wet sites, and can be found growing with American beech in rocky, stream-cut ravines. As you move west from New England, you'll begin to see more pines and balsam fir, white spruce instead of red spruce, and fewer hemlocks. Further west, Wisconsin's plentiful yellow birch begins to drop out, and beech gives way to American basswood. Some of these differences are caused by variations in climate or soil. In other cases, it may be that the migration of trees after the glacier is still occurring, and some species just haven't made it west yet.

Despite the slight variations, the overriding fact that distinguishes the sugar-maple forest from others is that it lasts. Foresters call it a "climax" forest, one that repeats itself over and over. The true test of this is to look in the understory. There you'll find an island of maple seedlings in every opening. The midstory is made up of the same trees that are in the canopy. Unlike the aspen-birch forest, which is quickly changing into something else, the maple-dominated forests (barring major upheaval) are here to stay.

THE INDOMITABLE MAPLE

One of the sugar maple's keys to success is its ability to wait, botanically speaking, for a position at the top. A major disturbance such as logging or fire may unseat the maples, but only temporarily. Within a few years, you'll

---

CHARACTERISTIC PLANTS:

Trees, Shrubs, and Vines:

		Herbaceous Plants:
alternate-leaf dogwood	prickly gooseberry	bluebead lily (yellow clintonia)
American basswood	white ash	Canada mayflower
American beech	yellow birch	crested wood fern
beaked hazel		downy Solomon's seal
black cherry		downy yellow violet
Canada yew		false Solomon's seal
eastern hemlock		hairy Solomon's seal
eastern hophornbeam		large-flowered bellwort
eastern white pine		large-flowered trillium
elderberry (red-berried elder)		partridgeberry
maple: mountain, red, striped, and sugar		rattlesnake fern
maple-leaf viburnum		shining club moss
mountain-laurel		stiff club moss
northern red oak		white baneberry

---

no doubt find a carpet of small maples (4,000 for every parent tree) waiting under the "nurse" trees that took over the cleared site (see Aspen-Birch Forest, page 225). As soon as one of the nurse trees falls, the patient maple will literally jump at the opportunity, growing by leaps and bounds to fill the opening in the canopy with its own leaves.

Once a maple makes it to the canopy, it may live as long as 400 years, providing seeds and shelter for wildlife, shade for other developing maples, and a mulch made from 2 tons of fallen leaves per acre per year. Maples are among the unusual tree species that function as "nutrient pumps." Their deep roots extract nutrients from the lower soil levels and transport them to the leaves. Unlike most trees that reabsorb nutrients from their leaves before shedding them, sugar maple leaves fall full of magnesium, calcium, and potassium. Because the leaves are alkaline rather than acidic, they break down quickly and return their nutrients to the soil. In this way, nutrients are "pumped" from the lower to the upper layers of soil, where they are then available for shallow-rooted plants.

THE REST OF THE TROOPS

Most of the associates in the transition forest are not as generous with their nutrients as maple are. American beech leaves are full of tannin, an acidic compound that makes it difficult for decay organisms to break the leaves down. In addition, the fallen leaves acidify the soil, stifling competing plants and giving beeches a monopoly on water, nutrients, and space.

Eastern hemlock needles are equally acidic, accumulating in a cushiony mat instead of breaking down to become part of the soil. The only plants that can break through this thick, acidic layer are members of the "heath" family, such as rhododendrons and blueberries. Not surprisingly, these are the same plants that you find in yet another rigorous habitat—the nutrient-poor bog (see page 161).

Hemlocks and beeches get a taste of their own acidic medicine when it comes time for their seeds to germinate. By the time the water-seeking root wends its way past the 2–3 inches of organic debris, it is often withered and dead. Thankfully, some seeds fall on more hospitable beds.

Moss-covered logs are a perfect nursery, and a large log may carry a whole row of young seedlings on its back. At first, the seedlings get their water and nutrients from the soggy moss. As they grow, they straddle the log with prop roots, eventually reaching soil on either side. Years later, the log finally decays, leaving a hole beneath the trunk of each tree. This is why log-grown birches and hemlocks seem to be leaping skyward, one behind the other, supported only by their bow-legged props.

Another good place for seedlings to get started is a tip-up mound, formed when a tree topples, tilting roots and all out of the ground. This newly exposed mound of soil is litter-free and perfect for tender seedlings. You can tell the trees that started on tip-up mounds by looking for the telltale dip next to their base where the old roothole used to be.

Other maple associates don't even try to fight their way through the leaf litter. Rather than depend on vulnerable seedlings, slippery elm sends out horizontal stems (like "runners" of grasses) from the base of the parent tree. A cutover American basswood sends out a circle of sprouts from its stump, all fed and watered by the large root system already in place. Each sprout becomes a trunk, forming the "fairy rings" of mature basswoods you sometimes see in the woods.

WHAT'S IN IT FOR WILDLIFE?

The needleleaf trees mixed in with the hardwoods are an added attraction for wildlife. "Supercanopy" white pines lift their whorls of graceful needles high above all the other trees. Hemlocks sweep their boughs almost to the ground. These densely needled evergreens provide feeding and nesting sites, as well as shelter from the wind. The cones are a source of food for seedeaters, and the swarms of larvae on the needles are a feast for caterpillar connoisseurs. The hardwood trees provide seeds and nuts (including beech-nuts, a favorite of ruffed grouse, tufted titmice, chipmunks, and squirrels), and the smaller shrubs in the understory bear fruits that are valuable for birds and mammals in both winter and summer.

The floor of the transition forest remains moist, thanks to the shade and fallen leaves of the larger trees. This moist realm is home to lungless salamanders (which must keep their skin moist in order to breathe), secretive reptiles, and all manner of small rodents. This forest floor life in turn feeds predators such as owls, hawks, and foxes.

Hollow logs as well as dead, standing trees are snug homes for a host of cavity-dwelling animals and birds. The insects boring through these decaying snags are expertly mined by the probing tongues of woodpeckers.

Broad-winged Hawk

Broadwings are quiet hawks; you have to listen carefully to distinguish their cries from the sound of branches creaking in the wind. And because they nest and hunt deep in the woods, most people speeding by on the highway don't get a chance to see them. That's why the last 2 weeks in September are such a great opportunity for hawk-lovers. The skies along the Great Lakes shorelines, the Appalachian Range, and the Atlantic coast

WILDLIFE LOCATOR CHART—TRANSITION FOREST

	Feeds from Air	Feeds in Upper Canopy	Feeds in Lower Canopy	Feeds on Trunk	Feeds on Ground	Feeds in Water
Nests in Tree Canopy or Shrubs	Sharp-shinned Hawk Northern Goshawk Broad-winged Hawk	Red-eyed Vireo Blackburnian Warbler Scarlet Tanager	Black-throated Blue Warbler	Yellow-bellied Sapsucker	Blue Jay	
Nests in Trunk			Black-capped Chickadee Tufted Titmouse	White-breasted Nuthatch	Gray Squirrel Northern Flying Squirrel Southern Flying Squirrel	
Nests on Ground		Ruffed Grouse (also feeds on ground)			Hermit Thrush Ovenbird Moose Redbelly Snake	
Nests Beneath Ground or Debris		Porcupine			Smoky Shrew Eastern Chipmunk Deer Mouse Woodland Vole Woodland Jumping Mouse Gray Fox Northern Dusky Salamander Redback Salamander Wehrle's Salamander Ringneck Snake	
Nests in Water				Gray Treefrog	Jefferson's Salamander Spotted Salamander (feeds beneath ground) Wood Frog	Red-spotted Newt

are full of hawks, tens of thousands of them, migrating to warmer climes for the winter. By stationing yourself at what are called "geographical bottlenecks"—places where the birds are apt to funnel through—you can see thousands of broad-winged hawks in a single day (the record was more than 21,000 in a day at Hawk Mountain in Pennsylvania).

Broadwings have mastered the art of traveling long distances with a minimum of effort. Like surfers searching for the perfect wave, they look for wind patterns that will lift them up and over obstacles, then drop them down farther along their route. Broadwings specialize in thermals: columns of warm air that rise over heat-reflective surfaces such as fields or towns. With their wings outstretched and hardly flapping, the hawks spiral to dizzying heights in these columns of air. From the ground, flocks or "kettles" of these hawks can look like a swarm of bees. When they reach the top of the column, they exit and begin to glide down, as if on a giant, diagonal sliding board, to the base of the next thermal.

Rather than risk going out over large bodies of water, where these upwellings may not occur, broadwings usually follow the shorelines of the Great Lakes and the coasts. They also stick close to mountain ranges to take advantage of "updrafts" that are formed when winds are forced up a slope. By riding a combination of updrafts and thermals, the hawks can efficiently soar all the way to their wintering grounds.

In the days when hawks were still considered "varmints," thousands of these majestic travelers were needlessly shot from lookouts such as Hawk Mountain. Thankfully, education has since changed many minds, and laws have been enacted to protect the birds.

Look for broad-winged hawks—perched one-third of the way down from the top of a tree, studying the forest floor for small mammals, snakes, frogs, etc. When they spot something stirring, they twitch their tail, catlike, and start to sway excitedly back and forth. At the perfect moment, they lunge forward, talons extended for the kill. They return to the perch to eat their prey, carefully removing the skin first. Also look for broadwings wheeling above the treetops. They are rarely found in open country, in pure needleleaf forests, or near human dwellings.

Length: 14–19 inches.

Look for migrating hawks—in mid-September or mid-April. The best time for hawk watching is just after a cold front has moved in, bringing sunny skies and winds from the Northwest or South. To find thermals, look for fluffy cumulus clouds that form at the top of the air column. After good flight days, look in the branches for stragglers that are taking a day off. Ask your local chapter of the Audubon Society for a list of the best viewing sites in your area.

Look for nests—loose stick structures, 14–21 inches in diameter, typically placed 24–40 feet up in the crotch of a broadleaf tree or the branch of a needleleaf tree. The parents gird the nest with dead spruce or hemlock branches, then line it with bark chips and lichen. Or they may simply refurbish an old hawk, squirrel, or crow nest. Periodically, the hawks bring fresh green sprigs to the nest, perhaps to cover wastes, perhaps to ward off parasites (biologists don't know exactly why).

Listen for—a wailing "su-eeee-oh" that has been described as the sound of chalk scraped the wrong way on a blackboard. This is their territorial warning to would-be intruders. When hurt, hawks issue a pain "chitter." Very young chicks "cheep" and older nestlings utter a food-begging call.

Eastern Chipmunk

Chipmunks are a popular menu item in the transition forest. Hawks circle the woodlands with eyes peeled for the dashing forms, and weasels make a habit of invading their burrows unannounced. It is only by virtue of their speed, their wary nature, and their stripes that these tiny rodents stay ahead of their enemies.

Chipmunks literally zip along the ground, covering up to 15 feet per second. They are intimately familiar with the ins and outs of their environment, and are never far from an escape burrow. An ideal habitat, in chipmunk terms, is one with plenty of brush piles, rocks, and shrubs, along with soil that is loose and easy to work.

From above, a dark-and-light-colored chipmunk is hard to pick out against a background of sun streaks and vertical shadows cast by branches and stems of trees. Throughout time, individuals that were striped survived longer and produced more offspring than those that weren't striped. Eventually, stripes became the official chipmunk pelage.

When they're not avoiding predators, chipmunks spend most of their time storing food; one cache may harbor up to 1½ gallons of tree seeds, nuts, and plant tubers. They gather them by the mouthful, carefully rounding off any sharp edges before packing them into their soft cheek pouches. They also eat leaves, buds, mushrooms, berries, fruit, insects (cicadas and grasshoppers especially), mice, frogs, slugs, and birds' eggs. When not storing food, they are defending their cache, delivering scolding sermons, and jerking their tails at potential food "pirates."

This protective stance is also a survival tactic. Unlike true hibernators, chipmunks still need to eat during the winter; they are merely in a deep, though intermittent, sleep. Having a bedside cache prevents them from having to brave the dangerously low temperatures and the white backdrop of snow that would make them boldly visible to predators. Chipmunks sleep on a nest that is built atop their pile of food; as winter drags on, their bed sinks lower and lower.

Look for eastern chipmunks—in mature forests of birch, maple, and nut-bearing trees. They are especially partial to forest borders where downed logs, rock piles, and brush provide important escape cover. They are active between 9 A.M. and 1 P.M., with a peak from 11 A.M. to 12 noon. This tends to decrease a possible conflict with red squirrels, whose peak hours are between 4 P.M. and 8 P.M. Although they spend most of their time feeding on the ground, you should also look up in the branches for these agile climbers. Chipmunks can develop a certain tolerance for people, especially if they learn that we can be easily convinced to share our food. They rarely abandon their wariness completely, however, and are quick to scurry for cover if you move too quickly.

Length: Head and body, 5–6 inches; tail, 3–4 inches.

Nests are underground—in complex burrows that extend 3 feet down and may be as long as 30 feet. There are many rooms for storage, toilet, resting, and nesting. The nest chamber is usually 10 inches in diameter and is underlain with a supply of nonperishable foods. The 2-inch-wide opening to this burrow is likely to be hidden under a log or rock pile.

Look for feeding debris—a pile of fruit pits, nutshell fragments, or seeds around their favorite eating perch— a stump, rock, or log. Nutshells are chewed open on one side.

Look for tracks—in mud, with the 1⅞-inch hindprint printing ahead of the smaller foreprint. The stride is 7–15 inches long.

Listen for—a soft "chuck-chuck-chuck" that chipmunks use to warn their neighbors. When speeding to safety, they give a high-pitched "chip" which, when repeated 130 times a minute, creates a songlike trill that can attract birds. Several trilling chipmunks will sometimes join in a chorus. They also whistle when aroused, fleeing with tail raised and flipping.

Redback Salamander

Unlike most salamanders, redbacks don't spend the early part of their lives swimming in a pond. They belong to a family of woodland salamanders that lay their eggs in logs and leaf litter, completely skipping the aquatic stage. Their young look like replicas of themselves, except for the large gills (a throwback to their watery ancestry) that disappear a few days after hatching.

Even so, this salamander's ties to water have not completely disappeared. Although they spend their entire lives on land, redbacks never develop lungs. Instead, they breathe in and out through their smooth, flexible skin. In order for oxygen to reach the capillaries just underneath, their skin must always be in contact with moisture, whether from wet leaves, dew, or moist soil. To help retain this moisture, they secrete a fine coat of mucous over their body. They absorb additional oxygen through the lining of their mouth by pumping water in and out. (This causes the characteristic "pulse" that you can sometimes see in the throat of a salamander.) In addition to oxygen, salamanders even take their drinking water through the skin!

Odors and tastes also come to them via water. Two thin grooves on either side of their face run from lip to nostril, transporting waterborne odors and tastes. It's no wonder that the best time to see these creatures is right after a soaking rain, when puddles and leaf drips make the environment good for breathing, smelling, drinking, and tasting.

Redbacks practice an interesting form of courtship that begins with "amplexus"—in which the male clasps the female in a bear hug while rubbing secretions from his chin onto her body. This not only puts her in the mood to mate but also prevents other males from attempting to mate with her. The male then creeps in front of the female, vibrating his tail. As she touches it, he deposits a "spermatophore," a blob of sperm set on a rigid pedestal. He then walks around in a tight circle until he is perpendicular to his original position. The female, who has followed him, is now centered over the spermatophore. She picks it up with the lips of her cloaca (an all-purpose opening under the body), and fertilizes her eggs. In other salamanders, a similar dance takes place underwater.

Look for redback salamanders—in the woods or crossing roads at night after warm rains, especially in the spring and fall when they are breeding. On wet nights, you may find them climbing tree trunks and shrubs in search of insects, spiders, and mites. At other times, look in rotting logs or lift rocks, moss, or bits of leaf litter to find them hiding (replace what you have overturned!). You'll rarely find them under birch logs, however, perhaps because of a chemical in birch that disagrees with them. When disturbed, they often curl up like millipedes, an imitation that may fool some predators that find millipedes distasteful. Prolonged dry weather forces them even deeper under the surface, and even though they are extremely abundant in woodlands, you may not be able to find them again until it rains.

Length: 2½–5 inches.

Look for eggs—3 to 14, hung in grapelike bunches in rotting logs or rock crevices. The female attaches the egg mass to the ceiling of the chamber with a gelatinous stalk. She watches over it for 2 months, protecting it from predators and rubbing it with skin secretions to keep it from drying out or becoming moldy.

In the winter—redbacks hibernate in the ground beneath the frost line, in rock crevices, or in a maze of decaying roots.

Shagbark Hickory

BLACK-THROATED BLUE WARBLER

WILD BOAR

MOUNTAIN DUSKY SALAMANDER

Mountain-laurel

Catawba Rhododendron

Appalachian Cove Forest

WHERE TO SEE THIS HABITAT:

Georgia: Chattahoochee National Forest
North Carolina: Pisgah and Nantahala national forests
South Carolina: Sumter National Forest
Tennessee: Cherokee National Forest; Great Smoky Mountains National Park
Virginia: George Washington and Jefferson national forests; Shenandoah National Park
West Virginia: Monongahela National Forest

Appalachian Cove Forest

BEGINNINGS

For someone who has just visited the diamond-sharp Tetons or the craggy Rockies, the not even-half-as-high Appalachians may seem anticlimatic. Until you get inside them. Walk one mile down any forested trail in these mountains and you will begin to understand the real majesty of this range. The spectacle is not a geologic one but, rather, a botanical one—a spectacle of greenery. Every square inch of hillsides, ravines, coves, and rounded tops are clothed in a rich robe of vegetation, more complex and varied than any on the continent. As the locals say, "We may not have volcanoes or Grand Canyons, but we've got our trees."

The greenery of the southern Appalachians is so lush that it creates its own weather phenomenon; the tons of water vapor given off by the trillions of blades, needles, and leaves create a smoky haze—the "smoke" in the Great Smokies and the "blue" in the Blue Ridge Mountains. This luxuriant vegetation is also very stable. Unlike most of the habitats in the East that are in the process of turning into something else, the cove or "mixed hardwood" forests of the southern Appalachians are "climax" forests, the pinnacle of millions of years of slow development.

Many of these forests have experienced their 200 millionth growing season! Unlike the northern forests that the glacier scraped bare less than 12,000 years ago, the southern Appalachians were never touched by the ice. They were, in fact, a refugium for northern species that were forced to retreat to southern climes. When the glacier finally melted, the Appalachians served as the "ark" of the plant world, providing the restocking supply for the newly uncovered lands. To this day, representatives of every eastern forest type can still be found in the Appalachians, including Arctic species on the tops of the highest peaks. All told, there are 130 tree species, 1,400 flowering herbs, 350 mosses and related plants, and 2,000 different kinds of fungi.

One reason all this vegetation still grows here is that there are so many different types of growing sites. The mountainous terrain has slopes exposed

CHARACTERISTIC PLANTS:

Trees, Shrubs, and Vines:

Allegheny chinkapin	fetterbush	
American beech	flowering dogwood	
American bladdernut	hickories: bitternut,	
American holly	pignut, shagbark,	
American hornbeam	and others	
birches	highbush blueberry	
black cherry	magnolias: bigleaf,	
black locust	Fraser, and um-	
black walnut	brella	
blackberry	maples: red, striped,	
blackgum	and sugar	
butternut	mountain-laurel	
Carolina silverbell	oaks: black, northern	
Catawba rhododen-	red, white, and	
dron	others	
cucumbertree	rosebay rhododendron	
eastern hemlock	slippery elm	
eastern hophornbeam	sourwood	
eastern redbud	viburnums	
eastern white pine	white ash	
	white basswood	
	witch-hazel	
	yellow buckeye	
	yellow-poplar	
	yellowwood	

Herbaceous Plants:

American ginseng
Canada violet
club mosses
common cinquefoil
cut-leaved toothwort
Dutchman's-pipe
false Solomon's seal
ferns: Christmas,
   crested wood, hay-
   scented, maiden-
   hair, and New
   York
foamflower
large-flowered tril-
   lium
large-leaved white
   violet
mayapple
round-lobed hepatica
Solomon's seals
spicebush
spring beauty
squirrel-corn
Vasey's wake-robin
wild geranium
wild ginger
wild grape
wild leek
wood anemone
wood-sorrels

to the sun in all directions, including those that are in the sun all day and those that don't receive sun all year. Cove forests are in sheltered hollows below 4,500 feet elevation. You can see the best examples in the Cumberland, Smoky, and Blue Ridge Mountains. Among the most common trees are yellow-poplar, sugar maple, white basswood, northern red oak, yellow birch, sweet birch, white ash, yellow buckeye, black, chestnut, and white oak.

THREE-HOUR WALK TO WINNIPEG

Though it may be a mild North Carolinian day at the base of Mount Mitchell, the plants on top (6,684 feet) will be experiencing a day more like that of Winnipeg, 1,000 miles north. The drop in temperature (about 3 degrees Fahrenheit for every 1,000 feet of ascent) is due to the fact that high-altitude air, being thinner, absorbs less radiation from the sun. In the Smokies, a hike from hollow to hillcrest may take you 3 hours, but you'll see as much landscape variety as someone driving due north for 3 days.

The soil underfoot is varied as well, derived from a mixture of ancient ocean sediment and millions of years of downwash from the mountains themselves. The long growing season, mild temperatures, and as much as 7 feet of snow and rain a year also contribute to the lushness and variety of these forests.

Water in the southern Appalachians is everywhere: dripping from the tips of the mountain spruces, cascading over moss-strewn boulders, and running down the trunks during a torrential downpour. Because the glaciers were never close enough to gouge out lakes or pile up rocky "dams," you're not likely to see much standing water in the mountains. Instead, the water flows from higher land to lower in the form of streams, runoffs, and underground springs. Because the land is so well padded (vegetated) against erosion, the runoff is usually crystal clear, even after a heavy storm. Rain falling in a cove forest is strained through the fine filters of millions of leaves, a thick layer of humus, and untold miles of roots and rootlets. Before it ever reaches the stream, much of the water is taken up and turned into something green.

WHAT'S IN IT FOR WILDLIFE?

There are five layers discernible in this junglelike forest. A top canopy, a midstory of trees that are aspiring to the canopy, an understory of smaller trees and shrubs, a ground layer of extravagant flowering plants, and a surface layer of lichens and mosses. In and among the layers, vines climb

WILDLIFE LOCATOR CHART—APPALACHIAN COVE FOREST

	Feeds from Air	Feeds in Upper Canopy	Feeds in Lower Canopy	Feeds on Trunk	Feeds on Ground	Feeds in Water
Nests in Tree Canopy or Shrubs	Cooper's Hawk Broad-winged Hawk	Red-eyed Vireo Cerulean Warbler Scarlet Tanager	Black-throated Blue Warbler		Wood Thrush	
Nests in Trunk			Carolina Chickadee Tufted Titmouse	Pileated Woodpecker	Gray Squirrel Raccoon	
Nests on Ground			Ruffed Grouse (also feeds on ground)	Black-and-white Warbler	Ovenbird Dark-eyed Junco Wild Pig	
Nests Beneath Ground or Debris					Northern Waterthrush Hairy-tailed Mole New England Cottontail Eastern Chipmunk White-footed Mouse Eastern Woodrat (rock crevices) Black Bear Northern Dusky Salamander Mountain Dusky Salamander Redback Salamander Slimy Salamander Jordan's Salamander Ravine Salamander Five-lined Skink Black Rat Snake	
Nests in Water					Spotted Salamander (feeds beneath debris)	Spring Salamander Red-spotted Newt

trees to gain access to the sun. This complexity provides abundant feeding, nesting, preening, singing, and resting places for a variety of wildlife species.

At the very top, perching hawks and owls scrutinize the floor for voles, mice, or rabbits. Flycatchers hunt from branches that have open space underneath, swooping into thin air occasionally for a winged meal. Many of their victims are drawn by the nectar of exotic flowers such as those of yellow-poplars and rhododendrons. Warblers pick off insects crawling in the tangle of branches and profusion of leaves. Bats roam between the branches after dark, using echoes to locate moths and other flying insects. In the fall and spring, thousands of migratory birds on their way along the flyway use the upper branches to rest, roost, and refuel.

Many of the trees in these sheltered coves live to be a ripe age (800 years for some oaks), and provide cavity homes for many generations of gray squirrels, raccoons, Virginia opossums, bats, treefrogs, woodpeckers, chickadees, owls, wrens, and nuthatches. Woodpeckers riddle the trunks of these trees, searching for grubs, wood borers, and beetles.

When the old-timers finally fall, they provide homes for salamanders, snakes, mice, voles, skunks, black bears, weasels, and bobcats. They also fertilize the soil as they decay, and sometimes support a crop of mushrooms that supplements the diets of deer, squirrels, and wild pigs. Ruffed grouse take these logs for their stage, performing drum solos designed to attract mates. Logs also hide the entrances to a great many burrows belonging to woodchucks, salamanders, chipmunks, moles, and others.

In addition to shelter, oaks and nut trees such as black walnut, butternut, and shagbark hickory produce a meaty mast that helps bears, turkey, and deer put on a winter blanket of fat. Squirrels cache the harvest to make it last the winter through. Black and yellow birch attract grouse and other birds that feed on catkins, and the sweet triangular nuts of American beech are relished by squirrels, white-tailed deer, raccoons, wild turkey, and ruffed grouse. Hemlocks supply cone feeders and evergreen connoisseurs with food reminiscent of forests farther north.

Just as the trees have had a long, uninterrupted time of development, so too has the wildlife community. Salamanders, which thrive in moist environments that keep their skin wet, number 2 dozen species, from the pigmy salamander that is less than 2 inches at maturity to the hellbender, which is nearly 30 inches. Some of these species are found nowhere else in the world. Cove forests are also renown for their snakes—those that slither on the ground, stream through the water, or climb straight up the trunks. Come see what you can find!

Pileated Woodpecker

If you stood beneath a tree that a pileated was working on, you'd literally need a hardhat (don't worry though—pileateds are shy and wouldn't let you that close). With their strong, stout bills and muscular bodies, these birds can chop right to the center of a tree, showering the ground with pieces of wood and bark as large as a human hand. To get full purchase on their target, they dig their sharp claws into the bark, prop their tail as a brace, and bring their gleaming scarlet head crest way back in an 8-inch arc. Their brain is encased in air, and their skull is fortified to take the pounding without shattering. Once they jackhammer their way into the soft and sometimes rotted heart of a tree, their tongue goes to work, probing the labyrinths of carpenter ant colonies. The ants are an obvious favorite; one biologist found 2,600 of these ants in one bird's stomach.

Pileateds have an uncanny knack for identifying trees infested with carpenter ants, even if there are no outward signs. They can unerringly hit the heart of these colonies even in the winter, when the ants are dormant and still.

Pileateds are a "pathfinder" species, that is, they open up cavities in trees that birds with weaker bills could not have made. These holes become nests and feeding sites for these birds and many other cavity nesters. Pileateds also speed the process of tree decay. As they rip off sheets of bark and tear out great loads of rotted wood, they "lift up the tent" for fungal organisms and insects that will break down the wood. By-products of this decay enrich the soil for a whole new crop of plants and trees.

Look for pileated woodpeckers—on trunks of large-diameter trees or tearing apart stumps, old logs, or stubs of dead trees. They may also root around in anthills. In the air, watch for them flying their straight-winged flight (different from the bouncing-ball flight of most woodpeckers). Despite their size, they are evasive and difficult to spot. Your best bet is dark, "primeval-looking" forests near water.

Length: 16–19½ inches.

Look for oval nest holes—3–4 inches wide, typically 45 feet up in a large-diameter (14+ inches) trunk or limb. The nest trees are usually dead and often near water. Look at the rim of the opening for cleavage marks made by the woodpecker's bill. The parents take turns incubating the eggs and feeding the young. At the end of 2 hours, the mate on duty will drum on the inside of the nest, signaling that it wants to be relieved. Pileateds use the same nest tree year after year, digging a new hole each time. Well-used trees will be honeycombed with holes.

Look for wood chips—strewn on the ground beneath woodpecker excavations.

Listen for—an accelerating, rolling tapping on the trunk, 11–30 beats per burst, repeated often. Instead of singing to announce their territory or attract mates, woodpeckers tap out a sound tattoo—the acoustic signature of the species. Pileateds will often "sign off" before entering a hole to roost for the night. Also listen for "mewing," "waaaaaa" calls, "whucker-whucker-whucker" calls that sound like a northern flicker, and a bugling call to greet the dawn. The sounds of excavation can be heard more than half a mile away on a calm day.

Wild Pig

Like domestic pigs, wild pigs love to wallow in the mud. They also have a long flexible snout that they use to root and grub for food. Their tastes, like their barnyard cousins', are catholic; they take whatever is edible and small enough: berries, tubers, acorns, nuts, insects, and carrion. Even poisonous snakes will tickle a wild pig's palate (and the snake's fangs won't puncture a boar's tough hide).

These relatively thin pigs stand 3 feet at the shoulders with a back that slopes like a bison's toward their small hind end. Their legs are long, and in place of a comic, upturned mouth, they have razor-sharp tusks. The tusks are actually canines that curve outward and up, growing as long as 9 inches. The small upper tusks (honers) rub against and sharpen the lower two (rippers).

These ivories come in handy when digging up roots or when defending themselves against a pack of pitbull hunting dogs. Male wild pigs are also aggressive with one another. They fight head on, hoping to get their opponent's tusks jammed up against the protective, 2-inch-thick skin of their own shoulder. Held thus, the active pig can reach down and slash open the competitor's soft underbelly.

These feisty animals were originally introduced to this country to stock game farms. It wasn't too long before they escaped their fences and began to populate the surrounding countryside. Now managers in the Great Smoky Mountains National Park must regularly transport wild pigs out of the park to protect rare plants from their rooting.

Look for wild pigs—abroad mainly at night, traveling in "drifts" of 3 or more through thickly forested areas in rugged mountains. They may travel several miles a night. Summer daytime resting beds are elongated depressions that they gouge out of the soil. When it gets cold, they resort to dense thickets, building large twig beds that look like huge bird nests. Several pigs may sleep head-to-toe here, and young will be born here. In cool weather, you're more likely to see boars up and about during the day. In hot weather, they like to wallow in mud or in water to protect themselves from insects and to keep cool. Like domestic pigs, they need to wallow when they are overheated because they have few sweat glands. In crossing streams, these surefooted mammals will "tight rope" their way across fallen logs, something their domestic cousins would never attempt.

Size: Head and body length, 3½–5 feet; shoulder height up to 3 feet.

Look for nests—large dishes of boughs and grasses, in secluded thickets. To protect the piglets from early spring cold snaps, the female may pile sticks and grasses atop the nest to form a roof. A piglet's coat is striped for the first 3 months to help it blend into the shadowy forest light.

Look for rooted-up ground—boars disturb up to 80 percent of the ground they forage in. One observer said it looked like a big Rototiller had been through.

Look for rubbing trees—small evergreens that wild pigs rub their tusks and mud-caked bodies against. Rubbing trees are usually near wallowing places and along trails. The trunk is often gouged and pig hairs are trampled into the ground at the base.

Look for tracks—in single-file trails. The 2½-inch-long prints are cloven, but not as sharply pointed as deer prints. Dewclaws print behind the main print. The hindpaws step on top of the foreprints.

Listen for—grunting or squealing to express contentment or pain. Members of a drift will growl or snort to warn each other that an enemy is near.

Black Rat Snake

The black rat snake looks like most other snakes, and on the ground, it moves like most other snakes. Its belly is covered with scales that overlap like shingles, with their edges facing backward. Each scale is attached to a rib with special muscles that can move it up, down, forward, or backward. To sneak up on prey, the snake "rows" with these muscles so that the edges of the scales dig into the ground and push back, moving the snake forward. When it wants to move faster, it "snakes" from side to side, causing a series of lateral waves to move through its body. As the outer sides of the "S" hit obstructions on the ground, they push off and the snake moves forward. So far, that's what all snakes do.

But when a black rat snake leaves the ground and climbs straight up a tree trunk or building, it moves into a class of its own, using special adaptations that belong only to climbing snakes. These adaptations solve two major problems that confront long, thin animals that climb. One has to do with blood flow to the brain; the other with blood that collects at the lower end of the body.

When a snake hangs, the heart must work against gravity to elevate blood to the brain. Climbing snakes have a heart that is placed far forward on the body, so the distance to the head is minimized. In aquatic snakes, where gravity is not a problem, the heart is centrally located to make it easier to move blood to either end of the body.

Of course, with the heart so far forward, blood returning from the tail has a long way to go. To give it extra "umph," the snake periodically wriggles while climbing, thus squeezing the blood upward in its veins. This is turn causes the heart to increase its output, thus increasing pressure throughout the system.

Tree snakes also tend to have a slender body, tightly attached skin, and firmer muscles than other snakes. These work to constrict the capillaries and keep them from stretching, along much the same principle as the G-suit of a jet pilot, support stockings for someone who stands all day, or the very thin legs of a giraffe. Without its tight suit, blood would have a tendency to pool in the lower part of the snake's body and leak plasma into surrounding tissue. This leakage is called edema, a condition that swells the ankles of human patients who have a weak heart. Perhaps further study of upright snakes can tell us something about treating or avoiding edema in human patients.

Look for black rat snakes—on moist, wooded north- and east-facing slopes. Look for them on the ground or in trees searching for mammals, nestling birds, or bird eggs. Rat snakes kill large animals such as rabbits by coiling around and strangling them, the way boa constrictors do. To escape their own predators, rat snakes may head into holes in tree trunks. When caught on the ground, they usually freeze, relying on cryptic coloration rather than a fast getaway. Threatened snakes will vibrate their tail, raise the upper part of their body, draw back their head in an "S," and strike. Their bite is not poisonous.

Length: 3–8½ feet.

Eggs are laid—in loose soil or sawdust piles in late June or July. Anywhere from 4 to 25 leathery eggs may be stuck together in a clump. Snakes may be seen mating while suspended in a tree.

Listen for—the hissing of a threatened snake.

HAIRY-TAILED MOLE

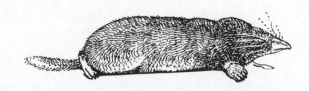

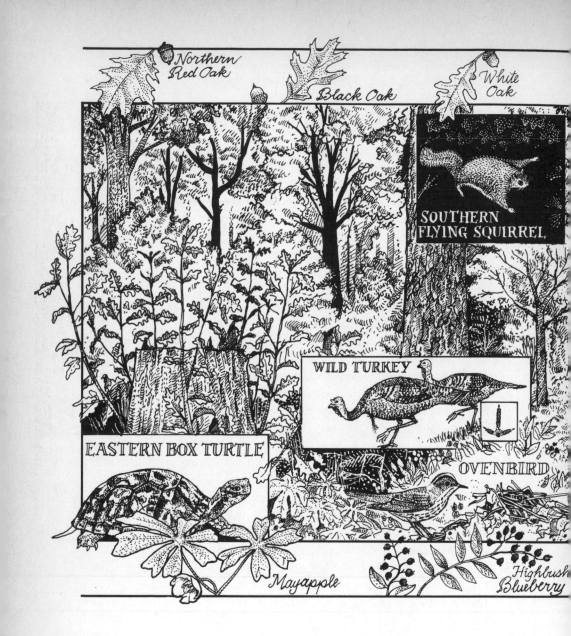

Shagbark Hickory

Bitternut Hickory

RED-BELLIED WOODPECKER

TIMBER RATTLESNAKE

GRAY SQUIRREL

Pussy-toes

Nannyberry

Large-flowered Trillium

Oak-Hickory Forest

WHERE TO SEE THIS HABITAT:

Arkansas: Hot Springs National Park; Ouachita, Ozark, and St. Francis national forests

Georgia: Chattahoochee National Forest

Kentucky: Daniel Boone National Forest; Mammoth Cave National Park

Mississippi: Holly Springs and Tombigee national forests

Missouri: Mark Twain National Forest; Mingo National Wildlife Refuge

North Carolina: Pisgah, Nantahala, and Uwharrie national forests

Ohio: Wayne National Forest

Tennessee: Cherokee National Forest; Great Smoky Mountains National Park

Virginia: George Washington and Jefferson national forests; Shenandoah National Park

West Virginia: Monongahela National Forest

Oak-Hickory Forest

BEGINNINGS

Oak forests are an eastern classic, covering one-fourth of all the forested land on this side of the Mississippi. They come in a multitude of species and sizes, from the pygmy oaks of Cape Cod to the ponderous wolf trees of the central states. Their widespread range is surprising, if you consider what it takes to move an acorn.

A tiny aspen seed can migrate a mile on a gust of wind, but an acorn can do little more than roll, if it's lucky enough to land on a slope. Most of the acorns in an average year's crop are digested by birds, mammals, fungi, or insects before they ever have a chance to germinate. Despite these odds, however, oak trees do manage to reproduce and spread.

Squirrels are their primary means of transport. A gray squirrel buries hundreds of acorns in underground caches and returns to them throughout the winter. Even with their uncanny memories, squirrels can't retrieve all the acorns they bury. In spring, the meaty hearts of the forgotten ones finance the first flush of seedling growth. After that, the seedling's fortunes depend on how much moisture is in the soil, how much shade is overhead, and whether a fire is likely to sweep through.

One of the greatest challenges the oaks ever faced was the ice cap that bulldozed the landscape down to the Ohio River. Like most other trees, oaks were chased out of their northern homes by the frigid wall of ice. They retreated to refugia in the Appalachians and to a tiny pocket of

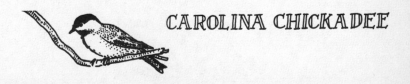

CAROLINA CHICKADEE

CHARACTERISTIC PLANTS:

Major Trees:

American basswood
ashes: green and
  white
black cherry
black locust
black walnut
blackgum
cucumbertree
hickories: bitternut,
  mockernut, pignut,
  and shagbark
maples: red and sugar
oaks: black, northern
  red, and white
slippery elm
sweetgum
yellow-poplar

North:

oaks: bur, northern
  pin, and shingle
pines: eastern white
  and pitch

South:

eastern redcedar
oaks: blackjack,
  cherrybark, chest-
  nut, chinkapin,
  post, scarlet, Shu-
  mard, and southern
  red
pines: shortleaf and
  Virginia

Associated Trees, Shrubs, and Vines:

beaked hazel
blackberry
blueberries
deerberry
downy serviceberry
eastern burningbush
eastern hophornbeam
eastern redbud
flowering dogwood
greenbriers
mapleleaf viburnum
mountain-laurel
poison-ivy
possumhaw
rhododendrons
sassafras
sourwood
spicebush
Virginia creeper
wild grape
witch-hazel

Herbaceous Plants:

asters
black snakeroot
bloodroot
common cinquefoil
common lespedeza
cut-leaved toothwort
Dutchman's-breeches
false Solomon's seal
goldenrods
indian cucumber root
jack-in-the-pulpit
mayapple
nannyberry
panic grasses
partridgeberry
pink lady's slipper
pussytoes
round-lobed hepatica
sedges
sessile bellwort
Solomon's seals
spotted wintergreen
spring beauty
tick trefoils
tickclover
trilliums
trout-lily
violet wood-sorrel
wild ginger
wild sarsaparilla
wintergreen (teaberry)

Pussy-toes

southwestern Wisconsin where the ice did not reach. In less than 15,000 years, they have managed to return to the North and West, advancing an acorn at a time.

THE MIGHTY, FLEXIBLE OAK

The oak family has members in every stripe of the spectrum, from the water oak that lives in swampy soil, to the turkey oak that thrives in sand and flames. They also vary widely in their ability to tolerate shade. Those that do survive shade—northern red, black, and white oaks, for instance—often play the role of "takeover" artists in the forest. They spend years growing beneath pines, aspens, and other sun-loving trees. When the overtopping umbrella finally dies, oaks are well established and ready to grab the reins.

Besides their ability to tolerate shade, many of the oaks can also survive ground fires, even when they're frequent. A classic case of this fire survival is at the forest-prairie border in the Midwest. For thousands of years, annual fires (started by Indians or by lightning) killed the tops of black and white oaks, while their roots kept on living and growing. These huge root systems, called "grubs," broke many a plow blade when settlers first tried to cultivate these lands.

When farmers finally gave up trying to share their fields with grubs, the long-suppressed oaks exploded, covering the ground with dense thickets. They bore the telltale signature of frequently "pruned" trees: each root developed 3 or 4 trunks in a bouquetlike cluster. Look for these multi-stemmed "coppice" trees next time you go strolling in an oak-hickory forest. You'll find them in areas that have been cut frequently for firewood, grazed by cattle, mowed for hay, or burned by frequent fires.

In the South, many of the oaks you'll find growing under the pines were also children of fire. They too had many eons of frequent fires to contend with, until the only oaks left were those adapted to sprout vigorously after a scorching.

WHAT'S IN IT FOR WILDLIFE?

Food and shelter, two absolute essentials for wildlife, are abundant in oak-hickory forests. Acorns and hickory nuts are the staff of life for many creatures, offering a lot of nutrition in return for a relatively small outlay of foraging energy. Animals that eat the tiny seeds of birch, for instance, must hunt longer to collect the same number of calories that they would find in an acorn. Acorns and hickory nuts are seasonal menu items, however, coming in large doses only in the fall. Those species that have learned to cache nuts and acorns are able to make the harvest last through winter.

For species that don't cache food, scattered yellow-poplar and white ash trees offer seeds that remain on the trees through winter. Dead oak leaves also remain on the trees, and though they are brown and not very palatable, they do provide a great shield from both winter winds and the eyes of winged predators.

When the leaves fall, they decay slowly because of the tannin (an acidic compound) in their cells. This creates a thick batting of leaves for amphibians, reptiles, and small rodents to tunnel around in, find food in, and keep either cool or warm in. Old, downed logs perform the same service, harboring a number of prey species that in turn feed predators such as hawks, owls, weasels, and bobcats. For night hunters such as owls that rely on their hearing for hunting, the millions of drying oak leaves are a secret weapon, as effective as a microphone for amplifying the sounds of scurrying prey.

Though their leaves may be slow to rot, the trunks of oaks are frequently stricken with heartrot. This is good news for the birds and mammals that build their homes in natural cavities, a community that includes 42 percent of all oak-hickory wildlife. In forests near farms and towns, practices such as burning and high-grading (harvesting only the best trees) have left an especially high percentage of dead or diseased trees. Be sure to check multiple-stemmed coppice trees for holes; they are particularly susceptible to heartrot.

In the summer, oaks and hickories sprout from their stumps, placing succulent leaves within easy reach of browsing animals. Around the stumps, blueberries, common persimmon, wild grape, and prickly pear cactus are devoured by a variety of mammals and birds. Insects that feed on the leaves and berries of these shrubs are also a menu item for a number of birds, including flycatchers, gnatcatchers, and warblers. Closest to the ground, bush clovers are relished by white-tailed deer, wild turkeys, and northern bobwhites.

BLUE
JAY

Wild Turkey

Wild turkeys are among the wariest and most elusive of all game birds, earning the respect of all who try to stalk them. Evidently, they were not always this sly. Turkeys were once plentiful as far south as Mexico, and were relatively easy to catch. Settlers of the New World hunted the great-tasting birds to near extinction in the East. Over generations, the survivors have developed a less trusting nature and assumed the cautious ways that they are now known for.

At breeding season, however, the normally shy bird becomes a show-boat. The males perform dramatic displays to show their dominance and impress their mates. As they strut, they spread their tail fans, drop and rattle their flight feathers, and swell their head ornaments, delivering a complicated repertoire of gobbles. On their chests, large swellings called sponges are filled with fats and oils to give them energy during these energetic courtship activities.

Before the breeding season, male turkeys fight with flapping wings and sharp leg spurs to establish their rank in the flock. Only the finalists will be able to mate; in one study, of the 170 males in a flock, only six mated. This pecking order is actually beneficial for the turkey population, however, because it ensures that only the strong individuals will mate, thus strengthening the genetic makeup of the future flock.

Look for wild turkeys—on the ground along edges and in mature forests with some understory. They are most active the first few hours after dawn and just before sunset. Like huge chickens, they scratch the ground or leaf litter to find seeds, nuts, or acorns that they grind up in their large, muscular guts. They also eat the fruits or seeds of junipers, dogwoods, grapes, pines, and grasses. In the summer they may eat grasshoppers, small amphibians, or reptiles to get quick protein. Turkeys prefer to run under bushes to escape from predators, but will flush into the air if need be. In the spring, watch for flocks strutting and breeding in woodland clearings.

Length: Male, 48 inches; female, 36 inches.

Look for flocks of roosting birds—heading for trees beginning at twilight. In lowlands, they often roost in branches over water for protection from ground predators.

Look for nests—leaf-lined scrapes on the ground near woodland roads or at edges of fields. Look in thickets (especially greenbrier) or under the branches of fallen trees. More than one female may lay eggs in the same nest.

Listen for—the deep bass gobble of older males or the higher-pitched gobble of juveniles. Tom turkeys gobble to attract females, and can "broadcast" their invitation up to a mile away. During the breeding season, any loud noise, even a car door slamming, may start turkeys gobbling. Listen

COOPER'S HAWK · GREAT CRESTED FLYCATCHER · EASTERN WOOD-PEWEE · WHIP-POOR-WILL · HAIRY WOODPECKER · BLUE JAY

WILDLIFE LOCATOR CHART—OAK-HICKORY FOREST

	Feeds from Air	Feeds in Upper Canopy	Feeds in Lower Canopy	Feeds on Trunk	Feeds on Ground
Nests in Tree Canopy	Cooper's Hawk Broad-winged Hawk Eastern Wood-Pewee	Gray Jay Blue-gray Gnatcatcher Red-eyed Vireo Summer Tanager Scarlet Tanager			Blue Jay
Nests in Trunk	Great Crested Flycatcher		Carolina Chickadee Tufted Titmouse	Downy Woodpecker Hairy Woodpecker Pileated Woodpecker White-breasted Nuthatch	Also feed in canopy: Gray Squirrel Fox Squirrel Southern Flying Squirrel
Nests on Ground	Whip-poor-will			Black-and-white Warbler	Wild Turkey Northern Bobwhite Worm-eating Warbler Ovenbird Kentucky Warbler Timber Rattlesnake
Nests Beneath Ground or Debris					White-footed Mouse Woodland Vole Gray Fox Black Bear Marbled Salamander Slimy Salamander Eastern Box Turtle Three-toed Box Turtle Five-lined Skink Black Rat Snake
Nests in Water					Spotted Salamander (feeds beneath ground)

at dawn to hear flocks gobbling in their roosting trees. Besides gobbling, they use a variety of calls for other reasons: a cluck or "cut" to assemble flocks, a "putt" or "pert" to signal alarm, and a "yelp" or "keouk-keouk-keouk" to keep in contact.

Gray Squirrel

Squirrels and oaks have an unusual relationship. Squirrels depend on oaks for lodging and food, yet they, along with other forest animals, completely devour most acorn crops, leaving precious little for reproduction.

Not to be outdone, the trees have evolved an offensive attack. They bear acorns sporadically; some years they bear in buckets, other times not at all. Bad crop years usually follow hard spring frosts, while good crop years are 1, 2, or even 7 years apart. In some localities, all the trees are synchronized to bear at the same time, through cues that scientists don't yet understand. By swamping the squirrels with more than they can possibly eat, the trees finally get a chance to germinate.

Squirrels ride this feast-or-famine cycle for all it's worth. They multiply quickly when the crop is fruitful, and when the crop fails, they switch to fruits, berries, tree sap, roots, etc. They'll even eat the poisonous amanita mushroom, which is potent enough to kill a human. Evidently their liver can handle this toxic substance—and may perhaps one day yield an antidote for humans.

Look for gray squirrels—in and around their nest tree. They seldom venture farther than 200 yards away from home. To find the nest tree, watch where they climb to get away from you. Once aloft, they may begin to play hide and seek with you, circling the trunk with a display of tail flicking. The more aggravated they are, the faster they flick. In encounters with actual enemies, these threats can save needless bloodshed. Squirrels, like many other animals, prefer to "settle out of court" rather than risk a physical injury. Besides being a message flag, the tail also serves as a swimming rudder, a sunshade, and a balance pole for their arboreal acrobatics.

Length: Head and body, 8–10 inches; tail, 7¾–10 inches.

Look for nests—in cavities in older trees, especially white oaks, elms, sycamores, and soft maples. Squirrels may finish what a woodpecker has started, gnawing the cavity opening to 3 inches in diameter. For summer resting places, they build leafy balls in tree forks close to the trunk, an average of 40 feet up. The ball rests on a platform of fresh leaves and twigs, and may be 19 inches wide and 12 inches high, with a hollow chamber in the center. Watch for the female moving young from a disturbed nest. She curls the young squirrels around her neck like a scarf.

Look for feeding debris—the clippings of twigs, dislodged fruit, or gnawed nutshells on the ground beneath a favorite tree perch or stump. Acorns stored by squirrels have the cups cut off; walnuts are shelled. They feast on 100 different kinds of plants, but their favorites are hickories, pecan, oaks, walnuts, elms, and red mulberry. Squirrels find and eat 80–90 percent of the acorns they bury.

Look for tracks—foreprints are round, 1 inch long, and hindprints are twice as long and more triangular. When bounding, the hindprints might register ahead of the foreprints, leaving tracks that look like exclamation points (!!).

Listen for—barking, "que, que, que, que."

Timber Rattlesnake

Biologists aren't sure why snakes evolved rattles on the end of their tail. One theory is that prairie rattlers used them as a warning bell to keep from being stepped on by hoofed animals. Another theory is that the rattle developed to lure curious victims into striking distance. Whatever the origin, the use of an auditory defense is ironic because rattlesnakes can't hear the high-frequency sound of their own rattles. Because they have no external ear membranes, their "hearing" is restricted to ground vibrations transmitted via their spinal cord and certain airborne vibrations transmitted via their lungs.

If *you* hear a rattle in the air, you'd be wise to go elsewhere. Although the bite is not likely to kill you, it can cause pain for several days. The venom in a rattler's fangs breaks down body tissue and blood cells, and is designed to start digesting its prey even before the snake swallows it. It also helps subdue a large animal so that its thrashing won't harm the snake. Rattlers deliver their venom through two hypodermiclike fangs that extend from the roof of their mouth. The fangs are curved backward like surgical needles to help the snake get a good grip on its prey, no matter how large it is.

A rattler eating a large rat would be like you eating a 40-pound pig in one gulp. Their tooth-lined jaws are not fused the way ours are, but are joined with an elastic membrane so they can unhinge and open them wide. Each half of the lower jaw as well as each of the six bones of the upper jaw and palate can be moved independently up or down, back and forth, or side to side. The snake moves alternating sides of its mouth up the victim, holding on with one side, and then "walking" up with the other, until the victim is completely engulfed. To enable the snake to breathe during this process, its windpipe has an outside extension that is reinforced with cartilage so it won't be crushed.

Once the prey is past the mouth, the snake puts a kink in its neck to push the "lump" down toward the stomach. The snake's skin along the entire body is pleated and elastic so it can stretch without tearing. It may take as long as an hour to swallow dinner, and even longer to digest it. Because a snake's metabolism is low (only one-tenth of a mammal's or bird's), however, each meal goes a long way. A rattler needs only 6–20 meals a year!

Look for timber rattlesnakes—on rocky outcrops of southwest-facing slopes in early spring or fall. They often try to soak up some sun just before or just after hibernating. Pregnant females stay on the bluffs through July and August, maintaining high body temperatures that help incubate their embryos. Other females and males spend most of the summer in the woods, feeding on small mammals such as white-footed mice, meadow voles, and eastern chipmunks.

Length: 3–6 feet.

Look for dens—deep rock fissures that ensure a warm hibernating spot below frost level. A hundred or more snakes may occupy one den, including fox snakes, racers, and black rat snakes. Traditional den sites are reused year after year, and some may stay in use for hundreds or even thousands of years. The young are born in mid-September in a secluded spot a quarter mile or so from the hibernating den. After going their own way for a few weeks, the young snakes reconvene at the den for the winter. Studies suggest they find their way to the den via odor trails laid down by adults.

Listen for—a sharp rattle indicating that a snake is riled and likely to defend itself.

GRAY FOX

Eastern White Pine

Red Pine

Pine Forest

RED-BREASTED NUTHATCH

GRAY JAY

BROWN CREEPER

PORCUPINE

Late Low Blueberry

Canada Mayflower

Northern Needleleaf Forest

WHERE TO SEE THIS HABITAT:

Maine: Acadia National Park; Moosehorn National Wildlife Refuge

Michigan: Hiawatha, Huron-Manistee, and Ottawa national forests; Isle Royale National Park; Seney National Wildlife Refuge

Minnesota: Agassiz and Tamarac national wildlife refuges; Chippewa and Superior national forests

New Hampshire: White Mountain National Forest

New York: Adirondack Forest Preserve

Vermont: Green Mountain National Forest; Missisquoi National Wildlife Refuge

Wisconsin: Chequamegon and Nicolet national forests

At high elevations only:

Georgia: Chattahoochee National Forest

North Carolina: Pisgah and Nantahala national forests

Tennessee: Cherokee National Forest; Great Smoky Mountains National Park

Virginia: George Washington and Jefferson national forests; Shenandoah National Park

West Virginia: Monongahela National Forest (high elevations)

Northern Needleleaf Forest

BEGINNINGS

For millions of years before flowering plants such as grasses, oaks, and dogwoods had evolved, needleleaf trees dominated the earth. They bore their seeds in scaly cones and depended on the wind to distribute their pollen. They were incredibly hardy, able to survive extremes of heat, drought, humidity, and cold. Today, two kinds of needleleaf forests persist in the North—spruce-fir and pine—and both are as hardy as their ancestors.

In the last glacial age, the spruce–fir forests of the Lake States and New England were herded from their homes by the bulldozer of ice. They found refuge in the deep South, where the climate, at that time, was cool enough to support them. When the glacier melted, these cold-weather species followed the ice cliff back up north. Remnants of that exodus can still be found on the highest, coolest peaks of the Appalachian Mountains, where a band of spruce-fir forest still grows.

Pines eventually returned to the newly uncovered North, and they stood in magnificent, towering groves that covered some 7 million acres. A logging boom at the turn of the century nearly wiped out these "tall pines," leaving a phantom forest of stumps under the boughs of their broadleaf successors.

Though they are not quite as extensive as they once were, you can still find spruce-fir and pine forests in New England, in the Lake States, and in a tonguelike extension along the Appalachian range. The stories of the two forests differ, but their adaptations to a demanding environment are ones they share with all needleleaf trees.

THE INGENIOUS EVERGREENS

Needleleaf trees grow in the harshest environments imaginable—scorching deserts, wind-ravaged mountain peaks, and even the far, frozen tundra. In our northern states, needleleaf trees dominate because they are built to handle the stress of low winter temperatures and a short growing season.

By the time winter locks the North in its frozen embrace, evergreens are already well winterized. Their trunks, filled with a concentrated "an-

---

CHARACTERISTIC PLANTS:

Major Trees:

Spruce-fir Forest:
balsam fir
black spruce
Fraser fir (southern
   extension)
red spruce (southern
   extension)
tamarack
white spruce

Pine Forest:
oaks: black, northern
   pin, northern red,
   scarlet, and white
pines: eastern white,
   jack, and red

Common to Both:
aspens: bigtooth and
   quaking
balsam poplar
birches: gray (east)
   and paper
eastern hemlock
northern white-cedar
red maple

Associated Trees and Shrubs:

Common to Both:
American fly honey-
   suckle
American mountain-
   ash
beaked hazel
bearberry
elderberry
evergreen
highbush cranberry
huckleberries
late low blueberry
lowbush blueberry
mountain maple
mountain-holly
northern bush-honey-
   suckle
prickly gooseberry
round-leaf dogwood
sheep laurel
sweet-fern
thimbleberry
trailing arbutus

Associated Herbaceous Plants:

Common to Both:
barren strawberry
bluebead lily
bracken fern
bunchberry
Canada mayflower
common wood-sorrel
cow wheat
false Solomon's seal
largeleaf aster
nodding trillium
northern white violet
oak fern
one-sided pyrola
pipsissewa
red baneberry
sedges
sessile bellwort
spreading dogbane
twinflower
wintergreen (teaberry)

---

tifreeze" of sap, are insulated from the cold by extra-thick bark. Their tiny leaves are coated with a wax to cut down on the amount of moisture escaping from their sunken pores. A cap of snow on the branches helps plug the leaks even further. This water seal is a lifesaver when water is frozen in the soil and there is no way for the roots to replace the moisture lost from the leaves.

When temperatures warm, evergreens can begin growing immediately. Their shallow roots start absorbing water as soon as the upper crust of soil thaws. Unlike the broadleaf trees that have to produce a full set of leaves before they can manufacture food, evergreens carry a set of leaves year round. They retain each needle for 2–3 or even 6–8 years. Even though a certain percentage of needles reach the end of their cycle each year, those that remain on the tree outnumber those that fall off. In an environment where nutrients are scarce, this thrift is a secret to survival.

THE SPRUCE-FIR FOREST

The northwoods tends to linger in your imagination long after you leave it. The landscape is wild and wet, still dripping from the glacier's last passing. The themes repeat—deep green spruce, snowy white birch, and loons silhouetted on a lake. This classic boreal forest, which nearly wraps around the world from Canada to Siberia, dips briefly into the northern tier of the United States. Here, the trees sit on a thin scalp of soil overlying an ancient shield of bedrock. White spruce and balsam fir are well adapted to live in this shallow soil because of a wide-spreading root system that keeps them from keeling over in the wind.

A good way to tell spruce and fir apart is to look at their cones. It would be convenient if spruce trees had their cones pointing up so you could remember "spruce up," but alas, spruce cones hang down. You'll have to remember "fir up" instead. Both trees have spire shapes and sloping branches that allow heavy snow to slide off before it breaks the branches. The needles are arranged in fanlike sprays that help to "comb" moisture out of fog; the mist condenses on the needles and then drips to the floor.

In areas where spruce and fir have been removed (by logging, insects, disease, wind, or fire), quaking or bigtooth aspen and paper birch will often sprout in dense thickets, crowding out any spruce and fir seedlings that try to come up. Once past the sapling stage, however, the aspen and birch begin to thin out as their canopies rise. They cast just enough shade to discourage their own seedlings, but to encourage young spruce and fir. Without aspen and birch to stop them, spruce and fir can once again begin their slow but steady climb to dominance.

EVENING GROSBEAK

HERMIT THRUSH

BOREAL CHICKADEE

THE PINE FOREST

Today's northern pine forest is a far cry from the legendary pineries that the settlers saw. At one time in New England, 400-year-old eastern white pines grew as high as 200 feet, and reached 7, 8, and even 10 feet in diameter. These were the "broad-arrow" trees, reserved by the king of England for the making of sailing masts. These giants were systematically removed from the forests, much to the chagrin of the colonists. The white pine in the flag that flew at Bunker Hill attests to the significance of this tree in early American history.

A logging boom that began in the mid-1800's leveled most of the red and white pines that had ruled the landscape as far west as Minnesota. Ravaging fires that followed the logging destroyed the seeds on the ground, and there were not enough seed trees left standing to compensate for the loss. In most places, hardwoods such as aspen and birch were quick to fill the gap.

In some instances, however, the fires actually encouraged the return of a certain pine. Jack pine is not as stately as its taller relatives, but it is far less choosy about where it will grow. Loggers often ignored the stubby jack pines, leaving them scattered here and there, their crowns filled with hump-backed, resin-sealed cones. The heat of the fires that followed the logging managed to melt open these cones, releasing the seeds onto the acres of cleared mineral seedbed. Having few competitors to stop them, jack pines rose up in the ashes. They are now common in the Lake States, second only to another pioneer tree—aspen.

Red pine came back in a few places, but on the whole, most of the stands you see today were either spared the ax or planted by the Civilian Conservation Corps. Efforts to replant white pines led to disaster when white pine blister rust was imported from Europe along with shipments of seedlings. This disease has stifled efforts to return the white pine to its once-princely status.

A few pine forests have sprung up despite the odds, but the likelihood of them lasting more than one generation is slim. The broadleaf trees in their understory seem certain to take over, unless of course, a fire turns the tables. Pines are remarkably resistant to fires, thanks to their thick bark and special buds that are hidden by tufts of needles. Ground fires may kill broadleaf saplings, but by the time the long, slow-burning needles of a seedling pine are consumed, the fire is past, and the bud is saved. Fires also clear away competition and in some cases let in more light, both of which favor pines.

WHAT'S IN IT FOR WILDLIFE?

The same tough, thrifty evergreen needle that helps conifers make it through the winter contributes to a relatively slim roster of wildlife in northern needleleaf forests. A thick duff of millions of these needles blankets the forest floor, piling up instead of being recycled into the soil. Ground plants and shrubs have a hard time getting established in this thick mat. Once they do, they must compete with the shallow-rooted evergreens for water and scarce nutrients. Consequently, there is not a lush offering of wildlife plant foods beneath the boughs of needleleaf trees.

There are, however, some insect fans of the evergreen needle that serve as a food source for birds and mammals in the needleleaf forest. These needle-eaters are most often seen clambering over the branches in their caterpillar stage. Millions of migrating birds come through the conifer forests in search of just such a snack.

Other wildlife species are more interested in the seeds of conifers, kept in intricate cones. Red squirrels and red crossbills are specially adapted to

REDBELLY SNAKE

SOUTHERN RED-BACKED VOLE

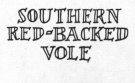

COMMON RAVEN · PINE SISKIN · LONG-EARED OWL · RUBY-CROWNED KINGLET · GRAY JAY · KIRTLAND'S WARBLER · MAGNOLIA WARBLER · PURPLE FINCH · HOARY BAT

WILDLIFE LOCATOR CHART—NORTHERN NEEDLELEAF FOREST

	Feeds from Air	Feeds in Upper Canopy	Feeds in Lower Canopy	Feeds on Trunk	Feeds on Ground
Nests in Tree Canopy	Long-eared Owl Red Bat Hoary Bat	Gray Jay Golden-crowned Kinglet Ruby-crowned Kinglet Solitary Vireo Blackburnian Warbler Pine Grosbeak Red Crossbill Pine Siskin Evening Grosbeak	Swainson's Thrush Magnolia Warbler Black-throated Green Warbler Bay-breasted Warbler		Common Raven (also nests on cliffs) Purple Finch
Nests in Trunk		Marten Fisher	Boreal Chickadee	Three-toed Woodpecker Black-backed Woodpecker Red-breasted Nuthatch Brown Creeper	Winter Wren (also nests in stump) Red Squirrel Northern Flying Squirrel
Nests on Ground		Spruce Grouse (also feeds on ground)	Kirtland's Warbler Canada Warbler		Hermit Thrush Dark-eyed Junco Redbelly Snake
Nests Beneath Ground or Debris		Porcupine			Louisiana Waterthrush Long-tailed Shrew Smokey Shrew Deer Mouse Southern Red-backed Vole Woodland Jumping Mouse Lynx
Nests in Water					Wood Frog

neatly extract the seed. Seeds that fall to the ground are hungrily devoured by rodents such as mice and voles. Owls and hawks keep their eyes peeled for these seed-eaters along the rather open forest floor. Porcupines prefer the sweet inner bark of conifers, and can be found nibbling trunks in the upper branches. Spruce grouse find needleleaf twigs to their liking during the winter, when other foods are scarce.

In addition to food, the dense overlapping branches of evergreens offer a unique wind and snow screen. Winter brings many animals such as white-tailed deer, moose, snowshoe hare, and grouse into needleleaf forests for protection and browse.

Come summer, an occasional broadleaf tree or berry-laden shrub in the understory provides a welcome alternative to the rough boughs of evergreens. Catkins, buds, seeds, and fruit are eaten by herbivores and omnivores alike. The leaves of soft-stemmed perennials such as grasses provide additional food for grazing rabbits, voles, and deer. Squirrels and deer seem to relish mushrooms, which are common in the low-light, high humidity conditions of the evergreen forest. Higher up, moose nibble patches of lichen off the bark.

Red-breasted Nuthatch

This upside-down bird sees things from a different angle. Instead of hopping up a tree like most woodpeckers, the red-breasted nuthatch climbs down headfirst. This allows it to see into crevices and insect galleries that its upright colleagues have overlooked. By dividing trees up in this way, woodpeckers and nuthatches can work the same patch of woods without actually competing for food.

To help it negotiate upside down, the nuthatch hangs from one foot while bracing itself in front with another. On horizontal excursions, the nuthatch can hang from the underside of a branch, gingerly making its way to the tips of the tiniest branches. When it reaches a dangling pinecone, it deftly pries a seed from the scales with its bill, then hops back to the tree trunk to wedge the seed into a crevice in the bark. Thus secured, the nuthatch may hack the seed open with its bill (hence the name nuthatch) or cover it with a piece of bark or moss for a later snack.

These acrobats are also fastidious parents. Nuthatches either dig their own cavities in trees or adopt ones that have been abandoned by wood-peckers. For security, they use mud to reduce the size of the entrance until it is just wide enough for the bird to squeeze through. Cracks and openings on the inside of the nest are caulked as well. Lastly, they smear the rim of the entrance with a glistening ball of pine gum to discourage predators and insects from crawling in. In the spring, look for males flying from the nest with bright strings of this sap stretching from their wings.

Look for red-breasted nuthatches—hopping jerkily up or down a trunk, out on limbs in the treetops, and even at the end of tiny twigs. They are combing the trees for needleleaf seeds, insect eggs, spiders, and insects such as beetles, wasps, caterpillars, crane flies, and moths of the spruce budworm. They occasionally feed on the ground, sometimes in stands of giant ragweed. In years when the pine and spruce crop in Canada is very poor, mass numbers of nuthatches may move southward in winter. These movements are called "irruptions."

Length: 4½ inches.

Look for nest holes—typically 15 feet up, in rotted stumps or dead branches. They dig cavities in pines, cottonwoods, birches, poplars, oaks, etc., preferring trees at least 12 inches in diameter.

Listen for—a tinny "yank yank."

Porcupine

Some people are surprised to find a porcupine riding the top of a tall spruce tree. Many want to rescue it, thinking it has been driven up there by a dog. For one thing, these large rodents don't need our protection, thank you, even from a pack of dogs. There are 30,000 good reasons not to fool with porkies, and any dog that has taken even one quill in the nose has learned to give them a wide berth.

Porkies climb trees on their own, and are as well equipped as tree surgeons to do it. Their paws are clawed, padded, and knobby, and their viselike leg muscles combined with all-over spurs (their downward-pointing quills) help them keep their place. For them, a treetop is a seat at the best restaurant in town. Porcupines eat buds, leaves, twigs, and the inner bark of trees. Their 21-foot gut takes up 75 percent of their body cavity, and is inhabited by an army of microbes that break down woody matter into digestible energy.

SPRUCE GROUSE

RUBY-CROWNED
KINGLET

The trees, for their part, seem to defend themselves from being the object of the porcupine's desires. Aspens, for instance, cluster their most nutritious parts on the outermost tips of branches, where the footing becomes too fragile to support a porcupine. Porkies counter with a neat trick of nip-twigging. They simply cut the twig close to them and bring the buds and leaves within reach, discarding the stripped twig like a well-picked bone.

As the leaves mature later in the summer, they accumulate tannin, an acidic compound that blocks the flushing of potassium out of the porkie's liver. Without flushing, potassium could build up and become toxic. When trees accumulate too much tannin, or are otherwise too high in acid, the porcupine simply meanders to another, more palatable tree. Its favorites, such as basswood, tend to be scattered throughout the forest rather than clumped and easy to find; could this be another tactic to avoid the porcupine?

The high potassium in their diet leads to another nutritional dilemma. As the liver flushes potassium, porcupines also lose what little salt they have in their system. This results in the porcupine's legendary passion for salt, which is all too familiar to resort owners in porkie country. Salty human perspiration on ax handles, canoe paddles, wooden porches, and even road salt on tires can entice porcupines to gnaw, often causing much damage.

Most folks aren't willing to tussle with a porcupine over a canoe paddle though. Those 30,000 bristling quills are a handy deterrent, foiling all but the fisher, a mammal that can flip a porcupine neatly to get at its quill-less underbelly. Contrary to popular wisdom, porcupines don't shoot their quills or throw them like darts. They simply deliver a bouquet of quills by swatting their enemy with their tail. The loosely anchored spears pull out of the porcupine easily, but stick with the recipient for days. The center of the quill is spongy. As it absorbs moisture, it swells, flanging out the backward-pointing barbules, and making it very painful to pull a quill out. Once embedded, quills are drawn deeper into the tissue each time the victim's muscles contract. A porcupine researcher who had a quill accidentally submerged in his upper arm was able to record its progress. By the time the quill finally poked its way out of his forearm, it had traveled an inch a day. Talk about occupational hazards!

Look for porcupines—hunched in a ball or draped on an upper branch, either munching on succulent leaves or dozing in the sun. They spend most of their time in trees, but may be seen on the ground as well, waddling from den to feeding grounds. Their only speedy move is when they pivot to display their tail full of spines. They are more active by night than by day.

Length: Head and body, 18–22 inches; tail, 7–9 inches.

Look for dens—in a deep rock crevice, a hole under a stump, an abandoned beaver burrow or fox den, a hollow log, or a cave. Brown, bean-shaped droppings may pile up so high inside the den that they spill out, evicting their owners along with them. Young porcupines are called por-cupettes.

Look for feeding debris—discarded twigs in sprays on the ground beneath where a porcupine is feeding. Look for a diagonal cut on the end of the twig and tiny parallel bites on the bark.

Look for gnaw marks—on anything made of wood, from saplings to buildings. Bright white scars higher up on trunks are the result of the porkie's habit of eating the inner bark. They shave off the outer bark first (look for it on the ground).

In the winter—porcupines will den together in crevices or caves. Hunger sends them out for food, and you'll usually find them feasting in the tops of trees.

Look for tracks—pigeon-toed, with a waddling stride of 5–6 inches, and a straddle up to 9 inches wide. The hindprint is more than 3 inches long, with five claw marks ahead of an oval-shaped pad. The quills may leave a broom-swept look on snow or soil.

Smell for—a strong urine odor near their dens, favorite feeding trees, or along the trails in between. The urine serves to mark these areas.

Listen for—an insistent sniffing as the porcupine tracks down food or senses danger. Mating includes a high-falsetto wooing song, a circle dance, nose rubbing, and face touching. Listen for a low-pitched meow during mating. They snort, bark, cry, whine, and chatter their teeth and quills when they are afraid.

Redbelly Snake

Snake-phobia sufferers take note: redbelly snakes will do anything they can to get away from you and stay alive. They have a large arsenal of tactics and distractions to deal with possible predators. First and foremost, they use whatever cover they can find to stay out of sight: logs, boards, rocks, or debris. If you do catch them out, they may curl their lips back in a sneer to discourage you. Or they may roll over to expose the red of their bellies, a bright color that often signals danger in the natural code. If that doesn't work, they've been known to stiffen their bodies straight as a stake, trying to look as dead as possible. Once they're sure you're gone, the "stiffs" come to life, slithering anxiously into the underbrush.

This extremely docile snake feeds almost exclusively on slugs and earthworms. Even if you touch one, the only characteristic mark you'll bring home on your skin will be a foul-smelling liquid that it exudes from its cloaca (an all-purpose opening on the underside of its body). Unfortunately, however, this small snake is often needlessly killed by people who think it is a copperhead.

Redbellies are most vulnerable in early spring, when they are just emerging from hibernation, and are usually groggy and cold. Snakes, like turtles and lizards, are ectotherms; they regulate their temperature from the outside rather than inside, and usually take on the temperature of their immediate surroundings. When first out of the chilly underground, they must bask in the sun a while to raise their temperature. Only a warm snake can move quickly enough to escape danger.

Look for redbelly snakes—under stones, boards, logs, and leafy debris, especially along forest edges. They are also known to inhabit mountainous terrain and sphagnum bogs. On warm summer nights after a rain, you may run across them (hopefully not over them!) on backroads.

Length: 8–16 inches.

In late September and October—they migrate by the hundreds to underground "hibernacula" such as ant mounds. They usually hibernate with a large tangle of other snakes, including brown, eastern garter, and rough green snakes.

Longleaf Pine

BROWN-HEADED NUTHATCH

PINE WARBLER

NINE-BANDED ARMADILLO

Post Oak

Large Gallberry

Slash Pine

Saw-palmetto

RED-COCKADED WOODPECKER

CORN SNAKE

GOPHER TORTOISE

SOUTHEASTERN POCKET GOPHER

Southern Red Oak

Yaupon

Southern Needleleaf Forest

WHERE TO SEE THIS HABITAT:

Alabama: William B. Bankhead, Conecuh, Talladega, and Tuskegee national forests

Florida: Appalachicola and Ocala national forests; St. Marks National Wildlife Refuge

Georgia: Oconee National Forest; Piedmont National Wildlife Refuge

Louisiana: D'Arbonnee National Wildlife Refuge; Kisatchie National Forest

Mississippi: Bienville, De Soto, and Homochitto national forests; Noxubee and Mississippi Sandhill Crane national wildlife refuges

North Carolina: Croatan National Forest

South Carolina: Carolina Sandhills National Wildlife Refuge; Francis Marion and Sumter national forests

Texas: Angelina, Davy Crockett, Sabine, and Sam Houston national forests; Big Thicket National Preserve

Southern Needleleaf Forest

BEGINNINGS

If succession has its way, the pine forests of the South will eventually change into broadleaf forests. In some areas, the change is already taking place, and dying pines are being replaced by oaks and hickories. For people who look at the forest in terms of timber, this change is not a welcome one.

Pines are a cash crop in the South—they grow quickly, and they can be harvested cheaply. For this reason, commercial forests are usually kept in a perpetual state of pines. Each time the trees are harvested, the successional clock is set back to zero, and the sun-loving pine seedlings eagerly take over the clearing. When the trees get a little older, foresters periodically set fires beneath them. This keeps the broadleaf understory from taking over, reduces the buildup of tinder-dry litter, and destroys some of the diseases that plague pines.

The reason fire works so well as a management tool is because it has been in nature's toolbox for eons. In the days before "prescribed burns," natural fires began with a lightning spark and spread swiftly in the sun-dried tinder. Indians also lit fires under the trees to facilitate hunting and travel and as a way of managing game. After a millennium of these fires, the only survivors were those plants that were specially adapted to live in this frequently scorched environment.

Longleaf pine and turkey oak are two excellent examples of fire-adapted species whose trees can handle a bark-blackening without dying, and whose seedlings can sprout again even if they are burned back to the ground. Longleaf pine made up much of the pine kingdom in the days of frequent fires. A carpet of wiregrass or saw-palmetto was sometimes the only cover between the ground and the lofty top of the canopy. Those species that were not fire-tolerant, such as magnolias and beech, were herded into the bottomlands where fires seldom traveled.

With fire to eliminate most of the broadleaf competitors, the pines were able to keep coming back generation after generation. Essentially, the program of prescribed burns on managed forests tries to replicate these conditions. As you will see, taking fire out of the equation leads to a very different kind of southern forest.

PUTTING OUT THE FIRE CHANGES THE FOREST

As our economy tightened during the Great Depression, the pines growing on old cotton fields suddenly appeared more valuable. More and more fires

---

CHARACTERISTIC PLANTS:

Major Trees and Shrubs:

Loblolly-shortleaf Forest:
loblolly pine
shortleaf pine

Longleaf-slash Forest:
longleaf pine
saw-palmetto
slash pine

Common to Both:
blackgum
large gallberry
hickories: mockernut, pignut, and others
red maple
sweetbay
sweetgum
oaks: blackjack, laurel, post, southern red, water, white, willow, and other oaks
winged elm

Associate Trees, Shrubs, and Vines:

Common to Both:
bayberry: odorless and southern
blackberries
buckwheat-tree
common persimmon
fetterbush
flowering dogwood
greenbriers
hawthorns
honeysuckles
lowbush blueberry
mapleleaf viburnum
shining sumac
southern arrowwood
swamp cyrilla
sweet pepperbush
tree sparkleberry
Virginia creeper
witch-hazel
yaupon

Herbaceous Plants:

Common to Both:
beautyberry
bluestems
Carolina jessamine
deer's tongue
grassleaf golden aster
longleaf uniola
panic grasses
partidge pea
paspalums
sedges
St. Andrew's Cross
tickclovers
wiregrass

---

were snuffed out to "protect" the mature trees and a campaign was begun to discourage the annual arson that had become a southern tradition. At that time, we didn't fully realize the beneficial role of periodic fires. Curbing these fires was destined to change the character of the southern pine region forever.

Finally, some of the fire-sensitive pines were able to spread from their hideouts in the swamps. Slash pine was able to join longleaf on many sites in the deep South. Loblolly pine (named after the muddy holes that pioneers called "loblollies") took over the northern part of the Southeast, occurring most often with shortleaf pine.

Without the vigilant groundskeeping of light fires, broadleaf trees from nearby forests began to seed in under the pines. The offspring of the pines themselves were no match for these vigorous young broadleafs; they proved frail in the heavy shade and died within a few short years. The broadleafs quickly took up the slack and grew into a solid underlayer beneath the canopy pines. Barring disturbance (or management for pines), these broadleafs will continue their ascent to the canopy, growing in spurts whenever an opening is created by the death of a pine. By the time the forest is 80–120 years old, the oaks and hickories will dominate, along with only a few relict pines.

WHAT'S IN IT FOR WILDLIFE?

Young pine forests between the ages of 10 and 20 years are dark places. The spreading tree crowns begin to intermingle, producing a near blackout on the forest floor below. In this stage, understory plants have no sun to grow in, and wildlife find very little ground cover and almost nothing to eat, with the exception of some mushrooms poking up amid the needles.

The good news is that tree trunks are now large enough to interest bark-insect feeders such as downy, hairy, and red-cockaded woodpeckers and red-breasted, white-breasted, and brown-headed nuthatches. In the shadiest part of the forest, trees lose their lower layers of branches, exposing their trunk to these birds. The trees along the edges of such young forests are exposed to the sun, and therefore may still have whorls of lower branches that provide cover for songbirds.

Middle-aged pine forests (15–35 years) go through a natural thinning that lets in enough light to support an understory. In areas where fires are routinely squelched, the broadleaf trees and shrubs begin their ascent. In all, there are nearly 80 woody associates of southern pines, many of which are invaluable to wildlife. The addition of this new layer in the forest provides niches for shrub nesters, singing posts for other songbirds, and

SCARLET KINGSNAKE

OAK TOAD

INDIGO SNAKE

FLORIDA PINE SNAKE

CAROLINA PIGMY RATTLESNAKE

FLATWOODS SALAMANDER

EASTERN DIAMONDBACK RATTLESNAKE

SOUTHERN SHORT-TAILED SHREW

WILDLIFE LOCATOR CHART—SOUTHERN NEEDLELEAF FOREST

	Feeds from Air	Feeds in Upper Canopy	Feeds in Lower Canopy	Feeds on Trunk	Feeds on Ground
Nests in Tree Canopy	Eastern Wood-pewee Northern Yellow Bat	Summer Tanager	Yellow-throated Vireo	Yellow-throated Warbler Pine Warbler (also feeds in canopy)	
Nests in Trunk				Red-cockaded Woodpecker White-breasted Nuthatch Brown-headed Nuthatch	Raccoon
Nests in Shrubs			White-eyed Vireo		Northern Cardinal Golden Mouse
Nests on Ground				Black-and-white Warbler	Bachman's Sparrow Eastern Diamondback Rattlesnake Carolina Pigmy Rattlesnake
Nests Beneath Ground or Debris					Louisiana Waterthrush Southern Short-tailed Shrew Nine-banded Armadillo Southeastern Pocket Gopher (feeds beneath ground) Florida Mouse Hispid Cotton Rat Gopher Tortoise Florida Box Turtle Eastern Fence Lizard Indigo Snake Corn Snake Scarlet Kingsnake Northern Pine Snake Florida Pine Snake
Nests in Water			Pine Woods Treefrog		Flatwoods Salamander Oak Toad

good rabbit cover. By the time they are 40–60 years old, mature pine forests have a distinct understory of broadleaf trees. These forests are ideal for wildlife in that they can provide the year-round shelter of dense-needled evergreen branches, along with broadleaf mast (nuts and seeds). Acorns are sought out by 185 species of southern wildlife. This energy-rich food becomes especially important in fall, when squirrels, black bears, raccoons, wild turkeys, northern bobwhites, and white-tailed deer are trying to put on weight for the long winter.

At age 70–80, pines begin to drop out, killed by lightning, red heart disease, southern pine beetles, or other stresses. This opens up the canopy and allows younger trees to get started in patches. This patchiness caters to the majority of wildlife that need all age classes to meet their needs.

Old-growth stands (up to 120 years) are a true mixture of pines and broadleafs, in the overstory as well as the understory. When mast-bearing broadleafs reach the overstory, they begin to produce even more than when they were in the understory: a boon to mast eaters. The broadleafs also provide cavities for at least 17 species of cavity nesters in the South.

In some managed forests, a program of prescribed burns keeps the understory open instead of letting broadleafs fill in. The frequent burning cuts down on the buildup of tinder-dry litter, reducing the chances of a runaway wildfire. Burns can also make travel easier for wildlife, expose pine seeds for hungry northern bobwhite and turkey, open dusting areas for songbirds, and encourage the growth of legumes and other nutritious plants. Some species are well adapted to these open-understory forests, including red-cockaded woodpecker, gopher tortoise, indigo snake, Bachman's sparrow, northern bobwhite, and cotton mouse. (The illustration features this type of forest.)

Clearings in the forest are also important to wildlife. The herbaceous plants in openings have been found to be an important aid to digestion in species such as deer. Fruit trees also bear more fruit in openings, and browse species are more nutritious and palatable when grown in ample light. The ideal wildlife watching areas will have a mosaic of (1) dense young pines for cover, (2) mature pines for cavities, (3) broadleafs for cavities and other nesting sites, mast, and other foods, (4) clearings for succulent browse, and (5) some open understories for wildlife adapted to frequently burned forests.

Red-cockaded Woodpecker

More than any other kind of bird, the red-cockaded woodpecker symbolizes the southern pinelands. For nesting, it looks for older pines that are infected with red heartrot, a fungal disease that softens the interior, making nest digging easier. The trees must be alive and solid on the outside, however, so that they are less likely to be consumed by fires. Light, frequent fires are the woodpecker's ally—they clear out understory vegetation, and create the open, parklike stands that the birds (and weary hikers) prefer.

In the timber-growing regions of the South, these aged, open forests are hard to come by. Most trees are cut down before they are old enough to develop the kind of rotted heart that the woodpeckers like. In other areas, natural ground-clearing fires are suppressed, giving the green light to a brushy understory that discourages the birds. Biologists estimate that there may be fewer than 10,000 of these classic pineland birds alive.

Birdwatchers are not the only ones who would miss the red-cockaded if it was gone. Flocks of Carolina chickadees, tufted titmice, pine warblers, and nuthatches often follow the red-cockaded on its feeding rounds. As the woodpecker scales off bark with its feet, it stirs up and exposes insects that these other birds eagerly pick off. Flying squirrels, owls, and other cavity nesters would miss the carefully constructed trunk holes that red-cockadeds create.

These nest holes may take as long as a year to complete. The entrances slant upward to the chamber, so that pitch or rainwater drains away instead of chilling the nestlings. Around the entrance to the nest, the woodpecker scrapes the bark and drills pits that dribble resin above, below, and on the sides of the hole. Tree-climbing rat snakes that come looking for breakfast eggs are bitterly repelled by this smooth, sticky "moat."

After many years of repeated nesting and drilling, red-cockaded nest trees are slathered with resin, and stand out like white columns against the darker trees. If you find one of the trees in the breeding season, you may be treated to a show. Feeding the nestlings is usually a family affair. Unmated males from the previous season stick around to help raise their parents' next brood. The efforts of these so-called helper birds can mean the difference between life and death for the nestlings. At a nest with helpers, the young are fed 5–27 times an hour. The helpers may feed the young directly, or pass food bill to bill to another helper that will feed the young. In nests without helpers, an average of 1.4 chicks are raised; but with helpers, the success rate rises to 2 birds per nest.

This seemingly altruistic behavior makes good ecological sense. The small number of nest sites in most forests are already claimed by the older, dominant males. Young males may not have the opportunity or resources to raise their own brood, but by increasing the number of their brothers and sisters, they can at least advance some of their own genes. In the meantime, they are gaining experience that will help them raise their own young someday.

Look for red-cockaded woodpeckers—bluebird-sized, spiraling around upper trunks or upper branches, using their two forward-pointing toes and two backward-pointing toes for traction. They use their stiff tail feathers to brace themselves for pecking, scaling bark, or drumming out a beat. In addition to combing trees for beetle larvae and ants, these wood-peckers also eat the fruits of southern bayberry, magnolias, wild grape, poison-ivy, pokeberry, blueberry, cherries, blackgum, and pecan. In the summer, they move to adjoining cornfields for a few weeks, eating up to 8,000 corn earworms (a damaging pest) per acre. A clan of as many as seven may be in the field.

Length: 8½ inches.

Look for resin-coated nest trees—with a westward-facing cavity that is usually 30–50 feet above the ground, depending on where the red heart infection is. The entrance is 2 inches wide and ringed with resin pits, scraped bark, and oozing sap. The woodpecker keeps these taps open by chipping away sap as it hardens. Traditional nest trees (reused for at least 20 years) may be entirely crusted below the nest. Sometimes, these wood-peckers nest close together (25–75 feet apart) with as many as six active nests on a third of an acre. These colonies may be spaced half a mile apart.

Listen for—"yank-yank-yank" that sounds like the woodpecker's as-sociate, the brown-headed nuthatch. Call notes "szreh" and "shrit" are uttered incessantly to communicate to family members or to warn intruders. Their soft drumming is seldom heard.

Nine-banded Armadillo

Texans have fallen head over heels in love with this leathery, peg-toothed charmer. Armadillos grace beer labels, restaurant marquees, and school team banners. But unlike the cuddly koala of Australia, the armadillo is not exactly a lap pet. This armored tank of the mammal world is covered with a series of shell-like plates layered with thick hide. The scapula at the shoulders is attached to the pelvic shield by an intervening set of nine hoops. Skin between the hoops allows the armadillo to twist and turn, just as the folds in an accordian allow the instrument to move.

Though they seem suited up for a joust, armadillos are actually docile creatures. The armadillo would rather flee than fight, and will usually zigzag one way or another to elude its enemies. It will gladly dart into a burrow if it can, arching its scaled back to wedge itself into the dirt of the roof. Trying to pull an anchored armadillo out of its snug-fitting burrow can be impossible without a shovel and the best part of an afternoon. If it can't get to a burrow, it will often take refuge in thornbushes, which are a prickly deterrent to predators, but which don't get under the armadillo's skin at all.

Despite their popularity with the public, most armadillos meet their death in the oily undercarriage of a speeding car. Armadillos have a peculiar habit of arching their back and jumping straight up in the air when alarmed—when, for instance, a car is roaring over them at 60 miles per hour.

The entire ecosystem is lessened when an armadillo dies. Many kinds of life find a cool home in armadillo-built burrows, including eastern cottontails, cotton rats, Virginia opossums, and striped skunks. Farmers benefit when these rooters go after crop pests, lapping up 60 or 70 insects with each swipe of their tongue. Believe it or not, medical researchers are also interested in the armadillo's well-being. Armadillos are the only North American mammals besides humans that suffer from leprosy, and are studied to help find relief for this disease. Another armadillo quirk that bears study is its four identical young. Each litter of four is derived from a single egg that splits into quadrants. The young are either all females or all males and are genetically identical.

Look for armadillos—grubbing for insects in shrubby, open woods at dusk, and moving into fields as night falls. They hunt by smell, pushing their long snout into the leaf litter, and digging a cone-shaped hole with their forepaws when they sense an insect below. They also eat frogs, snakes, birds, eggs, fruit, and carrion. They are active mostly at night, but rainy or cloudy weather will rouse them earlier in the day. During rainy periods they tend to seek higher ground, and in dry spells they seek out rivers and wetlands where moist soil is easy to dig. You may be able to get close enough to study them if they are preoccupied with foraging. Occasionally they may rise on their hind feet for a sniff around.

Length: Head and body, 15–17 inches; tail, 14–16 inches.

In the water—yes, armadillos do cross streams by walking across the bottom. Their specific gravity is 1.6 (heavier than water), and they can hold their breath for 6 minutes. For longer treks, they usually swim. They do a furious dog-paddle when they first get in, fighting to keep their snout above water. In a few minutes, however, their digestive tract absorbs enough air so that they can float. The longer they stay in the water, the higher they ride.

Nests are underground—in burrows. Armadillos gather a pile of leaves, grass, and twigs under their shell, balancing it on their hindpaws. They then lower themselves onto their forepaws, clasp the pile, and shuffle backward on a zigzag path into the burrow. The tail descends first; highly sensitive to touch, it tells them where they're going.

Look for grubbing furrows—3–6 inches deep, formed when the snout is pushed along the ground in search of insects. Look also for cone-shaped holes they dig to extract a morsel.

Listen for—a wheezy grunt when they are foraging. They buzz when running hard.

Gopher Tortoise

Rather than drag their shell-home, tortoises lift it clean off the ground when they walk (and we think carrying a suitcase through the airport is tough!). The stumpy hind legs are wrinkled and leathery like an elephant's. Their forelimbs are flatter and equipped with strong nails to help them dig their 30-foot burrows. At the end of the burrow, they hollow out a spacious chamber where they can cool off during the hottest part of the day.

A number of animals live in the burrows with the tortoises, including mice, rabbits, raccoons, foxes, Virginia opossums, rats, burrowing owls, skinks, eastern fence lizards, eastern spadefoot toads, and crawfish frogs. Insects of all kinds also live here, and there are as many as 14 species that are found nowhere else. The most dangerous snake in North America, the eastern diamondback rattler, is a regular resident. Hunters sometimes gas the holes to remove rattlers, inadvertently killing the innocent tortoise at the same time.

Tortoises work out the differences between themselves in a fascinating way. Males that are competing for mates or territory go through jousting competitions. The attacker runs at its opponent, ramming its side in an attempt to overthrow it. The other turtle tries to ram back, until they are both circling, looking for a broadside advantage. When patience runs out, they may meet each other head on. They pull their heads into their shells to reveal a spurlike extension that grows on the lower shell, just under the chin. They back up slightly, and then charge, using the spur as a crowbar to lift the opponent up and over. Once a turtle is on its back, it's out of commission for a while, and the winner can have its choice of mate.

The mating ceremony may also include some "persuasive" ramming. When the male finally gets on top of the female, his concave lower shell fits snugly against her convex upper shell. The male extends his head and neck as far as they will go and strokes the female with his foreclaws until she finally raises up on her hind legs (more weight to leg-press!). This exposes her cloacal opening so fertilization can take place.

Look for gopher tortoises—in scrub pine–turkey oak woods, especially where the soil is sandy and saw-palmetto is in the understory. The turtles emerge from their burrows in the morning to feed on grasses, leaves, and wild fruits and berries. They retreat to burrows when it gets too hot or too cold.

Shell Length: 9¼–14½ inches.

Look for burrows—in the southeastern side of sand hills, many of which were once dunes that are now covered with vegetation. The burrow dips down slightly for 30 feet, and may be 18 feet deep. The longest burrow ever found was 430 feet long. Be careful when looking down burrow holes—the eastern diamondback rattler may be at home.

Look for tracks—about 2 inches long and 1½ inches wide, with four or five long toes printing in soft mud. The middle three toes are longest. The drag marks of the shell may obliterate some of the tracks.

Listen for—grunting as turtles mate.

INDIGO
SNAKE

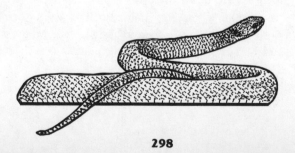

Resources for the Curious

GETTING INVOLVED

There are a number of ways you can help wildlife prosper in your area. Becoming a member of the following organizations will put you in touch with local chapters that are making provisions (through politics, research, and education) to keep wildlife habitats whole. These groups often meet to hear invited speakers or to take field trips to see wildlife. For a more complete listing of organizations, state and federal agencies, and universities involved in wildlife conservation, try the *Conservation Directory,* available through the National Wildlife Federation and many libraries.

National Audubon Society
950 Third Avenue
New York, NY 10022
Publications: *Audubon, American Birds, Audubon Wildlife Report, Audubon Adventures, Audubon Activist*
(212) 832-3200

National Wildlife Federation
1412 16th Street NW
Washington, DC 20036-2266
Publications: *National Wildlife, International Wildlife*
(202) 797-6800

Sierra Club
730 Polk Street
San Francisco, CA 94109
Publications: *Sierra, National News Report*
(415) 981-8634

The Nature Conservancy
Suite 800
1800 N. Kent Street
Arlington, VA 22209
Publication: *The Nature Conservancy News*
(703) 841-5300

The Wilderness Society
1400 I Street NW, 10th Floor
Washington, DC 20005
Publication: *Wilderness*
(202) 842-3400

World Wildlife Fund—U.S.
1250 24th Street NW
Washington, DC 20037
Publication: *Focus*
(202) 293-4800

Here are some other ways to get involved:
1. Participate in local censuses (studies that estimate numbers and locations of wildlife).
2. Volunteer to be part of a research project.
3. Take a class or teach one.
4. Keep a wildlife observation journal and share it with other wildlife watchers.
5. Write to your local Representatives about the need to protect habitats in your area.
6. Manage your own land for wildlife—be it backyard or back forty.

GETTING OUTSIDE

Next time you're dreaming about a vacation, envision yourself in wildlife habitats. How many do you think you could explore on your next outing? Could you see all 20 on an extended trip through the East? For vacation-planning maps and a world of wildlife information, contact the following land management agencies (the lands they manage are in parentheses):

U.S. Forest Service (National Forests)
United States Department of Agriculture
P.O. Box 2417
Washington, DC 20013
(202) 447-3957

U.S. Fish and Wildlife Service (National Wildlife Refuges)
United States Department of the Interior
Washington, DC 20240
(202) 343-4131

National Park Service (National Parks)
United States Department of the Interior
Interior Building
P.O. Box 37127
Washington, DC 20013-7127
(202) 343-6843

Your city, county, or state land management agencies (city, county, and state parks and forests). These agencies have different names depending on where you live. Begin by calling the capitol and asking for one of the following: Department of Natural Resources, Forestry Department, Fish and Game Commission, or Conservation Department. Direct specific wildlife questions to the Non-Game Specialist.

Your State University's Cooperative Extension Service. This is a good place to get advice about managing your own land for wildlife. The Extension Service is usually connected with an agricultural or forestry college.

RECOMMENDED READING

Natural history literature, ranging from the scientific to the poetic, can be found in back-pocket guides or lavish coffee-table books. I heartily recommend reading as a great way to explore habitats when you're cabin-bound and to better appreciate habitats when you're outside. I've included mostly area-wide books, but don't forget about local guides to birds, mammals, reptiles, and amphibians. Many states have their own, as do some of the larger parks. Visitor centers and sporting goods stores are good places to find these local guides.

Habitats

Amos, William H., and Stephen H. Amos. 1985. *The Audubon Nature Guides. Atlantic and Gulf Coasts.* Alfred A. Knopf, NY, 670 pp.

Barrett, John W. 1980. *Regional Silviculture of the United States.* John Wiley & Sons, NY, 551 pp.

Bishop, Owen N. 1973. *Natural Communities.* John Murray, London, 181 pp.

Braun, E. Lucy. 1985 reprint of 1950 edition. *Deciduous Forests of Eastern North America.* The Free Press, NY, 596 pp.

Burgis, Mary J., and Pat Morris. 1987. *The Natural History of Lakes.* Cambridge University Press, Cambridge, Great Britain, 218 pp.

Caduto, Michael J. 1985. *Pond & Brook, A Guide to Nature Study in Freshwater Environments.* Prentice-Hall, Englewood Cliffs, NJ, 276 pp.

Carson, Rachel. 1955. *The Edge of the Sea.* Houghton Mifflin, Boston, 276 pp.

Chabot, Brian F., and Harold A. Mooney. 1985. *Physiological Ecology of North American Plant Communities.* Chapman and Hall, NY, 351 pp.

Curtis, John T. 1971. *The Vegetation of Wisconsin.* University of Wisconsin Press, Madison, WI, 657 pp.

Daiber, Franklin C. 1982. *Animals of the Tidal Marsh.* Van Nostrand Reinhold, NY, 422 pp.

Daniel, Glenda, and Jerry Sullivan. 1981. *A Sierra Club Naturalist's Guide to the North Woods.* Sierra Club Books, San Francisco, 408 pp.

Evans, Keith E., and Roger A. Kirkman. 1981. *Guide to Bird Habitats of the Ozark Plateau.* Gen. Tech. Rep. NC-68, USDA Forest Service, North Central Forest Experiment Station, St. Paul, MN, 79 pp.

Eyre, F. H., ed. 1980. *Forest Cover Types of the United States and Canada.* Society of American Foresters, Washington, DC, 148 pp.

Farb, Peter. 1963. *Face of North America: The Natural History of a Continent.* Harper & Row, NY, 316 pp.

Flader, Susan. 1983. *The Great Lakes Forest.* University of Minnesota Press, Minneapolis, MN, 336 pp.

Gates, David A. 1975. *Seasons of the Salt Marsh.* Chatham Press, Old Greenwich, CT, 128 pp.

Gleason, Henry A., and Arthur Cronquist. 1964. *The Natural Geography of Plants.* Columbia University Press, NY, 420 pp.

Godfrey, Michael A. 1980. *A Sierra Club Naturalist's Guide to the Piedmont.* Sierra Club Books, San Francisco, 498 pp.

Hamel, Paul B., Harry E. La Grand, Michael R. Lennartz, and Sidney A. Gauthreaux. 1982. *Bird-Habitat Relationships on Southeastern Forest Lands.* Gen. Tech. Rep. SE-22, USDA Forest Service, Southeastern Forest Experiment Station, Asheville, NC, 417 pp.

Hay, John, and Peter Farb. 1966. *The Atlantic Shore.* Harper & Row, NY, 246 pp.

Hylander, Clarence J. 1966. *Wildlife Communities from the Tundra to the Tropics in North America.* Houghton Mifflin, Boston, 342 pp.

Jorgensen, Neil. 1978. *A Sierra Club Naturalist's Guide to Southern New England.* Sierra Club Books, San Francisco, 417 pp.

Karstad, Aleta. 1979. *Wild Habitats.* Charles Scribner's Sons, NY, 144 pp.

Kricher, John C. 1988. *A Field Guide to Eastern Forests.* Houghton Mifflin, Boston, 368 pp.

Larsen, James. 1982. *Ecology of Northern Lowland Bogs and Conifer Forests.* Academic Press, NY, 307 pp.

Neiring, William. 1985. *The Audubon Society Nature Guides. Wetlands.* Alfred A. Knopf, NY, 638 pp.

Page, Jake. 1983. *Planet Earth Series. Forest.* Time-Life Books, Alexandria, VA, 176 pp.

Perry, Bill. 1985. *A Sierra Club Naturalist's Guide to the Middle Atlantic Coast (Cape Hatteras to Cape Cod).* Sierra Club Books, San Francisco, 470 pp.

Platt, Rutherford. 1965. *The Great American Forest.* Prentice-Hall, Englewood Cliffs, NJ, 271 pp.

Sackett, Russell. 1983. *The Edge of the Sea.* Time-Life Books, Alexandria, VA, 176 pp.

Sanderson, Ivan. 1961. *The Continent We Live On*. Random House, NY, 299 pp.

Shelford, Victor E. 1963. *The Ecology of North America*. University of Illinois Press, Urbana, IL, 610 pp.

Stokes, Donald W. 1981. *The Natural History of Wild Shrubs and Vines*. Harper & Row, NY, 246 pp.

Stokes, Donald W. 1976. *A Guide to Nature in Winter (Northeast and North-central North America)*. Little, Brown and Company, Boston, 374 pp.

Sutton, Ann and Myron. 1985. *The Audubon Society Nature Guides. Eastern Forests*. Alfred A. Knopf, NY, 640 pp.

Thomson, Betty Flanders. 1958. *The Changing Face of New England*. Macmillan, NY, 188 pp.

Thomson, Betty Flanders. 1977. *The Shaping of America's Heartland; the Landscape of the Middle West*. Houghton Mifflin, Boston, 267 pp.

Vankat, John. 1979. *The Natural Vegetation of North America*. John Wiley & Sons, NY, 255 pp.

Walker, L. C. 1984. *Trees: An Introduction to Trees and Forest Ecology for the Amateur Naturalist*. Prentice-Hall, Englewood Cliffs, NJ, 306 pp.

Watts, May T. 1957. *Reading the Landscape: An Adventure in Ecology*. Macmillan, NY, 230 pp.

Whittaker, R. H. 1970. *Communities & Ecosystems*. Macmillan, NY, 158 pp.

Wildlife

Birds

Bent, Arthur C., et al. 1919–1968. *Life Histories of North American Birds*. 23 Volumes (various publishers).

Bull, John, and John Farrand, Jr. 1977. *The Audubon Society Field Guide to North American Birds*. Alfred A. Knopf, NY, 784 pp.

Burton, Robert. 1985. *Bird Behavior*. Alfred A. Knopf, NY, 224 pp.

Ehrlich, Paul R., David S. Dobkin, and Darryl Wheye. 1988. *The Birder's Handbook: A Field Guide to the Natural History of North American Birds*. Simon and Schuster, NY. 785 pp.

Harrison, Hal H. 1975. *A Field Guide to Bird's Nests (East)*. Houghton Mifflin, Boston, 257 pp.

Leahy, Christopher. 1982. *The Birdwatcher's Handbook: An Encyclopedic Handbook of North American Birdlife*. Bonanza Books, NY, 917 pp.

Perrins, Christopher M., and Alex L. A. Middleton. 1985. *The Encyclopedia of Birds*. Facts on File Publications, NY, 447 pp.

Savage, Candace. 1985. *Wings of the North*. University of Minnesota Press, Minneapolis, MN, 211 pp.

Stokes, Donald W. 1979 and 1983. *A Guide to Bird Behavior*. 2 Volumes. Little, Brown and Company, Boston, 336 pp. each.

Terres, John K. 1980. *Audubon Society Encyclopedia of North American Birds*. Alfred A. Knopf, NY, 1109 pp.

Welty, J. C. 1975. *The Life of Birds*. 2nd ed. Saunders, Philadelphia, 623 pp.

Mammals

Cahalane, Victor H. 1961. *Mammals of North America*. Macmillan, NY, 682 pp.

Forsyth, Adrian. 1985. *Mammals of the American North*. Camden House Publishing Ltd., Camden East, Ontario. 351 pp.

Godin, Alfred J. 1977. *Wild Mammals of New England*. The Johns Hopkins University Press, Baltimore, MD, 304 pp.

MacDonald, David. 1984. *The Encyclopedia of Mammals*. Facts on File Publications, NY, 895 pp.

Nowak, R. M., and J. L. Paradise. 1983. *Walker's Mammals of the World* (2 Volumes), 4th ed. The Johns Hopkins University Press, Baltimore, MD, 1362 pp.

Savage, Arthur, and Candace Savage. 1981. *Wild Mammals of Northwest America*. The Johns Hopkins University Press, Baltimore, MD, 209 pp.

Schwartz, Charles W., and Elizabeth R. Schwartz. 1981. *The Wild Mammals of Missouri*. University of Missouri Press and Missouri Department of Conservation, Columbia, MO, 356 pp.

Reptiles and Amphibians

Ashton, Ray E., Jr., and Patricia Sawyer Ashton. 1985. *Handbook of Reptiles and Amphibians of Florida*. Part Two. *Lizards, Turtles, and Crocodilians*. Windward Publishing, Miami, FL, 191 pp.

Behler, John L. 1979. *The Audubon Society Field Guide to North American Reptiles and Amphibians*. Alfred A. Knopf, NY, 718 pp.

Cochran, Doris M., and Coleman Goin. 1970. *The New Field Book of Reptiles and Amphibians*. G. P. Putnam's Sons, NY, 359 pp.

Conant, Isabelle Hunt. 1975. *A Field Guide to Reptiles and Amphibians of Eastern and Central North America*. 2nd ed. Houghton Mifflin, Boston, 429 pp.

Cook, Francis R. 1984. *Introduction to Canadian Amphibians and Reptiles*. National Museum of Natural Sciences, Ottawa, Canada, 200 pp.

Green, N. Bayard, and Thomas K. Pauley. 1987. *Amphibians and Reptiles in West Virginia.* University of Pittsburgh Press, Pittsburgh, PA, 241 pp.

Halliday, Tim R., and Kraig Adler. 1986. *The Encyclopedia of Reptiles and Amphibians.* Facts on File Publications, NY, 143 pp.

Obst, Fritz Jurgen. 1986. *Turtles, Tortoises, and Terrapins.* St. Martin's Press, NY, 231 pp.

Parker, H. W. 1977. *Snakes: A Natural History.* 2nd ed. British Museum of Natural History. Cornell University Press, Ithaca, NY, 108 pp.

Vogt, Richard Carl. 1981. *Natural History of Amphibians and Reptiles in Wisconsin.* The Milwaukee Public Museum, Milwaukee, WI, 205 pp.

General

DeGraff, Richard M., and Deborah D. Rudis. 1986. *New England Wildlife: Habitat, Natural History, and Distribution.* Gen. Tech. Rep. NE-108. USDA Forest Service, Northeastern Forest Experiment Station, Broomall, PA, 491 pp.

Grzimeks, B. 1972. *Animal Life Encyclopedia.* 13 Volumes. Van Nostrand Reinhold, NY.

Martin, Alexander C., Herbert S. Zim, and Arnold L. Nelson. 1961 reprint of 1951 edition. *American Wildlife and Plants: A Guide to Wildlife Food Habits.* Dover Publications, NY, 500 pp.

Ways of Seeing: Wildlife Watching

Brown, Vinson. 1972. *Reading the Outdoors at Night.* Stackpole Books, Harrisburg, PA, 191 pp.

Brown, Vinson. 1969. *Reading the Woods.* Collier Books, NY, 160 pp.

Durrell, Gerald M., with Lee Durrell. 1983. *The Amateur Naturalist.* Alfred A. Knopf, NY, 320 pp.

Farrand, John, Jr. 1988. *How to Identify Birds.* McGraw-Hill, NY, 320 pp.

Heintzelman, Donald S. 1979. *A Manual for Bird Watching in the Americas.* Universe Books, NY, 255 pp.

Kress, Stephen W. 1981. *The Audubon Society Handbook for Birders.* Charles Scribner's Sons, NY, 322 pp.

McElroy, Thomas P., Jr. 1974. *The Habitat Guide to Birding.* Alfred A. Knopf, NY, 257 pp.

Murie, Olaus J. 1974. *A Field Guide to Animal Tracks.* Houghton Mifflin, Boston, 375 pp.

Pettingill, Owen S. *A Guide to Bird Finding East of the Mississippi.* 2nd ed. Oxford University Press, NY, 689 pp.

Riley, W. 1979. *Guide to National Wildlife Refuges.* Anchor Press, Garden City, NY, 653 pp.

Roth, Charles E. 1982. *The Wildlife Observer's Guidebook.* Prentice-Hall, Englewood Cliffs, NJ, 239 pp.

Stokes, Donald and Lillian. 1986. *A Guide to Animal Tracking and Behavior.* Little, Brown and Company, Boston, 418 pp.

Thinking About Wildlife

Dillard, Annie. 1978 reprint of 1974 edition. *Pilgrim at Tinker Creek.* Bantam Books, NY, 279 pp.

Ehrlich, Paul R., and Anne Ehrlich. 1981. *Extinction.* Random House, NY, 305 pp.

Leopold, Aldo. 1966 reprint of 1949 edition. *A Sand County Almanac with Essays on Conservation from Round River.* Ballantine Books, NY, 295 pp.

Tributsch, H. 1982. *How Life Learned to Live: Adaptation in Nature.* MIT Press, Cambridge, MA, 218 pp.

Common and Scientific Names of Plants

(Page numbers refer to Characteristic Plants Charts for each habitat.)

Common name *Scientific name*

Alder, American Green *Alnus crispa* 228
Alder, Smooth *Alnus serrulata*
Alder, Speckled *Alnus rugosa* 105, 142, 152, 177, 228
Algae, Blue-green *Calothrix* spp. 67
Algae, Filamentous *Cladophora* spp. 105
Anemone, Canada *Anemone canadensis* 142
Anemone, Wood *Anemone quinquefolia* 252
Angelica *Angelica atropurpureo* 142
Arbutus, Trailing *Epigea repens* 276
Arrowhead *Sagittaria latifolia* 91, 105
Arrowwood, Smooth *Viburnum Molle* 105, 116
Arrowwood, Southern *Viburnum dentatum* 290
Arum, Arrow *Peltandra virginica* 105, 116, 129
Arum, Water (Wild Calla) *Calla palustris*
Ash, Black *Fraxinus nigra* 105, 165, 177
Ash, Carolina *Fraximus caroliniana* 177, 189
Ash, Green *Fraxinus pennsylvanica* 177, 189, 264
Ash, Pumpkin *Fraxinus profunda* 177, 189
Ash, White *Fraxinus americana* 105, 177, 214, 240, 252, 264
Aspen, Bigtooth *Populus grandidentata* 203, 214, 228, 276
Aspen, Quaking *Populus tremuloides* 203, 214, 228, 276

Common name *Scientific name*

Aster, Grassleaf Golden *Chrysopsis graminifolia* 290
Aster, Largeleaf *Aster macrophyllus* 214, 228, 276
Aster, New England *Aster novae-angliae*
Aster, Panicled *Aster simplex* 142, 152
Aster, Purple-stemmed *Aster puniceus* 142, 152
Aster, Salt Marsh *Aster tenuifolius* 67
Asters *Aster* spp. 203, 264
Asters, Golden *Chrysopsis* spp. 52
Azalea, Swamp White *Rhododendron viscosum* 165
Baccharis, Eastern *Baccharis halimifolia* 67
Baldcypress *Taxodium distichum* 129, 189
Baneberry, Red *Actaea rubra* 276
Baneberry, White *Actaea pachypoda* 240
Basswood, American *Tilia americana* 240, 264
Basswood, White *Tilia heterophylla* 252
Bayberry, Northern *Myrica pennsylvanica* 52, 203
Bayberry, Odorless *Myrica inodora* 290
Bayberry, Southern (Waxmyrtle) *Myrica cerifera* 52, 129, 203, 290
Bearberry, Evergreen *Arctostaphylos uva-ursi* 52, 276
Beauty, Spring *Claytonia Virginica* 189, 252, 264
Beard, Old Man's *Usnea strigosa* 52
Beautyberry *Callicarpa americana* 290
Bedstraw, Rough *Galium asprellum* 152

Common and Scientific Names of Birds, Mammals, Amphibians, and Reptiles

(Page numbers refer to Wildlife Locator Charts for each habitat.)

Common name *Scientific name*

Alligator, American *Alligator mississippiensis* 81, 132

Anhinga *Anhinga anhinga* 132, 192

Anole, Green *Anolis carolinensis* 81, 132

Armadillo, Nine-banded *Dasypus novemcinctus* 292

Badger *Taxidea taxus* 206, 218

Bat, Hoary *Lasiurus cinereus* 218, 280

Bat, Northern Yellow *Lasiurus intermedius* 292

Bat, Red *Lasiurus borealis* 218, 280

Bat, Seminole *Lasiurus seminolus* 192

Bat, Silver-haired *Lasionycteris noctivagans* 108, 180

Bear, Black *Ursus americanus* 108, 154, 254, 268

Beaver *Castor canadensis* 94, 108, 154, 230

Bittern, American *Botaurus lentiginosus* 70, 119, 132

Bittern, Least *Isobrychus exilis* 119, 132

Blackbird, Red-winged *Agelaius phoeniceus* 119, 132

Blackbird, Rusty *Euphagus carolinus* 168, 192

Blackbird, Yellow-headed *Xanthocephalus xanthocephalus* 119, 132

Bluebird, Eastern *Sialia sialia* 206

Bobcat *Felis rufus*

Bobolink *Dolichonyx oryzivorus* 144, 206

Bobwhite, Northern *Colinus virginianus* 206, 268

Brant *Branta bernicla* 70

Common name *Scientific name*

Bullfrog *Rena catesbeiana* 94, 108

Bunting, Indigo *Passerina cyanea* 218

Cardinal, Northern *Cardinalis cardinalis* 292

Canvasback *Aythya valisineria* 70, 119

Catbird, Gray *Dumetella carolinensis* 154, 218

Chat, Yellow-breasted *Icteria virens* 218

Chickadee, Black-capped *Parus atricapillus* 154, 230, 243

Chickadee, Boreal *Parus hudsonicus* 168, 280

Chickadee, Carolina *Parus carolinensis* 254, 268

Chipmunk, Eastern *Tamias striatus* 218, 230, 243, 254

Coachwhip, Eastern *Masticophis flagellum flagellum* 218

Coot, American *Fulica americana* 70, 94, 119

Cooter, River *Pseudemys concinna* 108

Copperhead, Southern *Agkistrodon contortrix contortrix* 192

Cormorant, Double-crested *Phalacrocorax auritus* 132, 192

Cottonmouth *Agkistrodon piscivorus*

Cottonmouth, Florida *Agkistrodon piscivorus conanti* 81

Cottonmouth, Western *Agkistrodon piscivorus leucostoma* 192

Cottontail, Eastern *Sylvilagus floridanus* 56, 119, 206, 218

INDEX